Action Research-Based Practices in Primary Education

ERZIEHUNGSKONZEPTIONEN UND PRAXIS
EDUCATIONAL CONCEPTS AND PRACTICE

Herausgegeben von / Edited by
Gerd-Bodo von Carlsburg

VOLUME 92

Daiva Jakavonytė-Staškuvienė, Jolita Kudinovienė and
Linas Jašinauskas

Action Research-Based Practices in Primary Education

Educational Contexts and Teachers' Experiences

PETER LANG
Berlin · Bruxelles · Chennai · Lausanne · New York · Oxford

Bibliographic Information published by the Deutsche Nationalbibliothek
The Deutsche Nationalbibliothek lists this publication in the Deutsche Nationalbibliografie; detailed bibliographic data is available online at https://dnb.dnb.de.

Library of Congress Cataloging-in-Publication Data
Names: Jakavonytė-Staškuvienė, Daiva, 1979- author | Kudinovienė, Jolita, 1974- author | Jašinauskas, Linas, 1977- author
Title: Action research-based practices in primary education : educational contexts and teachers' experiences / Daiva Jakavonytė-Staškuvienė, Jolita Kudinovienė and Linas Jašinauskas.
Description: Berlin ; New York : Peter Lang, [2026] | Series: Erziehungskonzeptionen und Praxis | Includes bibliographical references.
Identifiers: LCCN 2026019715 (print) | LCCN 2026019716 (ebook) | ISBN 9783631947166 hardback | ISBN 9783631947173 pdf | ISBN 9783631947180 epub
Subjects: LCSH: Education, Primary--Research--Methodology | Education, Primary--Lithuania | Action research in education--Lithuania
Classification: LCC LB1507 .J35 2026 (print) | LCC LB1507 (ebook)
LC record available at https://lccn.loc.gov/2026019715
LC ebook record available at https://lccn.loc.gov/2026019716

ISSN 0723-7464
ISBN 978-3-631-94716-6 (Print)
ISBN 978-3-631-94717-3 (ePDF)
ISBN 978-3-631-94718-0 (ePUB)
DOI 10.3726/b23445

PETER LANG
Open

Published by Peter Lang GmbH, Berlin, Deutschland

info@peterlang.com

http://www.peterlang.com

Contact for General Product Safety Regulation (GPSR): gpsr@peterlang.com

Reviewers

Prof Dr Rasa Braslauskienė, Klaipeda University, Lithuania
Prof Dr Ewa Filipiak, Kazimierz Wielki University, Poland
Prof Dr Daiva Malinauskienė, Vilnius University, Lithuania
Prof Dr Frédéric Torterat, University of Montpellier, France

The monograph was considered and recommended for publication at the meeting of the Department of Pre-school and Primary Education of Education Academy of Vytautas Magnus University on 14.02.2025 (Minutes No. IP 02-25-02).

The monograph was considered and recommended for publication at the meeting of the Council of the Academy of Education of Vytautas Magnus University on 22.04.2025 (Minutes No. ŠA-TA-N-12).

Contents

Figures

Tables

Preface

One of the components of a modern teaching qualification is the ability to initiate and implement research into pedagogical practice, to provide scientific ways of evaluating the educational process and solving problems, to improve educational practice and to innovate in the educational process. It is important that, from the first grade onwards, educators organise the educational process on the basis of students' experiences, taking into account their individual abilities, needs and dispositions. The application of action research in the educational process makes it possible to put this into practice.

The monograph identifies the theoretical concept of action research and describes empirical experiences that show in which contexts action research can be chosen as a way of solving problems. The authors believe that this book could mobilise school communities and researchers to collaborate in effectively addressing problems in educational practice and responding to global challenges.

The first part of the monograph provides a very detailed analysis of the research literature on action research. It describes different models of how action research can be applied in contemporary educational practice. As action research starts from the search for a problem situation and its solutions, it is hoped that this approach to education is the starting point not only for the present but also for the future of educational science and didactics, and that the need for action research-based practice will only grow in the future.

The second part of the monograph describes the methodology of action research in primary education, presenting the methodological framework of an empirical study conducted in Lithuania. The stages, process and participant characteristics of the empirical study, as well as the ethics of the study, are described and scientifically justified. This chapter enables the reader to understand the logic and implementation of the study.

The third part of the monograph is, in the opinion of the authors, the richest in didactic terms, as it provides an analysis of the results of the empirical study, which should be of interest to both educational researchers and educational practitioners. This part of the book presents the context of Lithuanian primary education practice, which highlights the strengths and weaknesses of educational practice. In addition, a detailed analysis of four years (2018–2021) of undergraduate theses from the Primary Education Pedagogy study programme at Vytautas Magnus University, where action research was applied, is presented, revealing the areas and didactic approaches to the selected educational problems. It also describes the experiences of primary education teachers who have been using action research as a basis for their work for a number of years and are advanced in the field of action research.

The authors hope that the new knowledge on action research in primary education presented in this monograph will be of interest to fellow researchers, to primary teachers, to parents of primary school children, and to any reader interested in action research and primary education.

We would like to thank the reviewers, whose comments were valuable in improving the monograph, the colleagues who shared their insights, and the primary school teachers who willingly collaborated in the empirical phase of the research and shared their experiences.

Daiva Jakavonytė-Staškuvienė, Linas Jašinauskas, Jolita Kudinovienė

Definitions of Key Terms

Bachelor's thesis (at university) is a student's independent research, project or creative work carried out at the end of the study programme and designed to acquire analytical, research, artistic and other cognitive and functional competences. At least fifteen credits are allocated for the preparation and defence of the Bachelor's thesis (Senate of Vytautas Magnus University, 2020).

Competence is the ability to perform a certain activity on the basis of a set of acquired knowledge, skills, and values (Law on Education, current consolidated version, 01-01-2025).

School is a legal person, a subdivision of a legal person or other organisation of a Member State, established in the Republic of Lithuania in accordance with the procedure established by legislation, whose main activity is formal and/or non-formal education (Law on Education, current consolidated version, 01-01-2025).

External evaluation of the quality of school performance (in the Lithuanian context) is a formative assessment of school processes that provides information for adjusting school performance and improving results. It can be organised as holistic (evaluation of the whole school activity), thematic (evaluation in depth of the school activity related to the topic (problem, issue) defined by the Minister of Education and Science), risk (identification, analysis of risk factors of the school activity, and the provision of opportunities for improvement of the activity) (Description of the Procedure for the Organisation and Conduct of the External Evaluation of the Activity of Schools Implementing General Education Programmes, 2018).

Pedagogue/teacher is a person who has acquired higher education and pedagogical qualification (Law on Education, current consolidated version, 01-01-2025).

Primary education is designed to provide a person with the basics of moral and social maturity, the foundations of culture, including ethnic culture, and basic literacy, and to help prepare him or her for the basic curriculum. Primary education is a compulsory four-year (grades 1–4) education programme leading to further education. It is the first stage of formal education, combining pre-primary and primary education. According to the International Standard Classification of Education (ISCED 2011), primary education in Lithuania is classified as ISCED level 1 (Eurydice, 2024).

Reflection is a way of philosophical thinking aimed at understanding and critically analysing one's own assumptions and forms of knowledge. It requires the consciousness to turn inwards – the thinker and the process of thinking are reflected upon (Universal Lithuanian Encyclopedia, 2025).

Socio-economic context is the social, cultural, economic environment of pupils, which is influenced by the characteristics of the locality, region, specificities and attitudes of the communities, the education of the pupils' families, parents' attitudes, employment, income, involvement in the child's learning, school affairs, cultural and educational resources available at home, etc. It is assumed that pupils living in more favourable social, cultural and economic environments achieve higher learning outcomes (according to PISA 2009, 2010).

Education is the cultivation of the spiritual, intellectual and physical capacities of the individual through communication and teaching (Law on Education, current consolidated version, 01-01-2025).

Content of education:

1. The content of education consists of what is taught and learned, how it is taught and learned, how pupils' progress and achievement are assessed, and what teaching and learning tools are used.
2. The content of education shall be designed to achieve the educational objectives set out in Article 3 of the Law on Education. The specific content of education shall be developed and systematically updated, taking into account the aims of education, teaching and study of the relevant group or type of school, the needs of Lithuanian society as a result of the changing socio-cultural environment, the needs of the local and school community, as well as the experience, educational needs and interests of pupils and students.
3. The requirements referred to in paragraphs 1 and 2 of this Article shall be complied with in the preparation of educational programmes or their modules for pre-school education, pre-primary education, general education, vocational training, studies at higher education institutions, curricula or regulations for fields of study, programmes for the examination of learning achievements, textbooks, virtual teaching aids, other teaching aids, supplementary educational materials (Law on Education, current consolidated version, 01-01-2025).

The process of education is a process of moving forward, a sequential process of change in a system or parts of a system. The educational process (or pedagogical process) is the purposeful process of human development through the direct or indirect interaction of educational actors with learners, based on values, educational tools, methods, techniques and organisational forms. Communication (exchange of experiences) is an essential component of the educational process. (according to Jovaiša, 2007, 218).

Action research is primarily participatory research in which the researcher is directly involved and determines the situation, and qualitative methods are used for research. In such research, the researcher is interested not only in the analysis of the problem under study, but also in the possibilities of changing the current situation, changing the behaviour or attitudes of the target groups, but doing so in a democratic way, where the course of the activity is agreed upon by all the participants in the process. Action research usually proceeds in the following steps: data are collected, a theoretical rationale is constructed from the information obtained, the data are interpreted, new questions are then raised, and additional data are collected again. The researcher goes beyond the collection of information, the research itself is the intervention, and at the same time the impact and results of the intervention are observed and interpreted. Often, a specific goal (usually to eliminate the problem) is set with a group or individual of participants and a joint search for a solution is undertaken, answering the question of *how to.* The researcher often uses a variety of methodologies in the search for a solution and monitors their impact together. Action research requires close interaction between the researcher and the research participants, mutual trust and a genuine rapport, which in turn requires the researcher to have experience, expertise and specific communication skills, as questioning and discussion are perceived as the driving force for learner development and educational quality (after Adelman, 1993; Lewin, 1948; Lewin, Lippett, & White, 1939).

Introduction

Relevance of the research. Action research in educational practice (synonyms include *action research, participatory research, participatory action research, praxis research*) is defined as the systematic study of how to change the status quo in educational practice, to find new ways of doing things that bring about positive change for all those involved in the educational process, i.e. to improve student learning and achievement (Anderson, Herr & Nihlen, 2007; Menter et al., 2011; Efron & Ravid, 2013; Fine & Torre, 2021; Ascroft, 2024; Middleton, 2024). It is an activity that enables the planning of an action strategy, which is then implemented, systematically monitored, reflexively reflected upon and modified (Adelman, 1993; Lewin, 1948; Lewin, Lippett & White, 1939; Dolbec & Clément, 2000; Mertler, 2009; Lafontaine, 2006, 2016; Clark, 2012; Carignan, Beaudry & Larose, 2016; Eden & Ackermann, 2018; Ascroft, 2024; Middleton, 2024). Action research involves the teacher as a researcher taking ownership of the solution to a particular learning problem (Adelman, 1993; Lewin, 1948; Lewin, Lippett & White, 1939; Macaire, 2007; Rönnerman & Nordberg, 2024). Action research enhances teacher capacity for professional development, autonomy, and the ability to assess and take responsibility for educational practice and its improvement (Efron & Ravid, 2013; Jakavonytė-Staškuvienė, Jašinauskas & Kudinovienė, 2024). It is important that teachers want to participate in such activity themselves, voluntarily. All education takes place in the context of active social practice, so action research is particularly important and relevant to solving learning problems (Macaire, 2007; Mertler, 2009; Fine & Torre, 2021; Ascroft, 2024; Middleton, 2024). Action research gives teachers the opportunity to step back and reflect on their professional practice (Cain & Harris, 2013; Ascroft, 2024; Middleton, 2024). In addition, action research is a way to bring about targeted changes in educational practice, which increasingly fails to meet the needs of the majority of pupils (Fullan, 2020; Fullan & Gallagher, 2020). This monograph is also important because of the constantly changing context in educational reality (in situations such as dealing with the consequences of the COVID-19 pandemic, integration of refugees in Lithuanian schools as a result of the war in Ukraine, inclusive education practices that adapt to the needs of the individual child). School leaders today have to be experts in understanding context (Fullan, 2019). In recent times, working at school brings a new context practically every week. From a change perspective, there is nothing more difficult to resolve than our current situation, and there is no indication that conditions will improve (Fullan, 2019; 2020). It is clear that education must become an essential element of solutions and change, because it is a factor in both individual and social development. The guiding principle is to create equitable public-school systems that become the lifeblood of prosperous societies, delivering both individual and collective benefits (Raby et al., 2013; Fullan, 2019; 2020; Fullan et al., 2020). The education system of the future should focus on the use of technology, innovative ideas for learning and well-being, and what we call systemicity, i.e. favourable drivers for change at local, regional and policy levels (Fullan & Quinn, 2020). Educational practice should be based on deep learning, developed in collaboration with practising school teachers, administrators and researchers. The following areas are integrated into educational content: development of individual character, citizenship, cooperation, communication, creativity and critical thinking. Education takes place in a physically and emotionally safe environment created within a learning partnership, with targeted use of digital technologies (Fullan & Quinn, 2020). We can say that action research-based education could serve as the foundation for building the school of the future.

Regardless of the field in which action research is performed, there are six principles that characterise it (McConnell, Conrad & Uhrmacher, 2020; Moosa, Salleh & Hamid, 2020; Rosen, Stoeffler & Simmering, 2020; Mertler, 2021):

- purposefulness of the action (the action is performed consciously and purposefully),
- critical reflection and assessment of the action,
- cooperation (participants in the action project are also researchers; the researcher is an active participant in the action),
- orientation to change (actions are flexible and open to modification),
- cyclicality (four main stages of action research, dynamically linked in a continuous cycle: planning, action, observation, reflection),
- unity of theory and practice (theory informs practice, practice refines theory, the process is oriented towards change).

It is important that everyone involved in the research has clear roles and tools assigned to them, and that they know the direction of the action. All this should be organised by the teacher. If action research is a whole-school objective, then all teachers, administrators and researchers should be involved in the planning and implementation of such action (Raby et al., 2013; Fullan & Quinn, 2020). Working in smaller groups, it is important to have a clear discussion of the pathway, the tools and the problem area, and to pool knowledge on certain key issues, such as the concept of general or subject-specific literacy. In the pre-implementation stage of action research, it is necessary to reflect on one's own knowledge in a given field.

For these reasons, this research aims to contribute to solving the identified problematic issues. **The research questions** of this research work: *how action research is organised in primary education, what educational problems are chosen to be addressed, how they are solved, what results are achieved, what are the reasons why teachers choose to perform action research in their classrooms, what challenges arise and how they can be managed.*

The aim of the research is to investigate action research-based practices in primary education, educational contexts and teachers' experiences.

The object of the research is action research in primary education practice.

Objectives of the research:

1. to theoretically justify the application of action research in primary education;
2. to identify the strengths and areas for improvement of the educational process, based on external evaluation data on the quality of performance of Lithuanian general education schools;
3. to analyse the issues, methodology and results of the bachelor's theses in which action research was applied;
4. to analyse the experience of applying action research in the educational practice of primary education teachers and revealing educational contexts.

As far as action research-based educational practices are concerned, it should not be forgotten that education is a social fact, and that conventional educational practices are shaped by historical and social factors. The moment when a teacher meets pupils and tries to help them acquire knowledge and abilities can be very difficult if the teacher fails to remember this. This encounter can become difficult if the teacher feels at the mercy of the pupils and if the pedagogical situation is not conducive to the pupils' development. However, the encounter will usually be successful if the teacher, because of his or her attention and concern for the pupil individually and for all pupils taken as a group, is able to guide them, creating the conditions for each pupil to learn a little more, to grow and to develop (Étienne & Fumat, 2014; Alexander, 2020; Akkari & Radhouane, 2022). Such learning practices, where significant moments/fragments of action are observed that help pupils achieve better results, are the essence of action research.

Theoretical and practical significance of the monograph. International education documents and scholars (Cerna, 2019; Fullan, 2020; Gudovitch et al., 2021; Keymeulen, Henry & Longlez, 2020; Schwartz et al., 2022; UNESCO, 2003, 2011, 2020, 2021, 2023; UNICEF, 2022) underline the changes in the world to which educational practices must respond and, in many cases, decisions must be flexible and quick, taking into account the realities of life, the children's cultural, social and emotional diversity and the well-being of everyone, every day and every lesson.

This is the environment that every school community, every teacher, must provide for. In this monograph, the authors show how qualitative action research can be applied in the implementation of the primary curriculum, which not only helps teachers to make a realistic assessment of the quality of their daily work and of the problem areas, but also demonstrates in an integral way how the flexible conditions created by teachers help to improve the educational process, and how they create an environment for each pupil (according to his/her needs, abilities, and interests) that helps him/her to achieve his/her own individual progress and the very best possible results for him/her (for that child). The monograph provides a detailed description of the Lithuanian context, showing how educational situations in Lithuania are progressive and what problems are encountered (this is the first sub-section of the empirical study, which analyses the data from the external audit). It also describes in detail what didactic problems and subjects were addressed by primary education undergraduates using the action research approach, which didactic approaches were chosen and how they managed to achieve certain results (this is the second sub-section of the empirical study, which analyses the data from the undergraduate theses). In addition, it was explored how the experience gained by primary teachers during their undergraduate studies in the field of action research is being developed and contributes to solving the problems encountered in the implementation of the educational content in their further work in primary education. The third and fourth empirical sub-sections of the monograph deal with the problematic issues and how primary school teachers address them through action research. The empirical part of the monograph substantiates and reinforces the didactical aspects of primary education that can be implemented and developed in the primary classroom when educational practice is based on research. We believe that this part of the work is not only relevant for practice, but also enriches theory by showing how and which theoretical elements contribute to the resolution of complex questions of practice.

In education science, it is important to develop practical knowledge that explains how children learn in particular settings and under particular conditions (Morin, 1985; 2004a; 2004b; Morin & Cardinal, 2004; Mondada, 2006). Action research is based on the need to solve problems in the educational process, but it is not applied science because it is in constant dialogue with reality. In education, action research does not only pose problems, but also discovers causes by investigating how to solve those problems. When researchers want to test relationships, they try to work in a natural way, seeking to find the right moments when relationships between situations and their context can be observed. It is important to capture the conditions under which these relationships emerge and when certain activities contribute to solving one or another of the problematic issues (Morin, 1985; 2004a; 2004b; Morin & Cardinal, 2004; Mondada, 2006).

Action research aims to bring about **change**. It seeks to change actions, which are as much about changing concrete reality as they are about changing a person's thinking, which is influenced by experience. Action requires creativity on the part of researchers in order to transform action. Our monograph therefore describes the experiences of prospective primary school teachers that allow them to transform their activities and achieve the desired changes, demonstrating their sustainability. **Context** is of particular importance in the concept of action research. **Therefore, the uniqueness and novelty of our monograph is that it presents the context of Lithuanian primary education practice and analyses the experiences when action research helps educators to solve educational problems and create individual, unique, child-enhancing, supportive contexts of educational situations that lead to better and more qualitative results.** The experience of teaching in science is central to all those involved in the education process, including the novice teacher (Houssaye, 2019). Experience includes elements such as knowing the situation in which the educational process is organised, the concepts that are analysed, the way in which the intended result will be achieved and the criteria from which it will be determined. It is a reflection on practical experience and, at the same time, a continuous process of reflection, involving all stages of action research. It is therefore a reflection on what and how needs to be further developed and transferred to another similar situation, and what and why needs to be adjusted. In this way, the concrete educational practices, situations and contexts reflected upon and described in our monograph enrich not only the practice of education but also the science of education, by showing what specific knowledge of educational science contributes to learning outcomes in twenty-first century contexts. It is also important to note that future primary teachers will be able to draw on this monograph in their analysis of educational science issues, as the content of this book will help learners to develop their pedagogical knowledge.

The conditions for conducting and analysing action research are shared governance. It is necessary both to plan and to respect the freedom of those involved. The researcher is not alone. Action research requires decisions to be made at all levels of application, participation and interpretation. Research is a cooperative endeavour between the researcher and the research participants, with a mutual search for meanings that go beyond the pure application of theory to practice, recognising the uniqueness of each situation. In the case of our study, the specific criteria are presented in detail in the research logic diagram (p. 56). The criterion of change is something that is particularly significant in didactic science, as it is important to improve practice and to think about the topic on the basis of concrete, changing contexts. Moreover, it must be kept in mind that researchers, teachers and pupils alike make their own decisions about change (Lafontaine,

2011; 2016). And our monograph highlights situations in which the changes we have adopted are successful and the results they produce. All of this shows the added value of this work for didactic science. The empirical part of the monograph allows the reader to understand and analyse how it is possible to create situational knowledge that is unique and useful to the practitioner when he or she can identify with it. Readers will be enriched by a deeper engagement with these descriptions of action research, both as educational researchers and as practising educators, and will be able to better refine their own ways of professional practice and reflection.

Research ethics. The analysis of Lithuanian educational practice and its changing trends (the monograph's sub-section "Linking action research to educational practice in Lithuania: external evaluation data on general education schools") was based on publicly available general data on external evaluation of the quality of Lithuanian general education schools' performance, reports summarising the external evaluation data (one of the monograph's authors, Linas Jašinauskas, was involved in the preparation of the reports), and the publicly available reports on the risk and thematic external evaluation of general education schools.

As the individuals and organisations involved in the research have the right to know not only the purpose of the research, but also the identity of the researchers, including who is conducting the research and how to contact the researchers (Denscombe, 2010), this was taken into account in the written communication to the participants of the focus groups. In line with this principle, focus group participants were provided with information about the research team (names of the researchers, contact details, name of the organisation they represent).

The monograph was prepared in accordance with the norms of scientific integrity in terms of a detailed description of the methods used to collect and process the research data, an objective and unbiased interpretation of the research results, and ethical citation requirements. Some of the findings of this study have already been published in scientific articles in scientific journals:

- Jakavonytė-Staškuvienė, D., Jašinauskas, L., & Kudinovienė, J. (2023). An analysis of prospective primary school teachers' action research: the case of Lithuania. *Educational Action Research*, 1–16. https://doi.org/10.1080/09650792.2023.2298744
- Jakavonytė-Staškuvienė, D., Jašinauskas, L., & Kudinovienė, J. (2022). Some principles applied to Action Research in Lithuania. *Lirdef*, (actes n°1). 10.34745/numerev_1799
- Some of the findings of this research have been presented at international or national scientific conferences:

- 14-03-2024/15-03-2024, at the International Scientific Conference "Teachers Heroes: What Helps a Teacher Grow?" of Vytautas Magnus University for pre-school and primary teachers, D. Jakavonytė-Staškuvienė, J. Kudinovienė, L. Jašinauskas presented a report on "Teacher's Experiences of Action Research: there is no error in pedagogy as in jazz, it is only calibration of thought.
- 23-02-2023 and 16/03/2023, at the national conference organised by Vytautas Magnus University for primary school specialists on the topic Primary Education in the Twenty-First Century: From Theoretical Assumptions to Best Practices, D. Jakavonytė-Staškuvienė, J. Kudinovienė, & L. Jašinauskas presented a report on "Activity-based Research in Primary Schooling: The Case of Lithuania".
- 21-10-2021, at the International Scientific Conference *Initiatives collaboratives pour la Petite Enfance* at the French University of Montpellier, D. Jakavonytė-Staškuvienė, J. Kudinovienė, & L. Jašinauskas presented a scientific report "La pratique collaborative basée sur l'activité en contexte lituanien".

Chapter 1 Theoretical Basis for Action Research-Based Practices in Primary Education

1.1. The concept of action research-based pedagogical practice

Research-based pedagogy has been a priority of Lithuanian education policy for many years and has been outlined in various educational documents and education strategies (*The concept of a good school*, 2015; *Lithuania's progress strategy "Lithuania 2030"*, 2012). Together with this practice, the endeavours of educators are emphasised – educators who are highly reflective and thoughtful, who reflect not only on their own activities as educators, but also on pedagogical activities based on the development of reflective abilities, i.e. enabling pupils to reflect on what they have done, how they have done it, why they have done it, and the result they have achieved. We recognise that the identified priorities are of great significance for education science and practice in Lithuania. However, we increasingly hear practitioners' concerns that there is not only a lack of abilities in this area, but also a lack of research to justify how such activities can be organised in a high-quality way. More and more countries are adopting research-based activities in the classroom, for example, the National Centre for the Evaluation of the School System in France (2017) identifies as priorities for education the strengthening of research-based practices, the development of a plan for problem-solving strategies, and the implementation of these strategies in the reality of education. The relevance of action research and its application to the renewal of pedagogical practices is highlighted by Canadian researcher L. Lafontaine (2016). She states that such practices make sense and are useful but are rarely based on scientific evidence. She presented a research study on how action research methodology-based practice trained educators working in small schools in disadvantaged social environments. The OECD (2011) identifies a number of criteria related to the quality of education: the *quality of the learning processes* (what children experience when they learn, the activities they perform); the *quality of the structured content of the education provided on the basis of which experience is acquired* (management of the educational process, educational environment, place in the community); and the *quality of the impact on the child* (at the cognitive level and at the level of general competences, i.e. health, socialisation, emotional control). All of these components operate in a specific situation and can therefore be explored and improved through action research. Action research has been identified by the European Commission as a valid educational intervention, taking into account the needs of children, especially in the early years, and as a highly supportive way of addressing educational situations in socially vulnerable settings (according to Eurydice, 2009). Teacher-training universities should follow the process of setting quality standards in the preparation of primary teachers and pay particular attention to the process of pedagogical practice, linking it to science (Mattavarat, Viseshsiri & Siribanpitak, 2017; James Long & Bae, 2018). Educational practice should be based on the psychology of learning. If pupils have little basic knowledge and abilities as tools for learning, especially in reading, writing and arithmetic, they tend to fail to progress to higher education, and these foundations are laid in the primary school years. Consequently, science-based practices that can be favourably implemented through action research are important for the future educational prospects of primary school pupils and teachers. However, it is sometimes difficult to implement such practices in a high-quality way for reasons such as lack of assessment arrangements, lack of resources and lack of time to plan and deliver inquiry-based lessons (James Long & Bae, 2018). Moreover, other problems are becoming more acute, most notably climate change and severe and rapidly growing inequality throughout the world (Fullan, 2020; Fullan & Gallagher, 2020). Action research-based education practices can be linked to the Finnish education system, because all children there are educated in schools, there is no selection based on achievement or other criteria, and there are no private schools (Varjo, Kalalahti & Silvennoinen, 2014; Kalalahti, Silvennoinen, Varjo & Rinne 2015; Varjo, Kalalahti, & Kauko, 2019). All children not only receive free education, but also all learning supplies and meals. The main feature of Finland's national education culture is equal opportunities for all (Simola et al., 2017). Individual support measures are put in place to ensure that each pupil is able to reach the pupil's full potential in all areas of their education. We mention these aspects of the Finnish system because the provision of basic necessities and meals are fundamental preconditions for changing any aspect of educational practice without negatively affecting the community.

Action research-based pedagogical practice is one of the most feasible ways for a teacher to implement the teacher's deep understanding and reflection on his/her own practice, which involves getting to know the learner, planning the action in light of learners' experiences and contexts, setting and implementing specific expectations and desired outcomes, and reflecting on the process and the outcome. It should be stressed that it is not only the teacher who should do this, but also the pupils who should be aware of all these stages. M. Miehakanda (2014) emphasises the organisation of education in the context of different cultures, and also points out that pupils still have only limited participation in the educational process, and that educators rarely choose educational methods based on the individuality of pupils. The criterion of individuality becomes particularly important when we live in a multicultural context. For these reasons, educational practices and the use of certain methods should change. Furthermore, education is seen as the construction of knowledge through active engagement, to which each pupil brings his or her own attitudes and values. For these reasons, it is necessary to take the learner into account and to provide the learner with the necessary support or activities in a timely manner. According to M. Miehakanda (2014), the educator should continuously perform action research in the context of his/her learners, which includes three essential interrelated areas: *the selection of the curriculum content and actions/methods, the creation of favourable conditions for interactive tasks, and the inductive dynamic development of knowledge/abilities*. An important role is played by the "permeation" of the entire pedagogical process with thinking procedures, i.e. inductive-deductive reasoning, whereby there is a continuous empirical monitoring of the activities, breaking them down into details and bringing them together, and summarising them as a whole. These reasoning operations enable the educator to make informed, reasoned decisions regarding the education of pupils. The aim of education is the development of each learner, and it is therefore essential to adapt teaching materials and methods to suit the pupils. It is also stressed that educational practice would be improved if teachers collaboratively examined their practice in light of the moral and ethical beliefs that underpin it (Cain & Harris, 2013). There are situations where educational practice demands excellence from teachers but does not provide the tools and training to create such conditions. Teachers then experience stress (Appay, 2005), psychological distress and discomfort (Maranda et al., 2013). Many action research studies focus on a change in activity, which requires careful democratic action because it is about decision-making and jointly agreed actions. The research explored the attitudes of teachers in implementing change, how they behaved in certain situations, and what motivated the implementation teams to act at the school level (Maranda et al., 2013). Engagement with activities is impaired if the administration proposes to inventory changes by introducing formal monitoring instruments and their documentation. The meaning of the educational work is undermined by the defensive strategy of the administration. Changes are only possible after taking into account occupational safety and mental health preventive measures to avoid psychological discomfort for educators and pupil-support professionals (Maranda et al., 2013). For this reason, action research should essentially be based on voluntary teacher engagement, positive support, encouragement and motivation, and good communication that fosters internal motivation and a desire to improve.

Action research is an appropriate approach because the educational process involves both pupils and teacher, so it is important to choose an appropriate, constructive path. An inductive posture allows the teacher to continuously analyse the situation and assess the appropriateness of the chosen instruments, which help to develop the learner's logical and critical thinking. Action research makes pupils take responsibility not only for their own learning, but also for the learning of their friends in the cooperating group (according to Ys & Mara, 2011). Action research is a systematic approach to investigation that enables people to find effective solutions to the problems encountered in the implementation of educational content and to solve them appropriately. This research helps to focus on a specific situation and to address it effectively. If the right tools are chosen, the effectiveness of the work can be increased. Action research is particularly useful in classrooms of learners, where teachers act as researchers, making decisions and changes to improve the quality of education. Unfortunately, if the chosen methods are not very advanced or appropriate, then the learner suffers because his or her reasoning processes are not developed (Miehakanda, 2014). Teachers, even after attending training courses/seminars, do not always understand how to organise education based on action research, which is why a culture of collaborative learning in the school is important in teacher training, where teachers discuss and perform action research together with pupils from the same class. In this way, strategies can be adopted and enhanced, the school culture can be nurtured according to the needs of the pupils in a particular class; thus, improving educational practice (Muijs, 2014; Kennedy, 2016; Johannesson, 2020). It is important that pupils are actively involved in organising the action research. And their involvement is still lacking in current practice. If the aim is to achieve action research-based educational practice, school teachers should agree to work towards this, to show each other successful cases, to analyse them, to support each other in doing so, and then it is likely that change will occur (according to Ys & Mara, 2011). For the pupil to develop, he/she should be offered different strategies from which, having activated his/her thinking/knowledge, he/she can choose, and can also give reasons as to why he/she is choosing that particular one. Presenting arguments allows the pupil to develop and summarise his/her views on one issue or another (see Figure 1.1.1).

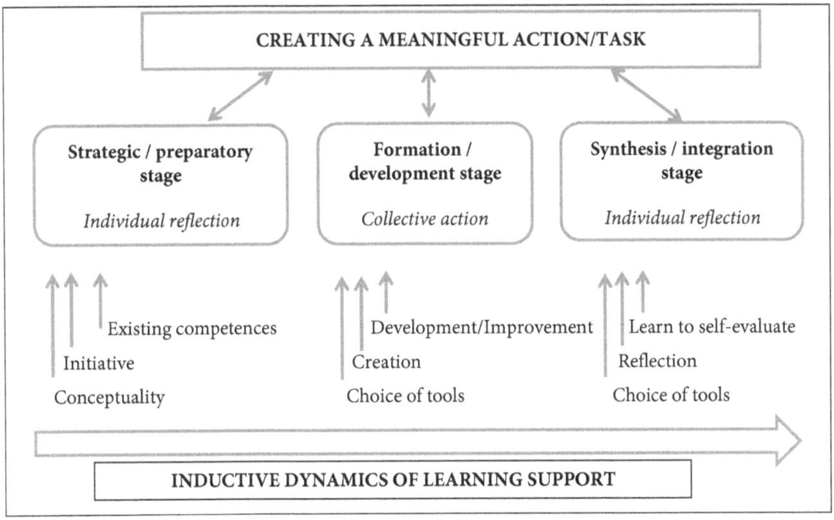

Figure 1.1.1: Diagram of action research-based learning

As can be seen in Figure 1.1.1., action research-based education goes hand in hand with active pupil engagement/participation. The key characteristics of such education are: 1) pupils are active participants in action rather than passive listeners; 2) there is a focus on developing/improving abilities rather than transferring knowledge or just listening to information; 3) pupils are engaged in a variety of actions; 4) pupils learn to reflect on how they learn (according to Ys & Mara, 2011). L. Lafontaine (2016) points out that primary school teachers tend to support primary school pupils and organise activities based on children's individual needs. Teachers look for appropriate ways to reach pupils who live in disadvantaged socio-economic environments, but teachers often doubt whether they are able to find such ways themselves and are therefore willing to collaborate with researchers. The search is not only for ways to develop academic abilities, but also to stimulate and support pupils' motivation. In fact, the elements outlined in the action research-based learning diagram are emphasised by most researchers (Gauthier, 2010; Riente, 2010; Lafontaine, 2016). Before performing a complex task/activity, the educator needs to think about the three stages of the learning and assessment activity: *preparation, implementation and integration*. In the preparation stage, a scenario is presented, outlining how, what and why learning will take place. All this allows pupils to activate their prior knowledge of the topic and their subject-area knowledge by reflecting on the objectives of the proposed activity, indicating the expected outcome/result and the provided instructions for implementation. The implementation stage is more oriented towards the learning activity, with the active participation of the pupils in relation to the learning and assessment objectives. Support is provided in this stage, by the teacher or by the pupils. In addition, feedback is given during this stage and one or more interim assessments may be carried out after each learning activity. These assessments provide an indication of how well the child is progressing towards the intended outcome. The integration stage provides activities that allow pupils to synthesise their learning and show the final result, which should also be evaluated. Time to celebrate and reflect on the activities completed by the pupils and to analyse all stages of the activity is very important in this stage. It is useful for the researcher and the teacher to be involved in the action research (Lafontaine, 2016), discussions can take many forms – classroom observation, analysis of video recordings of pupils' activities, online consultations with teachers. Action/activity is the key element, the link among research, teaching and learning. During the activity, there is interaction among teacher/pupils/researcher. Of course, the educator can play two roles at the same time: both teacher and researcher. The teaching component and the data gathered through learning allow research to inform and improve educational practice. Researchers L. Lafontaine (2016), A. C. Wennergren (2016), E. Wenger (2018), P. Johannesson (2020) point out that during professional development events, educators should reflect on their own practice, analyse and discuss what is going well, and look for ways of overcoming what is causing problems. Indeed, such activities, where participants reflect on their practice, adopt and experiment with new ways of working in their classrooms, bring lasting change. For this to happen, the training should last long enough, and educators should meet systematically to reflect on their experiences, discuss how they are doing and what has gone well.

Researchers B. Charlier (2005), L. Lafortune (2006), L. Prud'homme et al. (2011), M. Miehakanda (2014), L. Lafontaine (2016) also propose applying action research in the training of prospective teachers who have chosen to study pedagogy. This way of working allows for reflection and social networking, for going back and reflecting, and at the same time for deepening one's knowledge. With a deep capacity for reflection, teachers will have deeper insights into their daily practice and will make more reasoned, informed decisions. Such research combines academic research, reflective practice, educational innovation and teacher education (Cain & Harris, 2013). However, researchers A. C. Wennergren (2016), J. Davis et al. (2018) state that for prospective teachers, performing action research in educational practice is a challenging and complex activity that requires a great deal of time and professional skill. Therefore, school communities themselves should be involved in performing action research in the classroom, especially when the aim is to improve pupil learning (Dimmock, 2016; Johannesson, 2020). Teachers should have a good understanding of the conceptual foundations of pupil learning. It is recommended that teachers have a colleague in the school with whom they can engage in deep critical reflection and discussion about classroom activities. In this case, both educators can expect professional pedagogical growth if they not only consult, but also try out new practices that they reflect on (according to Wennergren, 2016). Otherwise, teachers tend to opt for a comfortable status quo, which does not lead to a qualitative change in the educational process. But if teachers spend too much time reflecting, then planning and quality of activities can also suffer (according to Johannesson, 2020), along with changes in the assessment system, where criteria are focused on improving each pupil's performance rather than their ranking (Rey, 2012; Rey & Feyfant, 2014; Béduchaud, 2021). N. Clerc & M. Agogué (2019) point out that teacher training in the university must enable teachers to know themselves and to define their relationship to the process of teaching another. Only after doing this can, they learn to take responsibility for teaching others and for planning and implementing different educational situations. It is also important to realise that the attitudes of prospective teachers may not coincide with the state's priorities or expectations of teachers' roles. All of this can be done if prospective teachers learn to reflect on their practice and ask questions (Agogué & Clerc, 2016a; 2016b). Indeed, the issue of improving the educational process is a complex one, with many interconnected factors that make it difficult to strike a balance that leads the community towards improvement. Moreover, if teachers do not have strong critical thinking abilities, action research can turn into mere evidence-based practice, but that will not help solve problems. This would undermine the concept of action research (Rey, 2012; Rey & Feyfant, 2014; Béduchaud, 2021). In fact, teacher communities should not only organise the educational process in the classroom, but also meet systematically (at least once every two weeks) to discuss action research experiences and examples. In fact, pedagogical work is based on questioning, constant inquiry, and the search for meaning and answers (Clerc & Agogué, 2019). It is important for every teacher to develop these abilities.

Action research-based education is intrinsically linked to the active engagement/participation of pupils (see Figure 1.1.2). Such education has the following characteristics: 1) pupils are active participants rather than passive listeners; 2) there is a focus on developing/improving abilities rather than transferring knowledge or merely listening to information; 3) pupils are involved in a wide range of activities; 4) pupils learn to reflect on how they learn (according to Ys & Mara, 2011).

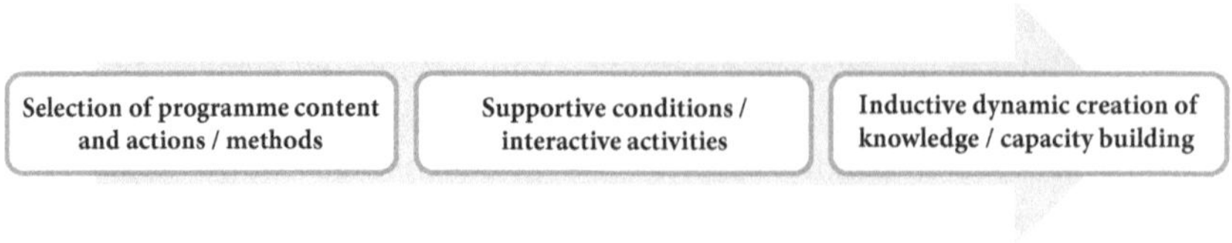

Figure 1.1.2: Diagram of action research-based education

L. Lafontaine (2016) highlights that primary school teachers are eager to collaborate with researchers because teachers want to update their pedagogical practices and are willing to support primary school pupils and organise activities based on children's individual needs (Cain & Harris, 2013). Teachers look for ways to accommodate pupils from disadvantaged socio-economic backgrounds, but often doubt their own ability to find such ways, so they willingly collaborate with researchers. The search is not only for ways to develop academic abilities, but also to stimulate and support pupils' motivation. In fact, the elements outlined in the action research-based learning scheme are emphasised by most researchers (Gauthier, 2010; Riente, 2010; Lafontaine, 2016). Before performing a complex task and/or activity, the educator needs to think about the three stages of the learning and assessment activity: *preparation, implementation and integration*. In the preparation stage, a scenario is presented, outlining how, what and why learning will take place. All this allows pupils to activate their prior knowledge of the topic and their subject-area knowledge by reflecting on the objectives of the proposed activity, indicating the expected outcome/result and the provided instructions for implementation. The implementation stage is more oriented towards the learning activity, with the active participation of the pupils in relation to the learning and assessment objectives. Support is provided in this stage, by the teacher or by the pupils. In addition, feedback is given during this stage and one or more interim assessments may be carried out after each learning activity. These assessments provide an indication of how well the child is progressing towards the intended outcome. The integration stage provides activities that allow pupils to synthesise their learning and show the final result, which should also be evaluated. Time to celebrate and reflect on the activities completed by the pupils and to analyse all stages of the activity is very important in this stage. It is useful for the researcher and the teacher to be involved in the action research (Lafontaine, 2016), discussions can take many forms – classroom observation, analysis of video recordings of pupils' activities, online consultations with teachers. Action/activity is the key element, the link among research, teaching and learning. During the activity, there is interaction among teacher/pupils/researcher. Of course, the educator can play two roles at the same time: both teacher and researcher. The teaching component and the data gathered through learning allow research to inform and improve educational practice. Researcher L. Lafontaine (2016) points out that during professional development events, educators should reflect on their own practice, analyse and discuss what is going well, and look for ways of overcoming what is causing problems. Indeed, such activities, where participants reflect on their practice, adopt and experiment with new ways of working in their classrooms, bring lasting change. For this to happen, the training should last long enough, and educators should meet systematically to reflect on their experiences, discuss how they are doing and what has gone well. Researchers B. Charlier (2005), L. Lafortune (2006), L. Prud'homme et al. (2011), M. Miehakanda (2014), L. Lafontaine (2016) also propose applying action research in the training of prospective teachers who have chosen to study pedagogy. This way of working allows for reflection and social networking, for going back and reflecting, and at the same time for deepening one's knowledge. With a deep capacity for reflection, teachers will have deeper insights into their daily practice and will make more reasoned, informed decisions. Such research combines academic research, reflective practice, educational innovation and teacher education. M. Toullec-Théry (2007) also points out that by reflecting on one's own experience, a teacher can also reflect on activities or educational processes that are not going well, i.e. to identify operational problems that prevent the achievement of higher results.

In summary, it can be said that action research allows teachers to explore and solve problems in an area of education in which they feel less advanced, in which they may know fewer methods to learn properly, and that action research naturally leads teachers to more in-depth study of these areas, to self-improvement, to greater initiative and more interest, and to attendance of professional development training courses (Soucy, Dumais & Moreau, 2020). For all these comprehensive reasons, the teachers themselves improve more, but at the same time the pupils learn more and pay closer attention, leading to more positive results for both the teachers and the pupils.

1.2. Issues that action research in the classroom/school could help address

L. Lafontaine (2016) and E. Soucy, Ch. Dumais & A. C. Moreau (2020) state that action research can be used to develop any general literacy skill. The researcher defines literacy as a general skill that enables everyone to explore the world around them, to communicate, to learn and to perform simple calculations. This is the understanding of the many forms of literacy needed to successfully navigate today's economic world. Primary school is focused on abilities such as reading, writing, speaking, arithmetic, learning about history and nature, music or drawing. It is the link between the learners' general abilities and language and the cultural environment. However, the development of literacy abilities goes beyond general abilities when it comes to reading and writing, which require a number of specific abilities related to analysis, interpretation and assessment, the recognition and understanding of attitudes, values, and writing culture. This concept thus illustrates how a person understands and conveys simple or complex information in different communication situations, both oral and written, in a variety of print and non-print media. In addition, action research is very useful and applicable when children live in environments that are not favourable to quality education, because such educational institutions have the highest proportion of children who need support in learning to read (Brodeur et al., 2011; Lafontaine, 2016; Soucy, Dumais & Moreau, 2020), to do arithmetic, and to explore the surrounding world. For example, the number of hours devoted to reading to children in the home in the socio-economic average/in favourable conditions before they start to attend school has been calculated. It was found that children from favourable backgrounds received between 1,000 and 1,700 hours of reading attention before the first class, while children from disadvantaged socio-economic backgrounds received only 25 hours of reading attention in the entire time spent at home before starting to attend school. A family's focus on the child and the attitude to reading is linked to the child's future ability to read (Brodeur et al., 2011; Lafontaine, 2016). Adult-child interaction during reading is also positively related to reading achievement in primary school. It is therefore important to provide appropriate learning environments to help children overcome difficulties, especially those from disadvantaged backgrounds. Action research-based educational situations/activities are most beneficial to children from at-risk families (Dion et al., 2010; Lafontaine, 2016; Soucy, Dumais & Moreau, 2020).

The question of accuracy in the methodology of action research in education. For data to be objective, they should be collected in accordance with a rigorous methodology (Lafontaine, 2016). Data collection includes video recordings, audio recordings, participant instructions, activity reports, pupils' work, reflection sheets, semi-structured interviews, group interviews, survey questionnaires, activity sheets, observation charts/protocols, etc. These different formats ensure the following of the triangulation principle and the transparency and accuracy of the research. Methods such as activity sheets, interviews, observation protocols, questionnaires, analysis of video and audio recordings can constitute triangulation. It is important that different methods are chosen. This can provide different levels of analysis in the research (Dolbec & Clément, 2000; Prud'homme & Guay, 2011; Miskovic, Efron & Ravid, 2012; Lafontaine, 2016). In summary, it can be said that the organisation of action research needs to take into account three aspects:

the educational methodology (how will learning take place, what actions will be performed?), the *innovation methodology* (what will be changed and how, what will be the pedagogical control/supervision?) and the application *of scientific principles* (the educational activities of pupils should be based on scientific knowledge). An action research project, involving teaching that combines theory and practice and the school environment in which the research will be performed, is the most appropriate way to implement change in educational practice.

For an educator to be able to perform action research, he or she should be competent in designing the content of learning activities. Researchers define pedagogical competence as the *ability to mobilise appropriate resources to successfully address a problematic situation* (Le Boterf, 2010; Roegiers, 2011; Rey, 2014; Kiffer, 2016), Such competence has the following components: the ability to identify problems and problematic situations, the ability to identify the appropriate resources to be used, the ability to apply such resources to a given situation, and the ability to ensure the successful resolution of the situation (Kiffer, 2016). The researcher found that young teachers tend to use combinations of several models in pursuit of educational goals and pupil learning. The dominant combinations are the following: observation/simulation – collaboration – independent learning; community of practice – collaboration – self-learning; observation/simulation – community of practice – independent learning. Not all educational practices are equally successful in developing pupils' abilities. The issue of the teacher's mastery is highlighted by V. Grosstephan (2015) & E. Maleyrot (2013, 2015), linking the quality of the educational process in action research with the master's degree. M. N. Schurmans (2009) & V. Grosstephan (2015) highlight another important role of the teacher in performing action research, i.e. epistemological knowledge of the field, the teacher's understanding of the role of the teacher as a researcher in a classroom of learners. Since action research takes place through one's experiential participation in social interactions, there is a need to be knowledgeable about the epistemic aspects that one wants to convey to pupils. This means that, regardless of the object of the research and the methodological approaches, the research is influenced by the teacher's attitude; the teacher both organises and participates in the research. The teacher's competence, mastery and in-depth knowledge of the problem being analysed are therefore essential.

In summary, it can be said that action research is defined as a methodology focused on solving a specific problem arising from a specific situation (Mayer et al., 2000; Prud'homme, 2007; Fortin, 2010; Guay & Prud'homme, 2011; Soucy, Dumais & Moreau, 2020). Action research brings together theory and practice, which are too often separated. In addition, when educators themselves explore theories more deeply, they are able to apply the theories more effectively in educational situations to bring about positive change. In this way, theory adds to practice, and vice versa – practice adds to theory (Mayer et al., 2000), and such situations allow a wide range of issues to be addressed, the root causes to be discovered, and knowledge to be created through the active participation of all those involved in the educational process. Theory becomes the backbone of practice, to understand and find the best solutions in a given situation. Educational practice based on action research provides a basis for using concrete evidence to organise the educational process and to take into account the needs and context of the pupils in a particular classroom. Research abilities are developed by educators, who through these experiences become even better educators who know their profession better and can not only make the right decisions, but also base such decisions on concrete data.

1.3. Instruments for implementing educational practices based on action research

It is important that everyone involved in the research has clear roles and tools assigned to them, and that they know the direction of the action. All this should be organised by the teacher. If action research is a whole-school objective, then all teachers and administrators should be involved in the planning and implementation of such action. Working in smaller groups, it is important to have a clear discussion of the pathway, the tools and the problem area, and to pool knowledge on certain key issues, such as the concept of general or subject-specific literacy.

In the pre-implementation stage of action research, it is necessary to reflect on one's own knowledge in a given field. Table 1.3.1 presents a sample questionnaire for teachers planning to perform action research (according to Lafontaine, 2016).

Table 1.3.1: Preparatory questionnaire to prepare for performing action research in the area of literacy

1. How would you define literacy practice?	*What I do...* *What I need...*
2. What are some of the potential barriers to literacy development in your community?	*What I know...* *What I need...*
3. How can we put pupils' literacy to use?	*What I know...* *What I need...*
4. What could be the positive contribution of parents to the development of pupils' reading abilities?	*What I know...* *What I need...*
5. What do learning and assessment situations in literacy mean to you? Which of your activities could you present as representative in the field of educational assessment?	*What I know...* *What I need...*

The responses of the action research participants to the questions in Table 1.3.1 are relevant for highlighting and discussing the strengths of the teaching team and for analysing the areas in need of support. In planning activities, it is necessary to take into account the areas where support is needed, and to provide support in these areas, it is possible to organise seminars or consultations for teachers to answer questions, to prepare certain techniques for presenting to pupils, to try out educational methods, etc. The planning also needs to consider how the action research data will be collected. It is also important to discuss and agree on the order in which activities will be implemented, how often the research participants will meet, etc. C. Dumais & G. Messier (2016) proposed an integrated model of verbal activities that would be suitable for the analysis of any subject. The stages of this model are shown in Table 1.3.2.

Table 1.3.2: A model of verbal activities to be used in action research

Activity stages	**Explanation**
1. Moment of stimulus/arousal of interest	At the beginning of the verbal activity, the subject to be worked on is introduced using questions and/or an example of the subject, without naming the subject itself.
2. Knowledge level	Knowledge is linked to the questions and the content of the pupils' answers, which are used to determine the weaknesses and strengths of the pupils' knowledge of the subject under analysis. The objective of the verbal activity is then decided.
3. Teaching	After the knowledge assessment, teaching is based on the pupils' answers. The subject is therefore taught and deconstructed in such a way that pupils have a good understanding of it and know how it is used in different contexts. The teacher models the subject and together with the pupils can create a frame of reference: what, how, why they will analyse, what problematic situations they will resolve.
4. Practical application	To promote learning and abilities development, pupils put their knowledge of the subject into practice. Learning can be done in small groups or as a whole class (e.g. by differentiating the content of activities).
5. Summarising the activity with the whole class	After each practice session, it is necessary to provide feedback to the whole class, as well as to summarise, to ensure that pupils have a good understanding of the topic and are able to communicate it themselves.
6. Metacognitive activity	Finally, one or more metacognitive tasks (written reflections, concept map, answers to written questions, etc.) are offered, in order to consolidate pupils' learning.

The flow of activities presented in Table 1.3.2 is appropriate as a framework for action research. In addition to the practical implementation of the teaching/learning process, the sequence also allows for the analysis of the verbal activities and the content of the tasks performed by the pupils. Oral comprehension is essential for learning any content. In order to ensure that the verbal content is understood as well as possible, it is important to develop listening abilities in an integrated way. Therefore, researchers (Dumais & Messier, 2016; Lafontaine, Dumais, & Pharand, 2016) recommend that pupils should be given opportunities to listen to a variety of works, to analyse documentaries, to contextualise (e.g. learning to prepare for a listening activity and to listen to the material even without the task, to discuss initial perceptions and then to listen again with the task), and to listen to each other in a targeted way, to formulate questions to their classmates, and to express affirmation, courteous disagreement, and interest. It is important to teach analysis by doing certain tasks after listening to a work, writing observations, formulating questions, etc. (Lafontaine, 2011; Lafontaine, Dumais & Pharand, 2016).

The process described in Table 1.3.3 is suitable for analysing the content of any subject within an action research framework. It is important to emphasise the in-depth development of teacher competences, which is anticipated in stages 3.3–3.4. Teachers not only become familiar with the changed didactic material, but also learn to create it themselves, collecting folders of work which are then developed in their work with pupils. Another very important point is that all activities are analysed and developed together with the pupils, in consultation with them, both on the outcome of the activity and on the process, public speaking situations, etc. Things to think about in the preparation stage are shown in Table 1.3.4.

When planning action research-based education, it is important to find out about the experiences of educators, to collect data on such experiences, and to reflect on the necessary tools and how to obtain them. In addition, it is important to consider how teachers themselves will collect data on changes in practice. L. Lafontaine (2016) presents a written questionnaire (Table 1.3.5) on literacy perceptions, reading and oral activity components. This questionnaire can be answered multiple times at key points in the research. It is then possible to see the change in educators' practices and opinions, to analyse the change in theoretical thinking and educational practice and to compare them.

Table 1.3.3: Didactic stages of the spoken language development cycle, where a problem in any subject is resolved

Stage 1: Communicative intent Discuss/explore what aspects of the subject might be of most interest to the children, justify their choice and create a collective set of pupils' preferences on the Didapage platform/mind map (a computer application that allows the creation of multimedia and interactive content).
Stage 2: Communicative situation – Integration of language abilities into any subject content: oral and written; – Meaningful subject: implementation of activity based on a programme that children like (TikTok activities or Minecraft, perhaps film editing in a final work); – Taking into account the interests of the pupils by agreeing on public or team speaking, viewing and listening to a product created by the children based on ICT; – Taking into account the audience: whether it will be peer and/or teacher assessment.
Stage 3: Planned speaking activity **Preparing for a speaking activity** – Setting situational criteria; – Stage 3.1: development of initial production; – Stage 3.2: the state of pupils' knowledge and abilities after viewing the initial works and selecting the subjects to be orally presented and assessed; – Presentation of the intended production (final output matching the communicative intent).
Realisation of speaking activity – Stage 3.3: practical implementation of the teacher workshops (presenting Stages 1–3.2 to teachers with didactic activities). – Justification for why pupils need speaking practice; – Listening techniques training workshop for listening to voice recording (without video material); – Workshop on language learning: communicating information by voice/orally; – General rehearsal: feedback in a large group at the end of the workshops, and links to the intended product (final work). – Stage 3.4 (a): formative assessment during workshops (teachers' portfolio of activities, worksheets, sample assignments, audio and video recordings, concept map, reflection sheets). – Stage 3.4 (b): the final output is assessed using an assessment grid based on the content of the subjects and the assessment system for learning/use of the Lithuanian language (according to *General Curriculum*, 2022).
Stage 4: Impact on the learner, enabling oral communication **Spoken language integration stage** – Assessment of pupils' performance by viewing the finished work; – Feedback on the final output: peer assessment, teacher assessment and feedback; – Discussion of challenges for future oral productions and selection of aspects to be improved; – Announcement of expected/final product.

Table 1.3.4: Example agenda for a preparatory meeting

Preparatory meeting................................. (date)
Area of preparation for action research
1. Presentation of the content of Teachers Workshop 2: reaction to the questionnaire data, follow-up, teachers' comments
2. Workshop 3: content and organisation
3. Organisation of Workshop 4: proposed speaker XXXX, preparation, materials, teachers' requests, reflection on activities.
4. Purchase of educational aids for the action research: follow-up
Area of activity
5. Workshop 3: discussion of teaching and assessment criteria, work on the integration stage and presentation to teachers
6. Essential complex problem-solving tasks for literacy development, analysis of 3–4 examples of tasks
Research area
7. Revisiting the XXXX meeting report, identifying key areas for improvement
8. Confirmation of researchers' functions: the role of each, timetable
9. Data collection: transcription of questionnaire and one group interview
10. Data analysis: content analysis using NVivo software
11. Follow-up actions after initial data analysis and presentation at the .... monthly meeting
Miscellaneous issues
Data registration in Dropbox
Date of next meeting, key content issues

Table 1.3.5: Written questionnaire on teachers' perceptions of literacy in the broad sense (reading and oral activities)

Literacy/reading area, written questionnaire .... (date)	**Oral activity area, written questionnaire .... (date)**
What do you think literacy is? Describe.	What do you think literacy is? Describe.
How do you think reading is integrated into the concept of literacy?	How do you think oral activity is integrated into the concept of literacy?
How do you think we can develop literacy through reading? And how do you do this in the classroom where you work?	How do you think we can improve pupils' oral literacy in your classroom?
What do you think is the learning and assessment situation in your classroom in the area of reading? Do you make links between these areas? How do you do this?	What do you think is the learning and assessment situation in your classroom in oral activity? Do you make links between these areas? How do you do this?

Semi-structured group interviews (see Table 1.3.6) can be filmed and conducted several times in different meetings. This approach to group interviews allows researchers:

to check participants' understanding of the concept of literacy reading and oral activity components and of the educational tool related to pupils' learning and assessment of their achievement; to check the support provided;

to gather new information on the pedagogical impact on literacy (reading and oral activity) from observation protocols of educational activities and examples of practical activities (children's work). Each participant in the research should be given a number that guarantees anonymity. Examples of group interview questions are given in Table 1.3.6.

Table 1.3.6: Group interview matrix

Literacy/reading area, ... (date)	**Area of oral activity, ... (date)**
1. What is your opinion on literacy after workshop/meeting 1? 2. Can you explain, after Workshop 1, how children should be taught to read, so that this area is included in the concept of literacy? 3. After Workshop 1, do you have any incentive to work in the classroom to develop pupils' reading literacy? What motivates you to do this? 4. After Workshop 1, how do you understand the situation of learning to read and assessment, when support is provided? 5. Do the workshop activities and content help you to better understand the concepts of literacy and learning and assessment, when support is provided? How? What? Why?	1. What is your perception of literacy in the area of oral activity after Workshop 5? Has it changed since Workshop 1? 2. Based on the material from Workshop 5, can you explain how oral activity can be integrated into the concept of literacy? 3. From Workshop 5, do you have any knowledge of literacy related to pupils' oral activity in the classroom? What motivates you to do this? 4. After Workshop 5, how do you understand the situation of teaching and assessing oral activity, when support is provided? 5. Have you changed the practice of teaching reading and speaking/oral activity in the time between Workshop 1 and Workshop 5? How? What? Why did you change?

When conducting action research, it is recommended that teachers keep individual and group journals to record specific observations about pupils' learning, assessment and the support provided. The individual journal is kept to support each teacher's positive observations during the research and to note problematic issues. The group journal should be completed at the end of each academic year in which the action research is performed, so that the teachers in each team can summarise their observations in order to better reflect on changes in performance and practice and to discuss them in the semi-structured interviews (see Table 1.3.7).

Table 1.3.7: Example of a teacher's individual journal

Action research stage	☐ Strategic/preparatory stage ☐ Formation/development stage ☐ Synthesis/integration stage
Name of activity:	
Pupils' response to the task and activity (emotional, cognitive, interpersonal, behavioural) Positive observations, difficulties, what needs to be changed, other	
* Keep the same journal for every activity and learning and assessment situation, where support is provided	

An individual journal can be kept to explore each teacher's positive observations during the research and to note problematic issues. A group journal can be completed at the end of the school year (during the workshops) to allow teachers in each team to summarise their observations, to reflect on changes in activities and practices, and to discuss them in semi-structured interviews (see Table 1.3.8).

Table 1.3.8: Example of a group journal

Preparatory stage: situation analysis **What? Why? When?**
Recall of prior knowledge (declarative/basic, conditional, procedural) • Activate pupils' prior knowledge related to learning and assessment on a given subject and their intention to read.
Taking into account my experience with the preparatory stage, I summarise my observations:
What I know about professional practice and the environment:
What I would do differently next time if applicable:
Realisation stage: learning experience How? Agenda changes
Taking into account my experience with the realisation stage, I summarise my observations:
What I found out/learned about professional practice and the environment:
What I would do differently next time if applicable:

Synthesis/integration stage: communication When? Agenda changes
Taking into account my experience with the synthesis/integration stage, I summarise my observations:
What I found out/learned about professional practice and the environment:
What I would do differently next time if applicable:

Individual semi-structured interviews should be conducted and recorded after 4 and 8 meetings and at the end of each project year, to understand the impact of the education system on literacy and the adaptation of the learning and assessment system, and to discuss updated teaching practices (see Table 1.3.9). Each participant has the same number as during the group interview to ensure anonymity and to track the evolution of the research participant's answers.

Table 1.3.9: Example of a semi-structured interview

Literacy/reading area, ... (date)	Area of oral activity, ... (date)
Area 1. Definition of the reading literacy component 1. What is your concept of reading literacy? 2. Do you feel satisfied with this idea? Explain how you are developing it. 3. How has your attitude and understanding of the concept of reading literacy changed/improved since the training?	**Area 1. Definition of the oral activity/speaking literacy component** 1. What is your concept of speaking literacy? 2. Do you feel satisfied with this idea? Explain how you are developing it. 3. How has your attitude and understanding of the concept of speaking literacy changed/improved since the training?
Area 2. Adapting the concept of learning and assessment to develop reading literacy 1. What is your concept of learning and assessment in the area of reading literacy? 2. Can you describe the overall impact of learning and assessment on reading? 3. Can you describe how you have been learning to put a learning and assessment system into practice? What tools have you used? How did you choose them? 4. Do you feel comfortable using this/these tool(s)? 5. How did the training help you to better understand this/these tool(s)?	**Area 2. Adapting the concept of learning and assessment to develop oral activity/speaking literacy** 1. What is your concept of learning and assessment in the area of speaking literacy? 2. Can you describe the overall impact of learning and assessment on speaking? 3. Can you describe how you have been learning to put a learning and assessment system into practice? What tools have you used? How did you choose them? 4. Do you feel comfortable using this/these tool(s)? 5. How did the training help you to better understand this/these tool(s)?

(Continued)

Table 1.3.9: (Continued)

Literacy/reading area, ... (date)	**Area of oral activity, ... (date)**
Area 3. Updating literacy teaching practices. READING 1. How are your pupils exceptional/excellent in the area of reading literacy? 2. Have you noticed from the beginning any significant abilities among pupils in the area of reading? In the area of learning support and assessment methods? Where did you see this? 3. What have you changed in your teaching practice in the area of reading since participating in the workshop? 4. Are these changes positive or negative? Explain why. 5. How do you now integrate reading literacy into everyday classroom practice?	**Area 3. Updating literacy teaching practices. SPEAKING** 1. Did the workshop encourage you to teach differently in the area of speaking? What? Have you put this into practice? In the classroom? How? Why? 2. What makes your pupils different in the area of speaking literacy? 3. Have you noticed from the beginning any significant abilities among pupils in the area of speaking? In the area of learning support and assessment methods? Where did you see this? 4. What have you changed in your teaching practice in the area of speaking since participating in the workshop? 5. Are these changes positive or negative? Explain why. 6. How do you now integrate oral activity/speaking literacy into everyday classroom practice? 7. What will you be doing next year in the areas of development of reading and speaking literacy? Do you have anything to add?

Research-action-teaching: the action/activity component. This component of the action relates to teachers' design of learning support and assessment, and their design during the workshop to modify/improve classroom activities. During the research, teachers formed inter-school teams of four or five members. Each workshop included design group/team activities to discuss how/in what ways learning support and assessment would be delivered when experimenting in thc areas of reading and speaking. The researchers were part of the core design team because they could answer a wide range of questions from the teachers and explain in a reasoned way why the activities should be organised in one way or another. This provided support to the workshop participants, analysing various problem-solving situations and highlighting certain aspects. This prepared the way for the changes in classroom activities (meeting 1), then a test run for the next month or even several months; and at the end of the semester, an analysis and self-evaluation of activities. Teachers performed practical tasks that were validated from a theoretical point of view. Six months later, the researchers met the teachers in the schools. Teachers appreciated this very much, because they could directly show the environments, the techniques used, ask questions and get useful advice. This supported the social-cognitive aspects, which are very important for changing particular practices. According to L. Prud'homme, A. Dolbec & M.-H. Guay (2011), research-action-teaching supports the researcher and the team by increasing reflective activity, all of which helps to make sense of the teaching experience.

Another very important component of action research is the change in classroom activities of the teacher and his/her pupils. This includes the development of new educational materials, a learning support system, and a system of self-evaluation and assessment. This encourages teachers to act, to rethink the importance of learning support and assessment, to deepen their understanding of literacy and the development of its elements in their daily practice.

Research-action-teaching: the teaching component. The teaching component allows for teacher development in a pedagogical situation and encourages reflection on educational practice and on what may be causing the problem(s) (Prud'homme & Guay, 2011; Lafontaine, 2016; Miskovic, Efron & Ravid, 2012). The change in educational practice took place in the following stages: theoretical presentation of the concept, knowledge transfer activities (modelling, practising, exercises, sharing of materials, etc.), clarification in a large group, teamwork in the development of a system of learning support and self-evaluation with integrated literacy activities. The reading literacy workshops led to the following concepts and their definitions: literacy, basic reading abilities, development of phonological and phonemic awareness among pupils, systematic teaching, explicit reading activities and reading strategies (decoding and graphophonic input), the development of a three-level model of intervention and the interrelationships between each level (Haager, Klingner & Vaughn, 2007), development and use of an orthopaedic pedagogical intervention model for reading, a learning planning tool including learning support and self-evaluation (content and strategic templates for reading). The content of the oral component of the workshop was related to phonological awareness, teaching clear strategies for speaking and listening, pragmatic/practical oral activities/tasks (Maurer, 2001; Dumais, 2011), a clear checklist for expressing thoughts orally (Lafontaine, 2006, 2016), and projects for listening and speaking activities.

After the discussions, during the workshops, teachers saw the need for more ways to support pupils, especially those with weak reading and speaking abilities. For example, if a pupil has an undeveloped spoken language ability and a poor vocabulary, he/she should get help from the teacher and prepare himself/herself with individual counselling before a performance/oral presentation to classmates. Indeed, at all stages of learning, there has been considerable investment in the design/development of learning support and assessment systems.

Advantages and limitations of action research. Action research is particularly relevant for a specific classroom, for specific pupils, because the educational content, the learning support and the self-evaluation system are tailored to them. In addition, such activities can continue over a long period of time until certain competences are developed. At the same time, the educator's understanding of the problem is deepened as he or she continuously collects data, reflects on activities and makes informed decisions. This means that the educator improves in the field of the problem being analysed. In addition, during the joint meetings, the research participants not only share their own experiences, but also hear about the experiences of their colleagues and their solutions. The whole community improves as a result. Working with data in this way influences changes in practice (Lafontaine, 2006, 2016; Miskovic, Efron & Ravid, 2012). When school and university teams work together, change is not just seen in one class of children, but in the whole community. Teachers see that they need to acquire additional competences in some areas in order to be able to successfully change the educational practice in a given classroom, i.e. developing new teaching materials, adopting teaching support techniques, different strategies and exposing pupils to those strategies, updating the self-evaluation and assessment system, re-designing it in light of materials and the system of support techniques. In addition to putting this into practice, educators also share the results of their work with researchers in workshops and develop tools based on scientific evidence. Limitations are seen if action research is desired without training workshops. The desired result may not be achieved because everyone will remain within their own knowledge, which may not necessarily be correct. Another limitation is if only theory is given, without practical examples or instruments.

In summary, it can be said that action research is characterised by both a flexible and a sophisticated methodological design, which allows for the collection of a large amount of data on actual pedagogical practices and classroom activities. This type of research has a high social relevance and significance, because activities are tailored to the needs of a specific group of pupils. Action research shows that the researcher is an actor in organisational development and social intervention, influencing the educational process and outcomes and empowering pupils to act autonomously.

1.4. Modelling action research

There are many different models of action research. D. Macaire (2007) stresses that two aspects can be taken into account when modelling action research, namely:

- the structural components of the data collection protocol and the implementation of the intervention (educational change);
- replication/duplication of the action research, i.e. describing the process of the action research in sufficient detail to be used by other researchers or teacher-practitioners wishing to perform the same action research in their own environment.

Action research is a qualitative rather than a quantitative approach. It uses tools to investigate direct educational practice (Soucy, 2019; Soucy, Dumais & Moreau, 2020). In many cases, semi-structured interviews and observation of participants in the educational process are chosen. It is useful to observe and analyse educational practice when the activity is filmed, and then it is possible to work with videos, photographs, pupils' work, drawings, etc. However, to be of research value, it must be based on a precise protocol that includes a variety of data collection tools and covers a clearly defined and manageable time period. Authentic situations are important, along with their detailed description (Dumais, 2015; Dumais & Lafontaine, 2011; Dumais & Messier, 2016).

One of the issues underlying deliberations on the value of action research is the question of its replicability/duplication. Do changes in performance and pupil learning remain stable over time? How can we ensure that changes are sustainable? Can we teach pupils performance strategies, attentiveness, etc.? attention to detail? Given the variety and specificity of the situations and contexts encountered, and especially given that we are dealing with people, it is realistic to ask whether the transfer of acquired knowledge, the action research project, is also possible in other teaching or learning situations. The added value of action research is seen when, at the end of the research, we see in the teachers' comments that they have objectively changed, if we compare with the way they thought at the beginning of the research (Dumais, 2015; Dumais & Lafontaine, 2011; Dumais & Messier, 2016; Macaire, 2007). The second indicator that teachers often talk about is the attitude towards certain theories: it has become clear to them, they are pleased…, they like… and wish…, they often take the whole practice more personally (reading, travelling, starting to work with a certain computer programme …) than professionally. The development of practices is usually based on concrete examples. Teachers are also aware of the values that underpin professional practice, their understanding of change, and the practical benefits. D. Macaire (2007) recognises the lack of clearly described methodologies for action research that can be applied to different practices and situations. The field of primary education is particularly suited to such research, given that primary school teachers, since they include all learners, must be particularly deep and responsible reflective practitioners. In addition, the teacher as researcher should also take responsibility for the epistemological and attitudinal formation area.

It is also useful to base innovative project activities on action research (Lacelle & Boultif, 2016). Projects can vary widely in content, depending on the context of the pupils, the teachers and the classroom context, the situations and the problems to be addressed. Project activities could include the targeted use of ICT abilities, ICT abilities development, the use of specific software. In addition, these activities include the need for meaningful collaboration opportunities with university researchers. Exposure to the latest research results, and joint work between university teachers and school teachers would help to meet the needs of teacher-practitioners and enrich them with deeper insights into what happens in the classroom. Putting innovative projects into practice is an effective way to increase teachers' theoretical knowledge and possibly motivate them to continue their research-based professional activities.

A proactive cycle of action research, consisting of two different models, has been developed by R. A. Schmuck (2006). Model 1 starts with the researcher's expectations rather than the problem itself, and immediately implements new or different classroom practices before collecting data (see Figure 1.4.1).

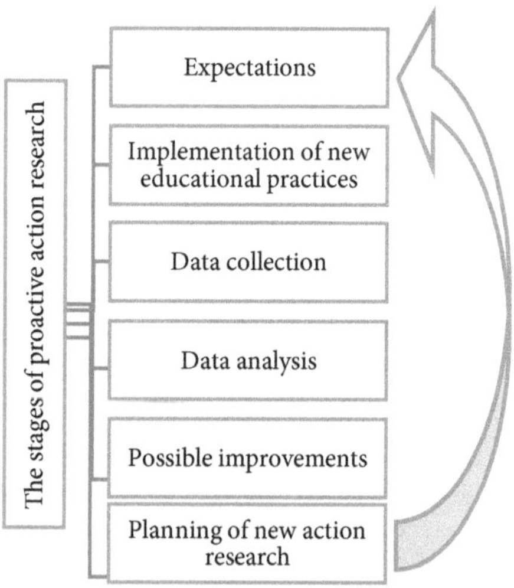

Figure 1.4.1: Stages of proactive action research

In Figure 1.4.1, we see that when planning a new action research, the researcher already associates it with new expectations. Expectations can be formulated in terms of questions that the action research will seek to answer. The questions can also be linked to the new activities and their performance indicators or attributes. The collection of data should be linked to the questions that have been asked in the expectations stage, because this will allow the data to substantiate the practices being implemented and to gather evidence on the elements of concern.

The difference between R. A. Schmuck's (2006) Model 2 and Model 1 is that the teacher-researcher collects and analyses data to find deeper reasons for the problematic situation, and then, after a change of activity, collects the data again and compares it with the previous data. The name of the model is related to this activity: the Responsive Action Research Model (see Figure 1.4.2).

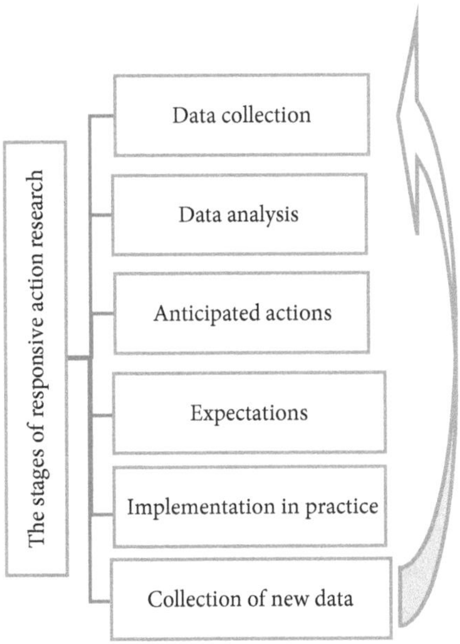

Figure 1.4.2: Stages of responsive action research

The directional arrow in the model in Figure 1.4.2 shows the data linkage and the need for deeper analysis using this model. This culture of thinking allows for deeper and different perspectives on a problematic situation. The increased focus on data collection and analysing a problematic situation is also reflected in the fact that it is only in Stage 5 of this model that the teacher implements a new activity in the classroom to try to solve the problem. This model is of interest to the practitioner-researcher because it assumes that he/she is constantly reflecting on his/her pupils' learning, which he/she seeks to improve by adjusting his/her own practice. However, this situation is also problematic, because the practice is implemented in a context of constant change, which often makes it impossible to pinpoint the causes and/or consequences of the problem (Soucy, Dumais & Moreau, 2020).

E. Soucy (2019), after analysing different models of action research, developed a hybrid action research model combining the insights of several researchers for his own action research (see Figure 1.4.3).

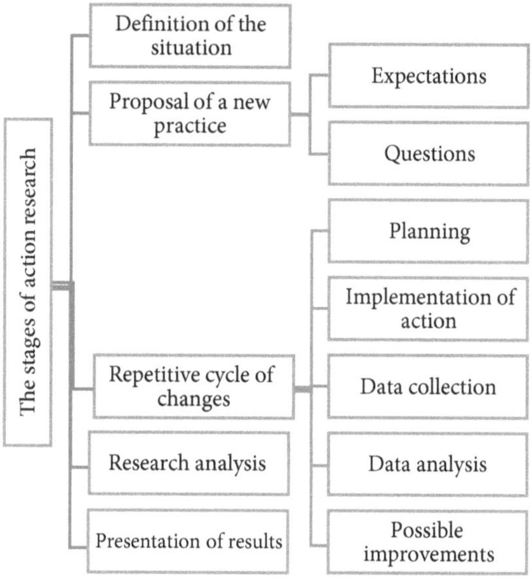

Figure 1.4.3: Hybrid model of action research

From the data shown in Figure 1.4.3, we can see that the first step is to define the situation in which the action research will be applied in the context of educational content. It is also important to reflect on the participants in the educational process and their experience in the field under analysis. It is then worth thinking about new innovative practices that incorporate the expectations and questions of the participants in the action research. The next stage consists of an iterative cycle of changes, including action planning, implementation, data collection, analysis and possible improvements. We have already discussed what practitioners can mark during the activity (implementation stage) in the sub-chapter of this book on *Instruments for implementing educational practices based on action research* (see Tables 1.3.1–1.3.9). Indeed, the instruments used to collect data can be very diverse, depending on the element of the practice to be changed and the attributes of the change to be monitored. The researcher can be involved in and observe the educational process as the new activity is developed. The improvement of the project can be discussed by both the researcher and the practitioner, based on an analysis of the results of the same activity that both have witnessed. To achieve the desired results, it is recommended to repeat this cycle several times until the pupils learn and understand the new methodology used. Finally, in the last stage of the model, it is proposed to disseminate the results of the activities, to share them with other educators and researchers and to publish the results in scientific journals.

Action research as an opportunity to provide students with individual support and to motivate them to learn a particular subject. Learning and teaching methods are important in this context, providing many opportunities for personalised support through differentiation of education, as well as levels of learning content, materials, timeframes and learning objectives, all of which can be used to adapt curriculum and conditions to meet the specific requirements and (learning) abilities of individual pupils (Roy, Guay & Valois, 2013; Knauder & Koschmieder, 2019). In addition, primary schools in particular – as schools for all children (UNESCO, 2021) – are encouraged to comply with these requirements, given the increasing heterogeneity of their pupils (e.g. due to the integration into schools of children with physical or mental disabilities, or those with an immigrant background). Individualised support is clearly considered to be a criterion for good teaching in contemporary educational practice (Knauder & Koschmieder, 2019). Acting in the educational process and thinking, practice and theory are linked in a continuous process of self-inquiry and transformation. Schools where the administration supports the efforts of individual teachers and genuinely values research have the opportunity to bring about school-wide change (Miskovic, Efron & Ravid, 2012). Action research is consistent with an approach to education as a means of realising the potential of each pupil to fulfil himself/herself. Educational practice promotes curiosity, care for others and the environment, perseverance and a willingness to learn: qualities that help people to lead happy and fulfilling lives. In this case, the curriculum is flexible to meet the interests and needs of each individual, and assessment helps to link learning to interests and needs (Cain & Harris, 2013; Kiffer, 2016). Moreover, research also shows that not all practices are effective (Kiffer, 2016).

In order to better provide personalised support in the classroom, two teacher characteristics are commonly discussed in the research literature: teachers' attitude towards the learning of every pupil, and teachers' beliefs about self-efficacy related to a personalised and differentiated teaching style (Kiely et al., 2015; Knauder & Koschmieder, 2019), when personalised support is provided. In addition, the research focuses on teachers' motivation and leadership in relation to innovation, as an individual characteristic (Hattie, 2009; Chapman et al., 2011; Helmke, 2012; Hargreaves, & Fullan, 2019; Fullan, 2019; Fullan et al., 2020). Teachers with an internal sense of motivation are more likely to provide targeted support to individual pupils in the classroom. Teachers' self-efficacy attitude and internal intention to provide support are the dominant factors that determine the specific behaviour or actual delivery of personalised support and lesson design (Knauder & Koschmieder, 2019). As one of the innovative activities enabling personalised activities, creative coding games in a Scratch environment can be used to develop children's computational thinking abilities, problem-solving strategies and abstract thinking (Panskyi, Rowinska & Biedron, 2019). Personalised activities, allowing both students and teachers to collaborate, are supported by the targeted use of tablets in the educational process (Al-Huneini, Walker & Badger, 2020). Activities in electronic formats that can lead to higher achievement among primary school pupils have been highlighted in action research by C. Raby et al. (2013) and S. Hubalovsky, M. Hubalovska & M. Musilek (2019). Action research-based activities in subject areas where a pupil or group of pupils have negative attitudes, e.g. reluctance to learn mathematics, help to meet pupils' basic psychological needs, and influence pupils' relationship with/attitudes towards the subject content (Samuelsson, 2021). If pupils are given the opportunity to make suggestions, express ideas, choose a method or make a proposal, they develop a more positive attitude towards the subject. The role of the teacher is very important when giving students the opportunity to make choices about the content, and the teacher should support and advise the student by explaining the content, the background, the key context, and the learning pathway (Samuelsson, 2021). If the teacher cultivates these elements, pupils develop the abilities of self-control and independent work. Positive attitudes towards the subject are an important predictor of academic success. To change pupils' attitudes towards mathematics, teachers focused more on individual, authentic support (based on the pupil's needs) and an authentic relationship with the pupil, and the environment created by this environment enabled pupils to change their attitudes towards the subject (Samuelsson, 2021). C. Eden & F. Ackermann (2018) presenting the action research cycle (see Figure 1.4.4).

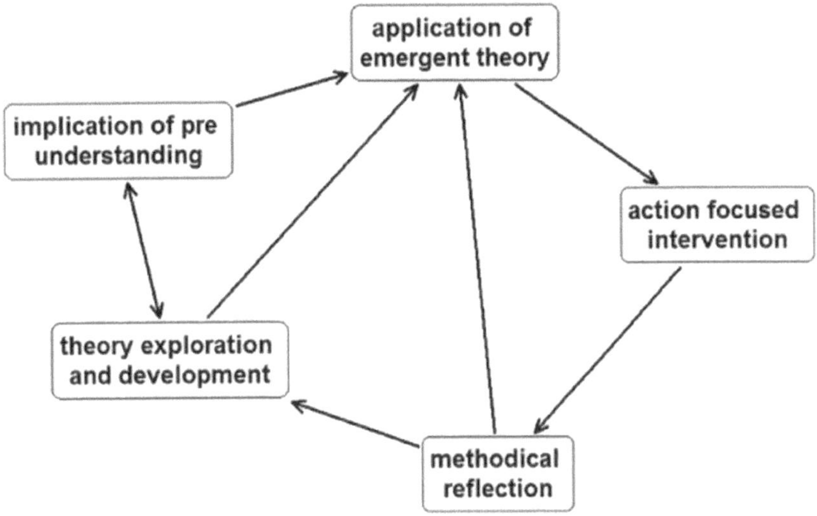

Figure 1.4.4: Action research cycle

C. Eden & F. Ackermann (2018) state that social discussion and the individual contribution of each learner or team member to solve the selected problems is important in addressing any problematic area highlighted during the action research. Reflection is an important aspect, once the activity has been performed. Integrated child development based on humanistic values, socialisation and support for pupils experiencing difficulties, and the tangible expression of the school culture are some of the school's tasks that are as important as cognitive knowledge (LeVasseur, 2012). Teachers may seek to reinforce a student's identity through a particular analysis of the chosen content, or they may choose to ignore the student's cultural identity and present the content in a neutral way. Nevertheless, it appears that science is to some extent leaving the realm of epistemology and entering the realm of morals and values that contribute to the construction of personal identity. The pupil should not only acquire a rational or scientific vision of the world, but also discuss world events in different contexts, analyse them from different perspectives and different points of view (LeVasseur, 2012).

Researchers who have performed action research on collaborative learning, where pupils work together to learn, include A. Toulia, V. Strogilos & E. Avramidis (2021). Teachers who participated in the research agreed that peer tutoring has a positive impact on the academic and social needs of pupils with special educational needs (Toulia, Strogilos & Avramidis, 2021; Duran et al., 2019; Cockerill, Craig & Thurston, 2018). During the action research, when pupils were tutoring their peers and preparing tasks for peers, it was important to allow high-ability pupils to create more complex activities, presenting them in a presentation or other interactive form (Toulia, Strogilos & Avramidis, 2021). This enhances the abilities and meets the needs of both learners.

In summary, it can be said that the modelling of action research can be very diverse, because it depends on the situation and on the experience, insights and decisions of the teacher-researcher, which particular situation he/she wants to change, and in which stages and through which elements it will be implemented. It is important that the teacher-researcher is willing to explore the problematic situation in more depth, from different perspectives, and is willing and able to gather as much data as possible, and to use it to draw appropriate conclusions and solutions, changing and improving educational practice.

1.5. The importance of reflection in action research

In educational practice, a learner/developing person is understood as an author or creator. A learner in the broadest sense is a person who thinks and creates. The essence of the quality of education is the capacity for reflection (both on process and on outcome) on the part of all those involved in the education process. This can only be achieved through the development of metacognitive abilities, which help to optimise experience, consisting of learners' knowledge and abilities, of the objects whose content has been learned, and to improve the quality of education and learners' achievement (Sagnier, 2013; Stalder, 2016, 2019). No problem can be solved without deep reflective abilities. In order to discuss any issue, we need to have basically answered for ourselves what is going well in this area, what I can do differently and how I can change things for the better and learn more. Some researchers regard deep reflective abilities (Macaire, 2007; Tardif, Borges & Malo, 2012; Morrissette & Charara, 2015; Stalder, 2016, 2019; Gohard-Radenkovic, 2017; Gohard-Radenkovic & Veillette, 2016; Blons-Pierre, 2016; Perez-Roux, 2017) as an essential pedagogical competence, which is also the basis for the development of pupils' reflective competence, an essential competence in action research (without the teacher's reflective abilities, it is impossible to develop pupils' abilities in this area). ***Continuous thinking before, during and after an activity creates the preconditions for achieving a high-quality result*** (Miskovic, Efron & Ravid, 2012). The teacher's ability to use the right learning strategies, at the right time, at the right pace, to support the pupil or group of pupils, is a prerequisite for achieving high-quality results. Educational didactics refer to the actions and decisions, including methodology, curriculum content, activity objectives and specific tasks, when designing the teaching/learning process for pupils in any field. The ultimate goal expected of a progressive educator is a daily educational practice imbued with a reflective approach based on theoretical foundations and methodological-strategic choices for the learner's learning. These reflective, action-oriented abilities are particularly important for identifying problematic areas in the educational process that can be adjusted on the basis of action research (Macaire, 2007; Jakavonytė-Staškuvienė, 2017).

In many cases, to create such practices, educators need mutual support, high-quality and constructive feedback, collegial communication and collaboration, where members of the school community can complement, advise and support each other, rather than compete. Colleagues can also provide the necessary support in the event of an unusual situation, where their professional experience can be helpful (European Commission, 2017). By the same token, a young, newly graduated teacher can also be helpful in the school community in certain areas, e.g. according to the European Commission (2017), only a quarter of children in European schools are taught by teachers who feel confident in their digital competences. Hence, providing mutual feedback and peer-to-peer guidance in a school's ever-learning and continually developing community is seen as one of the most essential and meaningful ways of learning. According to the European Commission (European Commission/EACEA/Eurydice, 2019), collegial feedback can take different forms: mentoring, working together to develop innovative practices in the school, mutual assessment (self-evaluation), and planned meetings with the head of the school to provide personal, social and professional support. Thus, learning among teachers with different pedagogical backgrounds and competences can take place in different forms and in different settings. High-quality, motivated and valued teachers are at the core of excellent education. Clearly defined competency levels and career structures enhance teachers' ability to self-evaluate their career prospects, and the opportunity to learn in an informal, supportive and motivating environment provides a favourable environment for long-term retention in the profession (European Commission, 2017; Jakavonytė-Staškuvienė & Ignatavičiūtė, 2022).

E. Maleyrot (2015) proposes focusing on the purpose or outcome of the reflection activity, which can be divided into seven categories of reflection purpose:

1. to think differently or more clearly, i.e. to develop new concepts and assessment procedures and criteria to bring clarity to the educational process;
2. to justify one's pedagogical orientation/position on the basis of evidence;
3. to reflect on actions or decisions on the basis of action analysis;
4. to change one's thinking by defining clear, evidence-based knowledge that can be "seen";

5. to perform or improve actions by clarifying, refining, redirecting or generally reformulating the course of action;
6. to improve pupils' learning by encouraging rich and meaningful activities;
7. to change one's activity or society through moral education of the individual and society.

Two aspects of this classification of reflection are worth noting. The first four categories focus on the internal aspects of pedagogical activity, while the last three focus on the external aspects of activity, which have an impact on society at large. The internal dimension of activity is linked to teachers' internal moral attitudes, including feelings, emotions, interests, attitudes and values. There is a difference between the expression of the first four categories, which are more oriented towards understanding, action and analysis, which are more concerned with the individual, and the expression of the last three categories, which are concerned with the movement beyond the self and into society. Mastering reflection requires not only the ability to detach and reflect, but also to link theoretical knowledge to practical activities. Reflective competence is presented as a skill or stance (Perrenoud, 2013), which the future or current teacher must gradually develop by learning to reflect on what he or she is actually doing and what he or she is mobilising by teaching others (Altet, 2013; Maleyrot, 2015). Therefore, a future teacher becomes a reflective practitioner only when he/she is able to organise processes such as action-reflection-return-to-action or practice-theory-practice cycles. A teacher who already has pedagogical experience is associated with mastery. The professionalism of the teacher's activity is changing, because it is no longer just a question of being a reflective practitioner, but even more so of being able to bring together knowledge from several different perspectives, i.e. practical experience, knowledge of the discipline (constant updating of subject knowledge) and knowledge of educational research, in order to be able to choose the best possible strategies in a given situation and to act as a competent professional. It is more important for the school leader to encourage the teacher to practise "critical analysis of his/her own performance" in order to improve teaching and consolidate his/her teaching abilities (Morrissette & Charara, 2015). The reflective stance is not constructed in the teacher's work, but presented as already existing, even when it might not yet be at a fully expert level. Pedagogical tools such as collective lesson/activity planning, where teachers can confer and discuss reflectively together (Morrissette & Charara, 2015); technical advice to develop pedagogical knowledge, as well as the development of teaching tools with a reflexive dimension (Altet, 2013, Maleyrot, 2015), help to develop reflective abilities. For example, French master's degrees in education are rich in integrated reflection activities. It is thought that such master-teacher training will lead to a return to the contextualisation of the knowledge taught and to the conceptualisation of the practices that give meaning to professional university teaching. Reflective mechanisms are one way of promoting this. However, it is recognised that these measures to promote the integration of different types of knowledge are quite costly and depend on a collegial culture which may not be widespread in universities (Pérez-Roux, 2013; Maleyrot, 2015), while reflection in a small group provides an opportunity to gain experience of the reflection process (Bourassa & Picard, 2014). However, the reflection process can also be ineffective if teachers are not prepared to take action in response to the issues raised, if the conditions for change are not met (Morrissette & Charara, 2015). Some prospective teachers, master's students, find it difficult to understand an open-minded approach, to embrace openness and uncertainty, to create an atmosphere of respect and mutual trust (Borges & Gervais, 2015). Moreover, some students do not attend classes and therefore cannot reflect objectively because they do not have a certain theoretical foundation. Participation in the classes of the final year of the master's degree seems to be a part of self-exploration, personal development and practice (Borges & Gervais, 2015). It is very important for teachers to self-evaluate their own experience and abilities before the activity, so that they are much more likely to achieve positive results without being disappointed. If the reflection exercise involves not only teachers but also university teachers, it is useful to find out at the first meeting what teachers' experiences, expectations and problematic situations are, for which they would like to receive help (Morrissette & Charara, 2015). It is likely that such a step would help to improve the quality of not only the planning, but also the implementation of the activities that teachers will reflect on. And the role of the university teacher in the reflection process can be seen as a safeguard to help develop the prospective teacher's capacity for discernment and critique (Borges & Gervais, 2015).

Principles of collegial work. It is best to start collaborating by working in pairs. There should also be no pattern of one colleague being the other's "teacher", i.e. the roles of one clearly weak and one clearly strong teacher. All team members should feel like equal partners. Positive interdependence and individual accountability are the basis for cooperation and a prerequisite for promoting engagement and participation among all members (Johnson et al., 2014; Johnson & Johnson, 2015; Slavin, 2014; Kazlauskienė & Gaučaitė, 2018). The reasons for collaboration must be clearly understood and identified by the collaborating team members. A common goal, formulated in the context of shared agreements (that each member understands, learns, meets a predetermined criterion, progresses), thus focuses on two key aspects: personal learning and partner/team member learning. The aspect/

criterion of positive interdependence can be useful in promoting collaboration between educators, but it needs to be done very carefully and deliberately. The school administration can also reinforce interdependence by using the tools at its disposal: allocating additional resources, assigning different/varied tasks, assigning additional roles. When individuals in a collaborative environment are aware of this positive interdependence, they are able to work towards team success. Interdependence emphasises the complementary nature of the work. When members perceive that they are positively interdependent, that one person's learning facilitates another's learning, they are more likely to embrace their responsibilities. The school leader helps to reinforce the individual sense of responsibility by organising activities in such a way that each team member's contribution is feasible and necessary to achieve the team's goal and that individual learning is visible (Hattie, 2009; Chapman et al., 2011; Helmke, 2012; Perez-Roux, 2017; Hargreaves & Fullan, 2019; Fullan, 2019; 2020; Fullan et al., 2020). Planning action research in an educational institution creates the conditions for building a school culture. Educators then have a dual responsibility: to strive to achieve the team's goal and to help their colleagues do the same. It is therefore important to focus on mutual and shared responsibility. The pedagogy of cooperative learning assumes that the members of the team (whoever they may be – two or more teachers, teachers and pupils) are able to trust each other sufficiently to be able to share responsibilities. Preparing for purposeful collaboration and teamwork requires careful planning of activities. In general, structuring cooperation not only promotes the quality of social relations, but also cognitive learning, too (Buchs, 2017). In addition, without deep experience in organising action research, a collaborative learning culture helps the whole school community of educators to learn new activities in a responsible way and to build on and share good practices. Individual teacher experience can be a source of new and useful knowledge (Miskovic, Efron & Ravid, 2012).

What are the necessary conditions for smooth pupil learning and for teachers to be able to perform collaborative action research? Cooperation cannot be imposed from the top down (Sahlberg, 2011; Søby, 2015; Education and Training, 2019). Shared leadership is a prerequisite for a collaborative educational institution (Supovitz & Christman, 2003; Mattatall & Power, 2014; Bryk, 2017; Jacq & Gibert, 2019). Responsibility should be shared among all teachers and administrators in the educational institution. Many studies emphasise the importance of maintaining a balance among all areas, and the ability to balance is the highest competence of a leader (Jarl, Blossing & Andersson, 2017; Robinson, Lloyd & Rowe, 2008; Tran & Buckman, 2017; Kelechukwu, 2011; Sanzo, Sherman & Clayton, 2011; Klevering & McNae, 2019). This is essential for teams to work in a focused and collaborative way (both in the process and the outcome). The involvement of school leaders in the introduction of projects is essential to enable sustained and whole-school research-based school improvement, involving all teachers in a professional and collegial working environment (Seiser & Portfelt, 2022). It is useful to promote collaborative learning throughout the community, with teachers who themselves are continuously learning, up-to-date with the latest research evidence, and able to make the best use of their classroom situation for educational purposes; there is a focus on improving the quality of interpersonal relationships, with professional abilities recognised and trusted, and with guidance for others who lack these abilities. It is important that the community is willing to learn and to achieve better results. It is recognised that there is a need for educational-context-appropriate and innovative approaches to leadership learning that will enable school leaders and teachers to lead well (Klevering & McNae, 2019). Teachers learn most when they reflect on how the educational process has worked and what the outcome has been. Constant reflection on what went well and what still needs to be improved is what "grows" a teacher the most; the deeper the reflection, the better the teacher becomes, because he or she can answer in every situation why he or she did what he or she did. The more complex the situation, the more teachers should trust and rely on each other. Research has shown that head teachers (directors, principals) who practise creative leadership, especially through positive cultural reinforcement, can achieve high levels of learning in primary school classrooms. The quality of classroom performance is linked to aspects of creative leadership practice, such as the vision, initiative and management of creative leadership (Wahl, 2015; Thaiwinkarn, Ngang Tang & Ariratana, 2018). The particular qualities that are seen among effective educational leaders are easily identifiable and include relational aspects such as trust, communication, cooperation and community building, and building strong relationships. In addition to empowering others, educational leaders should create an organisational culture based on collaboration (Klevering & McNae, 2019). G. Davitt & D. Ryder (2019) Research highlights the following leadership attitudes: communicativeness; orientation towards relationships; care and supportiveness; and behaviours that promote growth and change, where the leader is also a critical colleague as well as a friend. Responsible leadership should be purposefully developed and sustained throughout the culture of the educational institution so that it is felt by every teacher. For collaboration between school leaders and university researchers in action research, a relationship based on trust and respect is important to enable individuals to fulfil their professional roles (Seiser & Portfelt, 2022). The second aspect relates to the focus on the school's local infrastructure and the importance of an organisational environment that facilitates a holistic approach and a shared understanding of the objectives of research and collaboration. Prior agreements are essential for high-quality cooperation; otherwise, in the absence of such agreements, there may be different expectations, different points of view, and therefore the communication expected by the participants may not happen. Developing a common language and a common understanding builds interpersonal trust, which inspires a sense of belonging (Seiser & Portfelt, 2022). If the action research is organised in a school with the participation of only a portion of the teachers and pupils, it is important to agree that the research process, the results and the didactic material developed will be made available to other teachers in the school, otherwise the teachers may decide not to share the experience. It is important that research projects become part of the daily work and not a one-off experiment. Methods such as raising research questions collectively and conducting joint analyses are encouraged, allowing for a shared understanding of the research and collaboration.

In many cases, collaboration between teachers and university researchers is recommended when performing action research in an educational institution, but this is not easy to do in practice. When researching such collaboration, A. Olin, J. Almqvist & K. Hamza (2021) made use of recognition theory to explain how teachers, and to some extent researchers, understand and value their own and each other's participation and contribution. The research showed that such collaboration is very important for the development of innovative didactic knowledge, but that it only succeeds when all participants are accepted and perceived as equal partners who can share their insights and opinions. It is important that teachers and researchers can contribute to the solution of a given problem from different didactic perspectives/positions, building on each other's input and experience, thus both improving educational practice and building a research-based theory of educational science. When organising action research, it is important to pay attention to how teachers and researchers actually relate to and value their own and each other's contributions and participation in collaboration (Olin, Almqvist & Hamza, 2021). In a productive partnership, the experiences and differences of the different people working together are seen as strengths, and each is considered equally important based on his or her unique knowledge and competences. A culture of self- and peer-acceptance is essential for the well-being of all team members. If this culture is not present at the beginning of the work, it must be achieved in the course of the work through dialogue or reasoned discussion. A culture of discussion is essential, because in pedagogical practice there is no one-size-fits-all solution. On the contrary, teachers often find themselves in tricky, multifaceted situations which they have to deal with in their practice by making certain decisions. They have to choose one or another course of action, and the alternative of a single solution is not the optimal way to deal with it. Importantly, by talking/discussing, teachers reflect on their experiences, rethink their decisions, reflect on what has or has not worked, look for the reasons why, and therefore can "grow" as professionals, thus improving their competence. In this way, a deeper learning occurs, the adoption/recognition/testing/assimilation of certain didactic strategies. When teachers and researchers collaborate in this way, they enrich each other's experiences, and the expertise of both groups involved in the discussion is deepened. By talking, even when they disagree, and by expressing their insights based on arguments, there is scope for building common knowledge together (Bergmark et al., 2023; Olin, Almqvist & Hamza, 2021; Shotter & Gustavsen, 1999; Edwards-Groves, Olin & Karlberg-Granlund, 2016). It is important that all educators and researchers, when planning and implementing action research in particular contexts, at the same time develop self-acceptance in a new role (not in a state of denial, but willing to genuinely change the situation by accepting new roles and responsibilities), with different competences, and that they commit to acting in a responsible manner and to contributing equally (Olin, Almqvist & Hamza, 2021).

Mentoring plays an important role in action research when educators, researchers and students (future teachers) collaborate. Mentoring in action research is both situational and relational. It can thus be linked to the ethics of care, which states that caregivers base their care actions on the needs of the recipient (Noddings, 2012, 2013). In mentoring a fellow teacher or student, the mentor plays a variety of roles that can be described using the metaphors of gardener, shepherd, teacher and bridge builder (Bergmark et al., 2023). These roles can be practised by the mentor in the action research; they are often interchangeable, change throughout the action research and depend on the needs of the person being mentored.

In addition, cooperation between pupils and teachers is also emphasised, and for pupils to participate actively in the educational process, they need to feel safe and trust the educational environment and teachers, which is why it is important to create the right contexts for pupils to learn actively (Smit et al., 2022; Mahon, Francisco & Kemmis, 2017), to reflect on lessons learned after the activity, to think about what went well and what, how and why to improve. To have a lasting impact, such experiences of collaboration between teachers and pupils should be highlighted in the school's vision and long-term agreements (Smit et al., 2022).

Collegial feedback instruments/tools. These instruments cover different areas of pedagogical activity. Teaching/lesson observation covers the teaching and learning activities of the teacher and pupils in the classroom. The feedback meeting provides an opportunity to discuss the activities seen in relation to wider professionalism, responsibility and professional behaviour and growth.

Depending on the timing or nature of the feedback, certain themes can be highlighted. For example, it may be more important to discuss professional prospects or the mastery of a particular method/strategy. In each case, specific areas of interest/development can be identified, by mutual agreement (Quality Teaching in the European Schools, 2016; Professional Standards for Educational Leaders, 2015; Future of Education Skills, 2020).

One of the most important areas is peer observation of pedagogical activities/lessons. A colleague who is an observer may focus on certain aspects or may perform a general analysis of the activity, depending on the purpose of the observation and the prior arrangement with the observed teacher. It is recommended to observe the activities of selected pupils, how they behave in one or another case. It is recommended that the observer should pay attention to the following features/elements of pedagogical activity (Macaire, 2007; Quality Teaching in the European Schools, 2016; Professional Standards for Educational Leaders, 2015; Future of Education Skills, 2020):

- **Teacher activity related to pupil learning** (Quality of explanations, structure of activities/lessons, actualisation of content, strategies used, motivation of pupils, differentiation and individualisation of activities, etc.).
- **Pupil learning** (Pupil involvement (engagement), independent work, cooperative learning, targeted use of ICT, etc. Teacher's ability to organise, encourage and/or guide the pupils' learning process).
- **Pedagogical context** (Teacher's efforts to create a safe atmosphere, respectful interaction, rules of social behaviour, etc.).
- **Classroom management** (Teacher's efforts to create a classroom environment of goodwill, mutual support and understanding, and to provide the appropriate equipment and resources necessary for the educational process).
- **Time allocated to the activity** (Efficient use of time in the teaching/learning process, e.g. a good start to a lesson, smooth transitions between activities, individualisation and differentiation of the educational content, indicating the optimal time in which to complete activities).

In the context of observation, it is important that the observer compares what he or she might expect (under the circumstances) with what he or she actually sees. For example, at the beginning of a lesson, the observer might expect the teacher to explain the purpose of the lesson. The teacher either does or does not do this. This is quite easy to observe. If the teacher does explain, the explanation may be "sufficient" or "good quality". Therefore, before giving good-natured feedback, it is recommended to mark the comments according to whether a certain aspect is implemented/observed with good quality, implemented adequately, or inadequately (was expected, but was not observed) (Hattie, 2009; Chapman et al., 2011; Helmke, 2012). Some indicators may have been observed that were of very good quality, that were fulfilled as planned, as discussed before the lesson, but there may also be indicators that were not observed sufficiently. All these should be noted and discussed with the teacher when the activity/lesson is analysed. In addition, during certain activities/lessons, it may not be possible to observe certain because they are simply not relevant in a given context. For example, if the teacher presents a new project to be performed by the class, this information is relevant to all the pupils, so the observer should not expect individualised or differentiated activities. In this case, it is not necessary to talk about a particular indicator and to mark it (Buchs, 2017). If a colleague is observing and guiding a teacher who is working with pupils from different classes or even different curricula, it is useful to observe a few activities in different classes, and to note with which age group of pupils the colleague has more success.

In the context of collegial observation/guidance, after the observed activity/lesson, it is recommended to discuss certain aspects of the activity with the teacher, ranging from planning to evaluation (according to Buchs, 2017). It is important to comment accurately and informatively on each area, taking into account the focus of the observation/assessment. A colleague could refer to the following questions and indicators when talking with a teacher:

- Planning of the subject content
  - o *Has this topic been analysed in the past, will it be discussed in the future or is it included in the plan?*
  - o *Does the teacher have an annual, semester or other periodic plan (as agreed within the educational institution), a calendar of activities/lessons based on learning plans/curricula?*
  - o *Does the teacher coordinate planning horizontally (across the year) and vertically (across topics/sections) with colleagues?*
- Continuity of activity
  - o *Is the information needed for a substitute teacher to take over the teaching of a class in a well-organised form, in case the teacher is not able to carry out the planned activities himself/herself?*
- Assessment of pupils' achievements, instruments for giving feedback
  - o *Is a system of assessment and self-evaluation instruments used to measure pupils' achievements?*
  - o *How and how often are pupils' achievements assessed?*
  - o *With what instruments (observations, tests, portfolio, self-evaluation, etc.)?*
  - o *Which areas and subjects are assessed?*
  - o *When does the assessment take place? Is there a calendar?*

- Monitoring pupil progress, results
  - *Are progress and results properly recorded for each group and each pupil?*
  - *How are results recorded? Using marks, levels, abilities growth profiles, etc.?*
  - *Where are the results recorded? In a portfolio and/or in a digital system?*
  - *Who has access to the data?*
  - *How well is the information in the records conveyed? How often is this done?*
- Analysis of results
  - *Are the results analysed in more detail (e.g. type of errors, more in-depth research, diagnostic discussion, research on attitudes towards the subject of analysis, etc.)?*
- Further planning of activity
  - *Do pupils' achievement results lead to targeted action?*
  - *What will the teacher/classroom assistant do, what result(s) are sought, when, how, with whom?*
  - *Was this clearly stated?*

During the feedback meeting, colleagues should make constructive suggestions to each other, which can be made or modified depending on the purpose of the meeting, the aspect being assessed, the topic, etc.

Content of interest to educators, points of view, aspects relevant to a specific context: an overview of some particular educational subject content that should be addressed. In addition, a rethinking of what, why and how we would like to do things differently. It is important that schools create a learning environment that helps teachers to identify their professional development needs (Smith & Lindsay, 2016), encourages experimentation and exploration, and allocates resources to support teachers' learning. It is essential that the methods or strategies learned during professional development events are implemented in the educational process (Thoonen et al., 2011; Vanblaere & Devos, 2016; Postholm, 2018). Research has shown that teachers are interested in collaboration when they perceive that it supports their professional development and when they feel encouraged by their leaders (Silva, Amante & Morgado, 2017). Teachers' need for support for continuous professional development was also highlighted in a qualitative study performed in five Irish primary schools (King & Stevenson, 2017). Teachers in the study said they trusted their leader and the leader trusted them. In addition, time was allocated to plan and reflect on activities together. In this way, teachers developed an openness to working together and team learning. It is important that the development activities and the areas of development meet the needs of the teachers (Goodnough, 2016; Kyriakides et al., 2017; Mohan et al., 2017; Postholm, 2018). It should also be noted that teachers may have different motivations and expectations for attending professional development events, because they may have different levels of knowledge and experience in a particular area and in learning and practice (Skott & Møller, 2017). It can be said that sustainability is a key issue in the planning, implementation and analysis of existing action research. Action research is a good space for interdisciplinary aspects of educational content when teachers from several disciplines collaborate. The trajectory of sustainability becomes a shared commitment, with visioning, planning, activities, routines and assessment following one another in a continuously transformative process that engages both teachers and pupils in democratic processes and collaborative work, enabling deep learning and understanding of different perspectives (Wolff et al., 2017).

In summary, it can be said that action research is the basis for continuous reflection on the educational process, content, outcomes, context and all the other elements on which the situation depends. In our view, reflection is at the core of action research, but it is a mutually interrelated phenomenon, because during action research, educators and pupils develop deeper reflective abilities by reflecting on and discussing what happened, how and why. Hence, reflection and the quality of the results of action research are interrelated and interdependent.

Chapter 2 Research Methodology for Action Research-Based Primary Education

2.1. Methodological-theoretical framework of the research

Action research is a distinctive type of educational research that can be differentiated from other types of research by a number of features: social constructiveness, contextualised situational action, practical implementation, systematic inquiry and cyclicality (according to Efron & Ravid, 2013).

Social constructiveness. Educational researchers are perceived as creators of knowledge rather than recipients and implementers of knowledge produced by external experts. From this perspective, practitioners are professionals who are able to design educational content and make informed decisions based on the results of their research. Moreover, educators who develop such educational practices are able to take responsibility for action based on research evidence (Cochran-Smith & Lytle, 2009; Hendricks, 2012; Pine, 2008; Efron & Ravid, 2013). For sustainable change, the action research involves a large part of the school community, with teachers, pupils, school administrators, parents, and researchers discussing the identification of problems and solutions (Charlier, 2005; Lafortune, 2006, 2016; Prud'homme et al., 2011; Miehakanda, 2014; Cain & Harris, 2013; Wennergren, 2016; Davis et al., 2018; Dimmock, 2016; Johannesson, 2020).

Contextualised situational action. Action researchers seek to understand the unique context of the research and the people involved. The findings of such research should be understood in the context of the specific situation, its various nuances and the factors of that particular environment (Baumfield, Hall & Wall, 2008; Herr & Nihlen, 2007; Holly, Arhar & Kasten, 2009; Mertler, 2012). The results are therefore relevant for that particular educational institution and for improving its situation (Dolbec & Clément, 2000; Mertler, 2009; Macaire, 2007; Lafontaine, 2006, 2016; Clark, 2012; Efron & Ravid, 2013; Carignan, Beaudry & Larose, 2016; Eden & Ackermann, 2018), but not for an entire general set of such educational institutions.

Practical implementation. Action researchers choose the questions they plan to investigate in practice, based on their own insights and areas of professional interest. The results of action research are directly related to the improvement of the educational practice of the participants themselves (teachers and pupils) (Creswell, 2017; Altrichter et al., 2008; Bauer & Brazer, 2012; Dana & Yendol-Hoppey, 2009; Marzano, 2003; Charlier, 2005; Lafortune, 2006, 2016; Prud'homme et al., 2011; Miehakanda, 2014; Cain & Harris, 2013; Wennergren, 2016; Davis et al., 2018; Dimmock, 2016; Johannesson, 2020).

Systematic inquiry. Action research is targeted, well-designed, systematic and methodical. The research process must be systematic in order to produce reliable and meaningful results (Creswell, 2017; Burns, 2007; Burton, Brundelt & Jones, 2008; McNiff & Whitehead, 2010; Stringer, 2007, 2008; Silva, Amante & Morgado, 2017; King & Stevenson, 2017; Goodnough, 2016; Kyriakides et al., 2017; Mohan et al., 2017; Postholm, 2018; Skott & Møller, 2017; Wolff et al., 2017).

Cyclicality. Action research starts with a research question and ends with the application of the knowledge gained, which leads to new questions and a new cycle of research to identify other problems and solutions (Creswell, 2017; Mertler, 2009, 2012; Johnson, 2011; Mills, 2011; Sagor, 2011; Stringer, 2008; Efron & Ravid, 2013).

The theory of practice architectures, on which research into pedagogical practice is based. Developing a new theory requires rethinking existing practice. Practitioners around the world often ask themselves: how are we doing. how can we do it better? These questions are particularly relevant to education and educational institutions, where equity and human development/growth opportunities are sometimes compromised, for example, because of economic reasons, competing demands and external pressures. The task of addressing such issues and changing educational practice is a major ongoing responsibility and challenge for both practitioners and researchers. The theory of practice architectures (Mahon, Francisco & Kemmis, 2017; Kemmis & Grootenboer, 2008; Kemmis et al., 2012; Kemmis & Heikkinen, 2012; Kemmis et al., 2014; Kemmis, McTaggart & Nixon, 2014; Kemmis & Mutton, 2012; Kemmis et al., 2014;) helps to reveal the ways in which practice enables as well as the conditions that constrain. It is also a transformative resource for finding ways to change education when current practices and conditions are inappropriate, i.e. unjustified, unproductive or unsustainable, or are the cause of suffering or injustice. The aim of the theory of practice architectures is to help participants who find themselves in undesirable situations, or who are reacting to such situations; to decide how they might behave morally, for the good of the individuals concerned, and politically, in their own interests, for the good of humanity. The theory of practice architectures relates to the process of education by problematising practices, where a distinctive and authentic ontological approach is offered on what a practice is; how a practice is shaped; how practices relate to each other.

The theory of practice architectures states that the social world is composed of three dimensions (Mahon, Francisco & Kemmis, 2017; Kemmis et al., 2014). *Cultural-discursive arrangements* are implemented in a semantic space where people intersubjectively encounter each other in conversation (Kemmis et al., 2014). *Material-economic arrangements* are implemented in physical space-time, where people meet each other intersubjectively in a “medium of activity and work" (Kemmis et al., 2014). *Socio-political arrangements* are implemented in a social space where people intersubjectively encounter each other in a "medium of power and solidarity" (Kemmis et al., 2014). However, in these three dimensions – *cultural-discursive*, *material-economic* and *socio-political* – agreements do not take place in isolation from each other; they are always present in practice, in particular places, which are linked together. Together, they give people's social life an obvious materiality, tangibility, certainty, reality, relevance.

2.2. Logical framework of the research and its rationale

In order to objectively investigate the practice of action research in Lithuanian primary classrooms, we performed a qualitative study, following the principle of triangulation (Guion, 2002; Noble & Heale, 2019; Rupšienė, 2007), i.e. first, we analysed educational practices in the context of Lithuania as a whole (based on data from the assessment of Lithuania's external audits), then we analysed the content of action research used by prospective primary school teachers in their undergraduate theses prior to graduation from university, and finally, we investigated to what extent primary school teachers who have already graduated from university base their practice on action research once they are working on their own, with their own classes. The logic flow chart for this empirical research is shown in Figure 2.2.1.

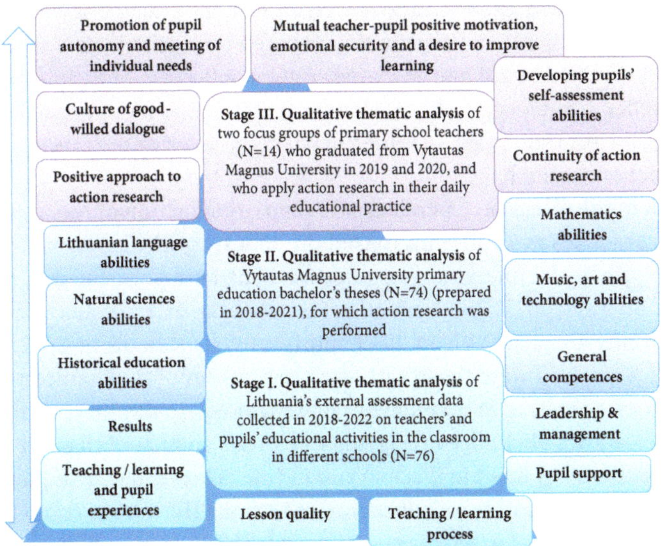

Figure 2.2.1: Logic diagram of the empirical study of action research-based primary education practice in Lithuania

For this research, we had several primary sources of information and applied several research methods. In the first stage of the research, a secondary thematic analysis of the external assessment data was performed, which helped to reveal the overall scope of Lithuanian practices, the content of learning, and the problem area of the learning environment (Mondada, 2005).

In the second stage of the research, the undergraduate theses in which the students/prospective primary school teachers performed action research were analysed in detail. The data from this stage of the research are described according to the themes of the qualitative content analysis (Braun & Clarke, 2006). The practice of a prospective primary teacher-researcher in the preparation of a bachelor's thesis is a practice that focuses on the pupils' performance in solving certain learning problems, i.e. on optimising this performance (Sensevy, Toullec-Théry & Nédélec-Trohel, 2006). The ability to analyse what we do depends on analytical abilities and the mastery of pedagogical concepts, the description and expression of which are sometimes difficult due to the different ways in which they are mastered and related in different situations.

In the third stage of the research, we organised focus groups with primary school teachers who had already graduated from university and who had done their undergraduate thesis on action research. We chose to interview a number of former students who should apply action research in their practical activities after graduation. This choice of research participants allows us to document the pursuit of a reflective approach and real changes in the practice of young teachers (Borges & Gervais, 2015). Data analysis is based on teachers' statements, which shed light on the essence and meaning of the application of action research in daily practice (Leutenegger, 1999; Mondada, 2005). The focus group discussion was based on a questionnaire designed in advance, covering the practical applications of action research.

Stage I of the research. Characteristics and organisation of research on educational practices in Lithuania (based on data from the external evaluation of school quality). Different types of assessment were performed in Lithuania between 2019 and 2022. The work analyses data from external assessments conducted in fifty-three schools in 2019 and twenty-six schools in 2022. In 2019, the schools assessed were those with weak expression of the characteristics of a good school, operating in an unfavourable socio-economic context (they had a higher percentage of children receiving free meals compared to other schools), with a prevalence of low pupil achievement (the achievement score for the first part of the primary and basic education was among the lowest, compared to all schools). The external assessment observed 2,487 lessons/activities organised by teachers (External Assessment Statistics of General Education Schools. 2019 Results of External Assessment of Risk, 2019). In 2022, the schools assessed as part of Lithuania's Quality Basket project received funding to improve their activities. The aim was to assess the progress made by the schools that received the Quality Basket. The type of external assessment was regarded as a repeated external assessment of risk, based on a set of criteria for the external assessment of risk, the school's progress and prospects were assessed using a variety of sources: previous external assessment reports, the results of the national pupil achievement tests and the state school-leaving (matura) examinations, reported data on pupils' achievements and progress, the data collected in the Education Management Information System, and the school's mandatory monitoring indicators, among others (Description of the procedure for allocating the Quality Basket to general education schools, 2018; List of schools with weak performance, 2018; List of schools applying for a Quality Basket to improve pupils' educational achievement, 2021). Of the 134 assessed schools, 26 schools were selected for analysis, because teachers' lessons were observed in these schools. A total of 1,418 lessons/activities were observed in the 26 assessed schools (External Assessment Statistics of General Education Schools. 2022 Results of External Assessment of Risk, 2023).

In addition, the work examines data from the thematic external assessment of sixty-one schools for the period 2021–2022. The assessment theme was established by Order No. V-1254 of the Minister of Education, Science and Sport of 9 July 2021: *Focus of the implementation of inclusive education in general education schools*. The aim of the assessment was to assess the focus of the implementation of inclusive education in schools, to answer the questions identified by the Minister of Education, Science and Sport on the development of a culture of inclusive education, its implementation in school policy and educational practice. When selecting schools for the thematic external assessment, priority was given to schools in various municipalities with at least 200 pupils, with a social, cultural and educational diversity of pupils, with at least 2 educational support specialists, including non-teaching staff, with at least 5% of pupils having moderate, severe and very severe special educational needs (hereinafter referred to as "SEN"), and with an external assessment having been performed in the period 2007–2014.

Although the systems of assessment indicators for thematic or risk assessment vary, most of the indicators are directly related to aspects of the quality of the teaching/learning process (see Table 2.2.1), which allows for a multidimensional analysis of the lesson and processes recorded by the assessors.

Table 2.2.1: Areas and indicators for assessing school performance

External assessment of risk		**Thematic external assessment**	
Areas of assessment	**Indicators**	**Areas of assessment**	**Indicators**
Results	Personality development Pupil achievement and progress	Leadership	Perspective and community agreements Leadership School self-governance Action together Collaboration with parents School networking Competence Continuous professional development
Support for the pupil	Focus on the pupil's personality Focus on pupil needs School community agreements for each		
Teaching/ learning process	Planning of (self-) education Learning expectations and pupil motivation Organisation of (self-) education Learning (Self-) evaluation for education	Teaching/ learning and pupil experiences	Planning of (self-) education Empowering leadership for learning and pupil learning experiences Assessment while being educated, results
Prepared according to: *Description of the Procedure for Organising and Performing External Assessment of the Performance of General Education Schools*, 2018; Order No. V-1254 of the Minister of Education, Science and Sport of the Republic of Lithuania of 9 July 2021, *Regarding the Establishment of the Theme, Issues and Indicators for the 2021–2022 Thematic External Assessment of the Performance of General Education Schools*			

In order to identify the aspects of the teaching/learning process in the classroom that need to be improved, a secondary analysis of the research data was performed using the deductive content analysis method (Žydžiūnaitė & Sabalauskas, 2017; Tight, 2019). Lesson observation protocols completed by external assessors and external assessment reports on the quality of school performance are analysed. The lesson observation protocols analysed the strengths and areas for improvement identified by the assessors, while the school external evaluation reports analysed the quality of the teaching/learning process in the lessons. The analysis of the data identified the numerical characteristics (frequency) of the aspects of lesson quality, and the characteristics of learning in the classroom.

Stage II of the research. Results of analysis of bachelor's theses of graduates of the Bachelor's degree programme in Primary Education of Vytautas Magnus

University in Lithuania according to performed action research. The research was performed using a thematic analysis strategy. The analysis was based on the reflective texts of seventy-four then-prospective primary school teachers, which were prepared as part of their undergraduate thesis on the basis of action research. The research data were analysed by discussing the themes of action research, the research questions/problems, the chosen problem-solving pathway (method), and the identified advantages and difficulties of action research. The development of a teacher's research competence relates to the ability to choose, in educational practice: *the educational strategy, the structure, the use of appropriate research methods and the organisation of professional research* (Description of Professional Competences for Teachers, 2007; 2018). The following action research flowchart was used for the writing of the bachelor theses (see Figure 2.2.2).

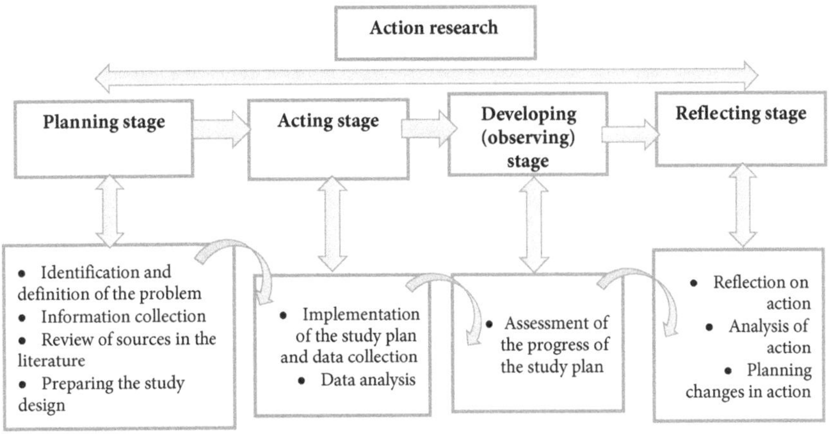

Figure 2.2.2: Flowchart showing all stages of the action research

The first step in the planning stage of an action research study is to define the research question or identify the problem the researcher wants to investigate (see Figure 2.2.2.). This is followed by information gathering, a review of relevant literature and a review of similar studies that have already been performed and which have explored a path to solving a similar problem. Once certain information is available, it is possible to specifically plan the methods of performing the research, i.e. how the children will be taught to solve the problem, and the methods of collecting the data, i.e. how the researcher will record the data. The action stage involves both the educational process and the collection of data. In the so-called developing (observing) stage, the researcher analyses and interprets the data, the available information about the educational process and the outcome.

In the reflecting stage, conclusions are drawn, shared, changes in activities are anticipated, new problems may be identified, and the same sequence of steps is repeated in a cyclical manner (according to Efron & Ravid, 2013). In order to perform the research activity (action research) according to the flowchart in Figure 2.2.2 and to solve the identified problem, the author of the bachelor's thesis, a future primary school teacher, collaborated with the supervisor (researcher) and a teacher-practitioner (see Figure 2.2.3).

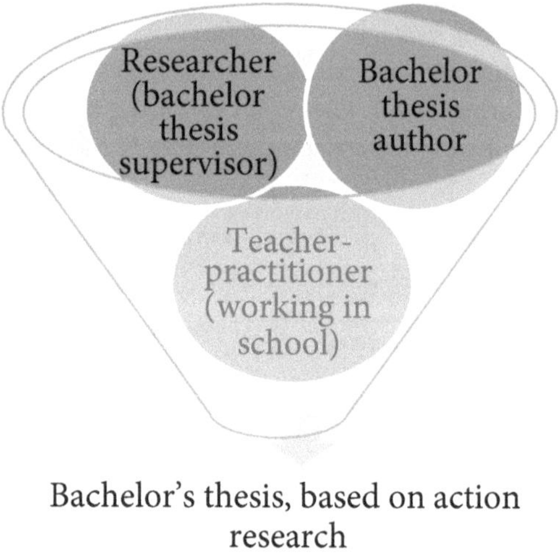

Figure 2.2.3: Diagram of collaboration among researcher, undergraduate thesis author, teacher-practitioner, when performing action research

The descriptions of pupils' interactions (behaviour, actions, intentions, emotional reactions), facts, events, reflections and reasoning recorded in the action research reports shed indirect light on the roles of the researcher and the teacher, and this likely provided a higher degree of reliability in the data (Bitinas, Rupšienė & Žydžiūnaitė, 2008; Norton, 2010). The qualitative thematic content (Braun & Clarke, 2006; Žydžiūnaitė & Sabaliauskas, 2017; Weber, 1990) helped to identify thematic categories/conceptual units: topic; research question-problem to be solved (subject); problem-solving method(s), assessment/reflection on the activity (advantages, difficulties); anticipated changes to the activity. These thematic categories provide a systematic assessment of the studied phenomenon.

In Lithuania, the bachelor's degree usually takes 4 years, and prospective primary school teachers have two specialities: they become both primary school teachers and teachers of early foreign language (Primary Education Pedagogy and Early Foreign

Language Teaching, Bachelor's Study Programme, 2023). Notably, students have a total of four internships, one in each year of their studies. In the first year of studies, students complete a teaching assistant practice (6 credits) in a school, during which they mainly observe the educational process in the school and keep a placement diary. In the second year of studies, students do the first cooperative practice under the supervision of a mentor (5 credits), during which the future teachers observe the educational process and assist the primary school teachers. In the third year of studies, students do the second cooperative practice under the supervision of a mentor (7 credits). During this placement, the student not only observes the educational process in the classroom, but also leads some of the activities for the children, each activity being carefully negotiated with the mentor. In the fourth year of studies, an independent pedagogical practice (12 credits) is performed, during which future primary school teachers work independently with pupils, carrying out all activities under the supervision of a mentor, i.e. conducting action research. For the bachelor's theses analysed in our study, empirical data based on action research were collected during the independent pedagogical practice. In addition, students learn the basics of the methodology of organising action research in the third year of studies, in the Pedagogical Action Research Technique course (3 credits). In Lithuania, primary school teachers are encouraged to carry out action research in their daily practice, and the experience gained at the university enables them to do so.

The research data was analysed by discussing the themes of the action research, the research questions/problems to be solved, the chosen approach to problem-solving (method), and the identified benefits and difficulties of action research. The development of teacher research competence is linked to the ability to choose in educational practice: educational strategy, structure, appropriate research methods and organisation of professional research (Description of professional competences for teachers, 2007).

The study was performed using a thematic analysis strategy. The bachelor's theses where action research was performed were analysed between June and November 2022. Each paper was analysed according to the following thematic areas: subject, method and solutions/outcomes for educational problems. The data was summarised by breaking down the results in Lithuanian language, history and science education. The analysis of descriptions of students' interactions (behaviours, actions, intentions, emotional reactions), facts, events, reflections and reasoning recorded in the action research reports took into account the alignment of the roles of the researcher and the teacher, and likely provided a higher level of data reliability (Norton, 2010; Mertler, 2009; Bitinas, Rupšienė & Žydžiūnaitė, 2008). Qualitative content analysis (Weber, 1990; Žydžiūnaitė & Sabaliauskas, 2017) allowed the identification of significant thematic categories/units: topic; research question/problem to be solved; method(s) of problem-solving, evaluation/

reflection of the activity (benefits, difficulties); anticipated changes in the activity. These thematic categories allow for a systematic assessment of the studied phenomenon. The qualitative method of thematic content analysis was chosen, focusing on interpretation, educational process and experience (Żydžiūnaitė & Sabaliauskas, 2017), where problematic educational situations in specific classrooms of students were resolved. The process of thematic content analysis was organised in a spiral fashion, continuously returning to the original data in order to identify details that may have been overlooked but are relevant to the study; in this way, the data is fed back into the data by describing the methods used in ever greater detail, and by justifying the results in terms of the problems that a particular method has helped solve (Żydžiūnaitė & Sabaliauskas, 2017).

The results of the study are based on the analysis of theses of graduates of the Bachelor of Primary Education programme at Vytautas Magnus University in Lithuania, based on the results of action research. The analysis included seventy-four reflective research texts of prospective primary school teachers, prepared during the writing of the bachelor's thesis on the basis of action research from the language, history and science thematic groups. The theses were selected from all undergraduate theses produced at the University that included action research in the period 2018–2021 (see Table 2.2.2).

Table 2.2.2: Breakdown of bachelor's theses selected by year and thematic group

Year	**Number of bachelor's theses**	**Thematic field**					
		Lithuanian language	**History**	**Natural sciences**	**Mathematics**	**Music, art and technology**	**General competencies**
2021	34	9	3	3	2	2	5
2020	6	2	1	2	-	-	1
2019	27	9	3	3	3	4	3
2018	7	2	1	3	-	1	-
	74	22	8	11	5	7	9
	In total:	62					

From the data in Table 2.2.2, it can be seen that the total number of theses produced in the context of action research is significantly higher, at seventy-four. However, due to the limited scope of this work, only theses in three thematic groups are analysed: Lithuanian language, history and natural sciences.

Each bachelor's thesis analysed a selected didactic problem and proposed a solution on the basis of action research. In order to ensure that the author of the bachelor's thesis (a prospective primary school teacher) was able to provide a high-quality solution to the problem identified from his or her practice, he or she consulted regularly with the primary school teacher (the practice mentor) and the academic supervisor of the bachelor's thesis (a university professor) during the research.

We present a summary analysis of the data from the different action research studies (sixty-two in total), highlighting the areas where didactic problems were identified, the methods chosen as a way of solving the problem and the results obtained.

Stage III of the research. We developed the research questions for the focus group members before identifying patterns in the application of action research in practice (Leutenegger, 1999). Focus group interviews are important for our research because focus group participants reflect on their experiences and put them into words, which allows us to create a representation of how action research is performed/understood in the practice of the research participants (Maurel, 2008; 2009). The questions that were asked of the focus group participants are shown in Table 2.2.3.

Table 2.2.3: Theoretical basis for focus group questions

Question for focus group members	Rationale for the question
1. In your bachelor's thesis, you performed action research. Do you apply this experience in practice? How? What? Why? How often?	This question asks participants to recall and reflect on both their own pedagogical experience and to try to relate it to the experience of conducting action research. The question allows the research participant to give examples of experiences and arguments about what was applied and how it was applied, from which the researchers will be able to judge whether the research participant is more advanced in action research design or more of a novice (Maurel, 2008; 2009).
2. Can you give some examples, in your experience, of how often you base your pedagogical practice on action research?	The examples provided by the participants will allow the researchers to find out in which activities teachers are able to put action research or its elements into practice (Leutenegger, 1999; Mondada, 2005).

(Continued)

Table 2.2.3: (Continued)

Question for focus group members	Rationale for the question
3. What motivates you to organise action research-based pedagogical practice? What encourages you to do so?	This question is designed to investigate whether action research-based practice is based on teachers' internal motivation (Thoonen, Sleegers, Oort, Peetsma & Geijsel, 2011; Vanblaere & Devos, 2016; Goodnough, 2016; Kyriakides et al., 2017; Mohan et al., 2017; Postholm, 2018), a desire to improve their own educational practice, or external motivation, such as the motivation provided by the leader of the educational institution when building a learning community in the educational institution (Silva, Amante and Morgado, 2017; King & Stevenson, 2017).
4. How do you prepare for inquiry-based activities? What aspects of the activity do you think about in advance? Do you prepare specific tips/reminders/strategies for children on how to learn certain aspects, how do you provide support? Please give examples.	The question is designed to reflect on the elements of a teacher's preparation for action research, and the examples will reveal whether teachers are able to reflect accurately and choose the right words to describe certain stages of preparation (Skott & Møller, 2017; Wolff, Sjöblom, Hofman, & Palmberg, 2017). We expect that the question will also allow educators to express the problems encountered when planning action research activities (Knauder & Koschmieder, 2019; Panskyi, Rowinska, & Biedron, 2019; Hubalovsky, Hubalovska & Musilek, 2019; Al-Huneini, Walker, & Badger, 2020).
5. How else do you integrate inquiry-based learning into children's everyday activities? What percentage does inquiry-based learning represent in the general educational field?	The question is expected to shed light on whether research participants are already using action research as a routine practice, or whether it is relatively rare (Hattie, 2009; Chapman, Armstrong, Harris, Muijs, Reynolds, & Sammons, 2011; Helmke, 2012; Hargreaves, & Fullan, 2019; Fullan, 2019; 2020; Fullan, Quinn, Drummy, Gardner, 2020). Frequency of performance of action research reflects teachers' ability to base practice on research (Roy, Guay & Valois, 2013; Knauder & Koschmieder, 2019; Knauder & Koschmieder, 2019; UNESCO, 2021).

Question for focus group members	Rationale for the question
6. With pupils from which social context do you work? How would you describe your pupils? Are there children from other cultures, such as speakers of other languages who have come to Lithuania from other countries?	The question will help to identify the kinds of environments of the pupils with whom the research participants work (Dolbec, & Clément, 2000; Lafontaine, 2006, 2016; Eden, & Ackermann, 2018). Action research gives teachers the opportunity to step back and reflect on their practice (Cain, & Harris, 2013). It will also be possible to investigate whether action research is being used to overcome difficulties (Fullan, 2019; 2020).
7. Do you have any other observations on inquiry-based learning that you would like to make?	The question is intended for research participants to add to or clarify their views (Maurel, 2008; 2009).

Focus group interview data analysis method. The qualitative thematic content analysis (Braun & Clarke, 2006; Žydžiūnaitė & Sabaliauskas, 2017; Weber, 1990) was chosen. This approach uses concepts or phrases and a description of the relationships between them. It groups empirical data into categories based on the language of the research participants and the revealed experiences (Jørgensen & Phillips, 2002; Žydžiūnaitė et al., 2009; Lambert & Lambert, 2012). The data analysis approach is *insight-driven*, the analysis process *is interpretive*, based on the researchers' *expertise, experience* and takes practice into account. The main data analysis strategy chosen was *comparison:* an interpretative comparative analysis of the data was performed according to categories covering the reasons for the teachers' chosen action research, examples of motivation, aspects of planning and reflection (prior to the action research), the forms in which the inquiry-based activities are developed, the timing of these activities in relation to the entire educational content, and with whom the teachers in the school can consult and confer regarding the planned and implemented activities. The qualitative thematic content analysis is a valid method for drawing specific conclusions based on the text being analysed. We used both inductive and deductive analytical strategies in an iterative cyclical manner to investigate and integrate teachers' application of action research in primary classrooms when teachers are advanced in this field. Categories and statements were developed directly from the data, taking into account the scientific literature to identify the prevalence of action research use, the reasons for it, and the design aspects of the educational process (Merriam & Tisdell, 2016). The text provided by the informants is the research material for the content analysis, reflecting the process of personal reflection (according to Mayring, 2019). The process started with an analysis of the teachers' interview material. The insights generated from the interview data were based on teachers' activities in educational practice, highlighting examples of emerging practice and the prerequisites for the development of a culture of action research-based pedagogical practice.

Location and timing of the focus group interviews. Two focus group interviews on the Microsoft Teams platform were conducted at the following times:

- 23-03-2021, interview recording time 2 h 15 min. (Group 1);
- 31-03-2021, interview recording time 1 h 53 min. (Group 2).

2.3. Characteristics of participants in focus groups

Research participants. The sample of informants is qualitative-targeted. A qualitative (targeted) sample of informants is achieved when experts in the field are chosen who are capable of responsible reasoning about the problem under study, so it can be expected that in addition to statements and conclusions based on theory, there will also be new ideas that can serve as a starting point for the investigation of the theory of the research subject (according to Bitinas, Rupšienė & Žydžiūnaitė, 2008). *Criterion sampling* was used because the research participants were selected purposefully, all the participants in the focus group discussions are alumni of the Vytautas Magnus University Education Academy, who prepared their bachelor's thesis on the basis of action research. The analysis of their theses was performed in the sub-chapter of this research paper entitled *Analysis of Bachelor's Theses in Primary Education in which action research was performed.* We selected these teachers in both focus groups purposefully, knowing their level of competence (Patton, 2002; Merriam & Tisdell, 2016; Hesse-Biber, 2017). All research participants were invited to take part in the study by direct email contact. All teachers agreed to participate of their own free will, were informed of the aims of the study and that the interview would be recorded. In the work, the participants are referred to by names other than their real names, such as Cecile, Zita, Clareta, Ana, Elzė, [...] Liza. The characteristics of the research participants are presented in Table 2.3.1.

Table 2.3.1: Characteristics of Focus Group 1 participants, who had been VMU full-time bachelor's degree students and had graduated 3 years ago, and now work in primary school classrooms

Teacher's name	Work experience	School
Cecile	3 years	Urban state school (Vilnius)
Zita	3 years	Urban state school (Šiauliai)
Clareta	4 years	Urban state school (Klaipėda)

Teacher's name	Work experience	School
Milana	4 years	Urban state school (Vilnius)
Oksana	3 years	Urban state school (Klaipėda)
Ilona	4 years	Urban state school (Vilnius)

Focus Group 1 consisted of primary school teachers currently working in different cities in Lithuania, all of whom were former students in the Primary Education study programme at the Education Academy of Vytautas Magnus University. This focus group included two teachers who had chosen to continue their studies in the master's degree programme in Educational Management and Leadership at Vytautas Magnus University, and at the time of the research were finishing these studies at the end of the semester.

Table 2.3.2: Characteristics of Focus Group 2 participants, who had been VMU part-time first cycle students and had graduated 2 years ago, and now work in primary school classrooms

Teacher's name	Work experience	School
Ana	7 years	Urban state school
Elzė	6 years	Urban private school
Johanas	6 years	Urban private school
Violeta	5 years	Urban specialised school (deaf and hard-of-hearing)
Elė	6 years	Urban state school
Liza	3 years	Small-town state school, in which the language of instruction is a national minority language (Polish)

All the teachers listed in Table 2.3.2 have a qualification in Primary Education Pedagogy from Vytautas Magnus University. The data shows that they have been working in schools for longer than they have had a bachelor's degree. In Lithuania, due to the severe shortage of teachers, students of pedagogical studies receive job offers while still in university and for this reason they sometimes change the form of their studies, i.e. they switch from full-time studies to part-time studies, which last 1 year longer. The table shows the data of the participants who studied at the university for 5 years (they had chosen a part-time sessional study programme) and throughout their studies were able to work in a school. For this reason, the length of service of the participants ranges from 3 to 7 years. In addition, some of the teachers work in private schools and others in public schools. The majority of the participants work in urban areas. One teacher works in a specialised school for deaf and hard-of-hearing children. Another teacher works in a national minority school located in a small town.

2.4. Research ethics

The study was guided by the general principles of research professionalism and ethics: credibility, integrity, respect and accountability. The principle of ensuring the voluntary participation of research participants in the study was respected by ensuring that research participants are aware of and can withdraw from the research at any time without giving a reason and without feeling pressured to participate in the research (Carling, 2019; Guillemin & Gillam, 2004; Israel, 2015; Kardelis, 2005; Žydžiūnaitė & Sabaliauskas, 2017). In addition, the study committed to comply with requirements relating to the protection of personal data and transparency in declaring the source of funding for the performance of the research and the publication of its results.

All research participants participated in the study on a voluntary basis, were informed about the nature of the study, the ethical principles of the study, and verbal consent was obtained from each participant to take part in the interview and to have it recorded. Informants were informed that confidentiality and anonymity of the informant would be guaranteed. During data collection, the text of each focus group interview was recorded, transcribed and filed in separate computer files, while maintaining the confidentiality and anonymity of the participants. The research was carried out following the provisions which underline the basic principles of professionalism and ethics of research, approved by Resolution No. SEN-N-17 of the Senate of Vytautas Magnus University on 24 March 2021. The study was conducted in accordance with the principles of reliability, integrity, respect, and accountability. The data are presented after translating the participants' responses into English.

Chapter 3 Analysis of the Results of Empirical Study of Action Research-Based Primary Education

3.1. Linking action research to educational practice in Lithuania: evidence from external assessment of general education schools

When analysing educational practice and its changing tendencies in a Lithuanian context, it is important to pay attention to the anticipated and modelled directions of educational practice and their expression in organised teaching/learning activities. Taking as a starting point the attempts to conceptualise agreement on "a good school" and its creation in the middle of the second decade of the twenty-first century, we can observe a persistent gap between theory and practice in what is developed and declared to be a school, inclusive education or a specific lesson. The question is raised whether agreement on what constitutes "a good school" is explicit, or rather, how is it to be created (Targamadzė, 2017) or having outlined guidelines for the implementation of the principle of inclusion, whether concrete steps are anticipated on how the elements of an inclusive culture written in a school's documents should reach a particular pupil. Data from the external assessment of the quality of school performance show that schools often declare a culture and attitudes of inclusive education, and this is reflected in school planning documents, but these processes are not monitored in teaching/learning practice, in the organisation of education, in the assessment of pupils' achievement and progress (Jašinauskas et al., 2021).

The documents regulating the updating of the content of education in Lithuania, and its implementation, outline a teaching/learning process that focuses on meeting the teaching/learning needs of all learners, providing for their individual learning opportunities, and creating the conditions for each pupil to make personal progress and reach higher levels of achievement ((Self-) education in a paradigm shift, 2017; Guidelines for Updating the General Curriculum, 2019). Educational documents and methodological guidelines state that the educational process should be based on active cognition, the application of acquired knowledge in practical activities, the involvement of pupils in active and conscious learning, the development of an active interpretive relationship with the subject material, and the development of meaningful and coherent learning (Curriculum for pre-school, primary, basic and secondary education, 2022; Towards inclusion. What does a school need to know?, 2022). In the Good School Concept (2015), Methodology for self-evaluation of the quality of a general education school (2016), the aspects identified as defining successful learning are related to self-directed learning, constructivist learning and social learning (see Table 3.1.1).

Table 3.1.1: Creating learning experiences for pupils in a general education school

Self-directed learning	**Constructivist learning**	**Social learning**
With the teacher's support, pupils are able to set learning objectives, choose their own way of doing tasks, find the information and tools they need, ask questions and ask for help, discuss and evaluate their learning, and plan and manage time. They are aware of, recognise and try to solve learning problems. They are able to provide evidence of personal progress (individual work or achievement folders, learning diaries) by observing and reflecting on their progress. By reflecting on individual learning experiences, pupils help teachers to assess the depth and relevance of learning.	Pupils are encouraged to link what they have learned and their personal experiences with the unknown, creating meaningful connections. They are taught to visualise and explain how they think, demonstrate abilities and ways of doing things. By constantly revisiting what they have already learned, they learn to make connections between ideas, to grasp, to test and to reconstruct their understanding, thinking or way of doing things.	Pupils are able and motivated to learn cooperatively in a variety of contexts, in groups of varying size and composition, and in partnership (pairs). They help each other to learn. They are able to express themselves publicly and to listen to others, to question, to debate, to defend their opinions, to explain a point of view (orally, textually, pictorially), to analyse and solve problems together, and to develop a shared understanding, solutions or work.

However, data from the external assessment of general education schools in Lithuania, which has been organised for more than a decade, show that the changes in educational practices outlined in the national education documents have been very slow to take place, or that the problems in school performance identified for more than a decade have not yet been solved. In a report prepared by the former National School Assessment Agency (now the National Agency for Education), Quality of performance of general education schools (2015), four school activities that need to be improved are related to monitoring and assessing pupils' progress and achievement in the classroom. The authors of the report point out that "the plethora of national projects initiating change in the teaching/learning process in Lithuania, which have taken place and are still ongoing, suggests that educational quality in all educational institutions should improve significantly year on year. However, according to recent external assessments, educators have a wealth of knowledge about teaching/learning methods, paradigms and other aspects of education and learning, but their knowledge is not always successfully applied in practice."

The 2017–2018 external comprehensive assessment of the quality of school performance revealed that the lessons observed by the assessors were dominated by a teaching process centred on the teacher, with the pupil as a passive receiver of information, taught according to the teacher's objectives and plan, and often using traditional methods of teaching (explaining, demonstrating, narrating, writing, reading, etc.). As a result, in some lessons, pupils were not encouraged and taught to monitor and adjust their learning independently and to plan their next steps. In half or more of the lessons, the components of the lesson relating to each pupil's progress and achievement, assessment while being educated and learning experiences were rated as satisfactory by the assessors (Quality of performance of general education schools. Annual report 2018, 2018). The assessors' conclusions and recommendations to schools suggested moving away from an "instructional culture" and emphasised the importance of providing continuous feedback to help students solve learning problems in order to develop a sense of responsibility for their own learning and self-management of their learning. For example, external assessment reports indicate: "[…] it is worth pointing out that following teachers' instructions in a responsible way does not, however, give pupils the opportunity to develop their learning competences, as they are not encouraged to plan their own learning in a meaningful way, nor are they given the opportunity to choose the tasks, the sources of information, the type of activities, etc." (External assessment report of Kurmaičiai Primary School in Kretinga District, 2018, 12) "[…] teachers do not make enough use of discussing pupils' learning and sharing progress data as a way of improving pupils' learning outcomes. […] pupils are not sufficiently involved and/or engaged in reflecting on their own performance in the lesson" (External Assessment Report of Rimantas Stankevičius Primary School in Marijampolė, 2018, 10). In only a few lessons did the assessors record activities that would encourage students to systematise their experience, to understand the multidimensionality of the cognitive process, to know themselves better as learners, to understand the features of their individual perceptions and to use them as a basis for completing tasks and solving problems (Learning in a general education school:

what does the data from the comprehensive and external risk assessment show?, 2019).

The analysis of the protocols of the lessons observed during the 2018 external assessment revealed that the lessons identified by the assessors as "modern", based on the paradigm of freestyle education and learning, i.e. the teacher acts as an adviser and consultant in the organisation of the educational process, relying on the pupils' experience, the environment, and using individual and group work methods, only partly provide opportunities for the pupils' development of self-directed learning abilities (Jašinauskas, 2019). In most cases, lessons focus only on some aspects of the self-directed learning process, such as discussing and formulating learning objectives and criteria for assessing performance with students, encouraging them to work collaboratively in groups and pairs, checking and self-evaluating whether they have achieved the intended (by the teacher/themselves) learning goals and objectives. However, in some lessons pupils are not encouraged and taught to plan, monitor and manage their own learning process. In lessons, teachers tell pupils (usually without class discussion) what the learning objectives will be, the criteria for assessing learning outcomes, how the lesson will be taught, how pupils will have to self-evaluate their performance, or summarise the lesson themselves, giving a whole class/individual assessment of pupils' achievement and progress. In research published in the last decade, self-directed learning is primarily associated with the learner's personal initiative to take responsibility for his/her own learning, which becomes the basis and starting point for planning, implementing, monitoring and managing as well as assessing his/her own learning and performance. In self-directed learning, learners, with the support of others or on their own, identify their learning needs, formulate learning objectives, identify the resources needed to achieve them, select and implement learning strategies and self-evaluate their performance (Thornton, 2010; Žydžiūnaitė et al., 2012; Conradie, 2014; Dubosas, 2016). We take this opportunity to draw attention to a study performed in 2012 by a group of researchers at Šiauliai University on the experience of self-managed learning in general education schools. The results showed that in schools, self-directed learning is most often seen as an end result, but not as a process that should provide opportunities for pupils to learn, to gain experience of self-directed learning (Gaučaitė et al., 2012). Action research would help to address this situation by taking into account the problems that arise in a given environment and by seeing education as an ongoing and changing process.

Similar problematic areas have been highlighted in recent years when analysing the quality of the teaching/learning process and the assessment of pupils' achievements in general education schools. One of the objectives of the national educational content update is to ensure coherence among educational objectives, content implementation and performance assessment (Lithuania. Education in the country and regions, 2019; Guidelines for Updating the General Curriculum, 2019). However, despite the projects that have been prepared and implemented, or even launched, to improve, develop and implement the educational content, the problems of the teaching/learning process in schools, such as teaching/learning planning, assessment of pupils' progress and achievements, and provision of feedback, have only been partially resolved (Kazragytė & Kudinovienė, 2018; Juškevičienė, 2019; Šarckuvienė, 2020; Implementation of the National Education Strategy 2013–2022. Material for discussion, 2024).

In this context of constantly rethinking and re-setting the goals of general education, which very often do not "reach" educational practice or are only partially implemented, it becomes essential to take a fresh look at the lesson in the classroom. The question is: can we successfully implement the new general education goals, the priorities for updating content and its implementation, and the directions to be taken, when it becomes clear that we are facing the same problems we faced five, seven or even more years ago? Therefore, based on the data from the 2019, 2021–2022 external quality assessment of the performance of general education schools, it is important to identify key aspects of the classroom teaching/learning process that need improvement. In examining individual issues of lesson quality, given the nature and scope of the available external assessment data, the work also focuses on school-based research activities as a basis for teachers' planning, implementation and adjustments to the classroom teaching/learning process.

External assessment of Lithuanian schools and a look at lesson quality. Data from the National Agency for Education's (NAE) external assessment of the quality of the performance of general education schools enables researchers to analyse the performance of the country's schools from a variety of perspectives. The data collected during the external assessment allows us not only to assess the quality of teaching/learning, to plan and anticipate priorities and directions for improvement of schools' activities, but also to talk about the expression of the features of the teaching/learning process defined in educational documents and the desired features of teaching/learning process in the practice of education, and to analyse the problems of the quality of teaching/learning process that have become apparent.

External assessment of the quality of school performance in Lithuania has been performed for several decades and is an integral part of education monitoring. Lithuania is a member of the Standing International Conference of Inspectorates (SICI), which brings together nearly forty members from twenty-seven countries with specific bodies established for the external assessment of schools and the external assessment of educational institutions (SICI members map, 2024).

Since 2018, the external assessment of general education schools in Lithuania has been defined as a formative assessment of school processes and is organised in three types of assessment: comprehensive (assessing the whole-school activity), thematic (assessing the school's activity by looking at a relevant topic (problem, issue, question) identified by the Minister of Education and Science), risk (identifying and analysing the risk factors of the school's activity and identifying opportunities for improvement) (Description of the procedure for organising and performing external assessments of the performance of general education schools, 2018). External assessments collect and refine data on the quality of the school's performance and observe teaching/learning activities organised by teachers, which account for at least 75% of the assessors' time at the school. The performance of the school as an educational institution and the performance of each teacher working there is monitored in accordance with the Quality Assessment Indicators for general education schools.

The school's performance is assessed on a 5-level scale in a comprehensive, thematic or risk assessment: level 4 (very good): the activity is effective, outstanding, focused, distinctive, creative; the experience of such activity is worth disseminating outside the school; level 3 (good): the quality of the activity is above average, relevant, impactful, promising, flexible; the experience of the teachers so rated is worth disseminating within the school; level 2 (satisfactory): the activity is mediocre, fair, unsystematic, unexciting; the school has room for improvement and is worth strengthening and developing; level 1 (poor): the performance is unsatisfactory, ineffective, inadequate, unspecific; the performance needs to be improved and the school needs external help; level N (very poor) – the performance is unacceptable; radical changes are needed and the school needs urgent external help (Description of the Procedure for Organising and Performing External Assessment of the Performance of General Education Schools, 2018).

Problematic areas related to the teaching/learning process in the classroom. The external assessment data from recent years show that, despite the different types of school external assessments, assessment indicator systems, methodologies and scopes of assessment used, there are certain problematic areas that are related to the teaching/learning process in the classroom (Figure 3.1.1).

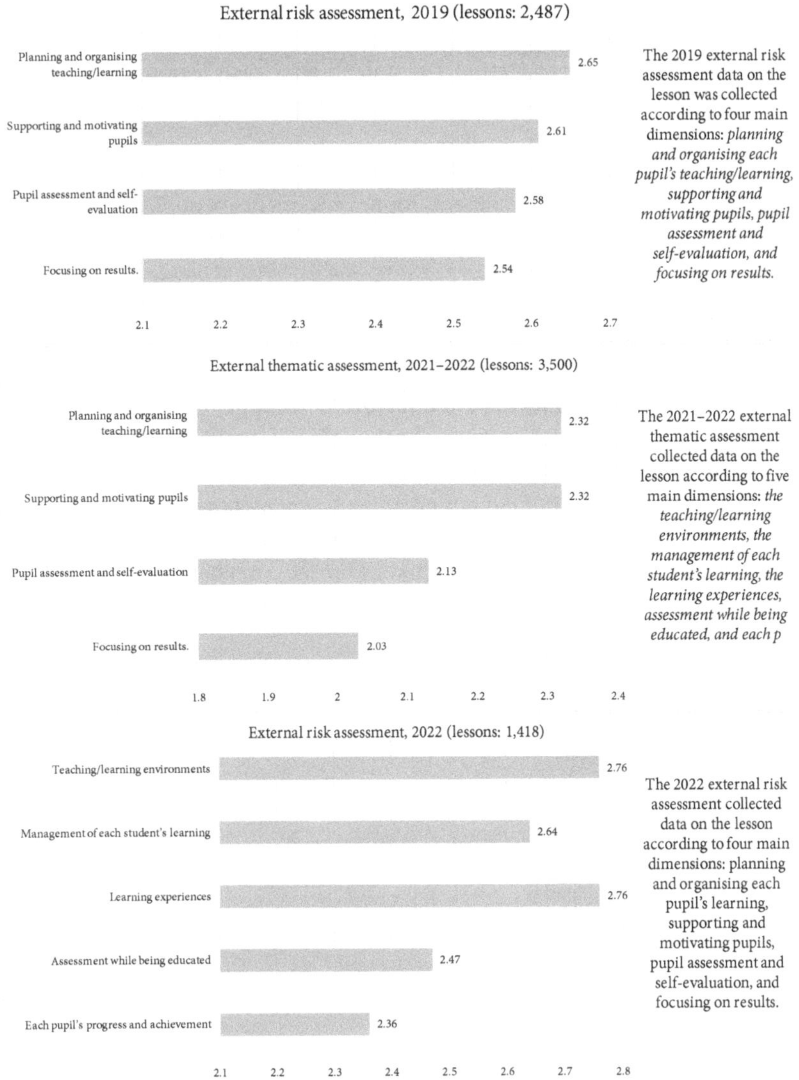

Figure 3.1.1: Average scores for the quality of the lessons observed during the external assessment, according to different aspects of the lesson

The aspects of the lesson that scored the lowest in the 2019 external risk assessment were *the progress and achievement of each pupil, and the assessment while being educated.* These aspects of the lesson were the worst-assessed in the 2021–2022 thematic assessment, compared to other aspects. The lowest scores in the 2022 external risk assessment were in the *focusing on results, and in pupil assessment and self-evaluation.* In the external assessment, after each lesson observed, the assessors discussed the lesson with the teacher and identified the strengths and the areas for improvement of the lesson.

The data from the quality assessment of the observed lessons show that the most frequently identified components for improvement are pupils' performance in the lesson, *planning of teaching/learning, pupils' involvement in the teaching/learning process, self-management of learning, and assessment and self-evaluation of progress and achievements.* The aspects of the lesson to be improved are discussed in more detail in the sub-chapters of this work, in the context of the external assessment data of schools in certain years.

External risk assessment, 2019: a lesson for schools with "weak expression of the characteristics of a good school". The external risk assessment data revealed that the assessed schools *encourage pupils to collaborate with each other, to participate in joint activities, to design their personal futures, and to engage in activities in different contexts.* These are identified by the assessors as strengths of these schools (Statistics on the external assessment of the performance of general education schools. Results of the 2019 external risk assessment, 2019).

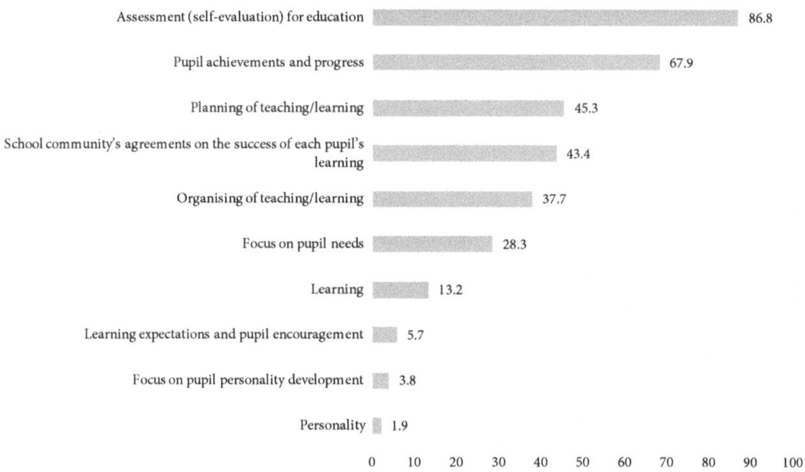

Figure 3.1.2: Aspects of performance to be improved in schools assessed in 2019 (%, N=53) (Data source: NAE, 2019)

However, monitoring, assessment and self-evaluation of pupils' achievements and progress, systematic and consistent focus on pupils' progress, planning of teaching/learning, school community agreements on the success of each pupil's teaching/learning, and the organisation of teaching/learning are the most frequently identified by the assessors as aspects of school performance that need improvement, and are associated with risky school performance (Figure 3.1.2).

Of the fifty-three assessed schools, ten had risk factors identified by the assessors that were related to assessment (self-evaluation) for education. Involving and engaging pupils in the assessment and self-evaluation process in the lesson, providing and applying assessment criteria, and providing feedback in the educational process are the most frequently identified by the assessors as areas for improvement that provide satisfactory conditions for pupils' achievement and progress. Lesson aspects pupils summarise the material they have learned and the results of their learning, pupils are informed and the expected assessment criteria are discussed with them, the learning objective is revisited and the result is discussed, pupils are encouraged to reflect and analyse the assessment information and to learn to understand what is helping or hindering their progress are the worst-rated by the assessors (mean score 2 (satisfactory)) (Statistics on the external assessment of the performance of general education schools. Results of the 2019 external risk assessment, 2019).

Pupils' achievement and progress is the second most problematic area of school performance identified by assessors, after self-evaluation for education. In thirty-six of the fifty-three assessed schools, the assessors identified risk factors related to pupils' achievement and progress. The external assessment reports of the schools indicate that the level of general and subject competences acquired by some pupils is not always in line with the objectives and learning experiences for their age group and the requirements of the general curriculum, and that pupils' academic achievement is low. The assessors point to the problems of recording pupils' achievements and individual pupil progress, the fact that very often there is no agreement in schools on a system for monitoring and measuring individual pupils' progress in lessons, or on measures to improve pupils' performance in order to achieve progress. Goals and targets for further learning are rarely based on information about pupils' achievements and progress, which does not encourage pupils' self-directed learning.

The organisation of pupils' learning in lessons is also rated as satisfactory (in the aspects of the lesson "teacher-led learning is combined with self-directed learning" (mean score 2.24), "teaching material is linked to other subjects, to life experience" (mean score 2.48), and "everybody is provided with the conditions for learning and success according to their abilities, and is able to co-operate with each other" (mean score 2.39).

External risk assessment reports on schools indicate that classroom activities are mostly based on the (traditional) teaching paradigm. What, how and for how long in lessons is mostly planned and decided by the teacher alone. The assessors noted that in more than half, and in some schools in most, of the lessons, the learning objectives were set by the teacher, while a minority or a proportion of pupils were able to choose the way in which tasks were carried out. Activities to encourage pupils to plan their learning, to choose their own way of doing things, to find the necessary information and tools and to self-evaluate their learning were observed by the assessors in only a few lessons.

Of the forty-six schools assessed in the first half of 2019, thirty-four schools (73.9%) were identified as having risky activities related to students' self-directed learning. For example, not systematically informing pupils about the expected criteria for assessing learning objectives, not often encouraging pupils to meaningfully reflect and analyse assessment information, not systematically involving pupils in reflecting on what they have achieved, and rarely allowing pupils to assess each other's work, to summarise their learning in class and to set further targets and guidelines for activities (see Figure 3.1.3).

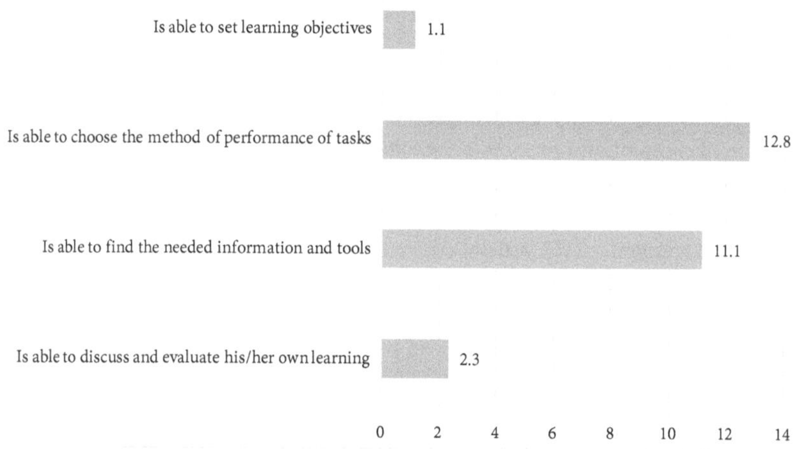

Figure 3.1.3: Self-directed learning in the classroom in 2019 (% of lessons, number of lessons N=171) (Data source: NAE, 2019)

It is only possible to talk about the expression of certain elements of constructivist learning in schools where an external risk assessment was performed. The reports indicate that, in most cases, pupils are encouraged in lessons to relate what they have learned to personal experiences, other subjects and life situations. Sporadic, fragmented activities were observed where pupils had to demonstrate their abilities, visualise their understanding or revisit what they had already learned. In some lessons, teachers' assignments provided opportunities for pupils to inquire (24.9%), solve problems and build on knowledge or abilities developed in other lessons (23.2%). It should be noted that although in a number of observed lessons teachers provided opportunities for students to work in pairs and groups, to help each other and to confer with each other, the majority of pupils have insufficient ability to work together in groups and pairs of different compositions (see Figure 3.1.4).

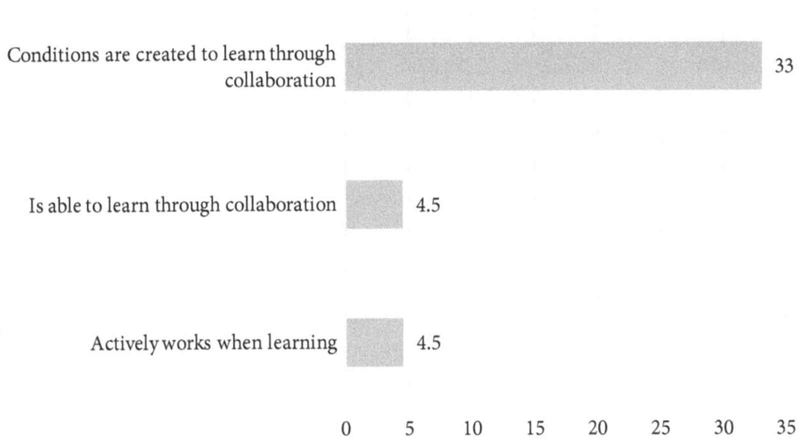

Figure 3.1.4: Social learning in the classroom in 2019 (% of lessons, number of lessons N=871) (Data source: NAE, 2019)

The reports state that "in lessons, efforts were made to create conditions for collaboration, but only some pupils were able to collaborate because pupils lacked social competences, i.e. to learn by discussing, finding joint solutions and demonstrating a joint result – the collaborative tasks partially promoted higher-level thinking/perception" (from a 2019 gymnasium external risk assessment report, 25). "Pupils are willing to participate in joint activities, but they are not always able to communicate, cooperate, take responsibility, and resolve conflicts in a constructive way" (from a 2019 primary school external risk assessment report, 7). "In the majority (89.1%) of the observed lessons, pupils' willingness and ability to communicate and cooperate was not effective, and the majority of pupils lacked social abilities and teamwork abilities" (External Risk Assessment Report on the Performance of Balsiai Primary School, Pakruojis District, 2019, 6–7).

The external risk assessment reports for schools assessed in 2019 show that pupils' ability to develop their understanding of issues solves problems, plan, monitor, adjust and self-evaluate their learning independently and in collaboration with others is developed only in a fragmented way in lessons. The assigned tasks and situations show that teachers are trying to raise pupils' awareness of the importance of learning how to learn, of relating new knowledge and abilities to existing experiences, of working in a collaborative way, but there are no step-by-step procedures, no tasks, no system of learning-oriented assessment that would not only help pupils to understand the importance of these things, but also to involve them in activities that encourage them to take decisions about their learning and their own performance.

External assessment reports highlight important issues related to *planning of teaching/learning* in the lesson. Assessors report that lessons do not systematically return to the lesson objective, rarely discuss with pupils how the objective was achieved, how pupils' achievements compare to the objective, and do not involve pupils in summarising the lesson's results. Planning of learning is identified in nineteen of the fifty-three schools assessed as a risk factor that has a strong impact on the quality of the lesson, pupils' achievement and progress. External assessment report data show that teachers often face difficulties in planning the potential achievements and progress of pupils, in defining assessment criteria, and in envisaging how the assessment and self-evaluation of pupils' achievements will be organised. One school's external assessment report states that "[…] the observed lessons did not record the extent to which the learning objective had been achieved, and there was no clear summary of the lesson, so that teachers and pupils were not in a position to plan the next lesson's teaching/learning achievement and progress in a targeted way. There was also insufficient focus on assessing individual pupils' progress against the learning objective and setting assessment criteria. Teachers themselves often described the success of the whole class, and rarely organised pupils' reflection on self-evaluation" (External risk assessment report for Palomenė Primary School, Kaišiadorys District, 2019, 3). This suggests that in some of the assessed schools, planning of teaching/learning, assessment and self-evaluation of pupils' achievements and progress constitute a kind of "vicious circle", with the teacher spinning the wheels of his/her activities, and pupils learning without a clear sense of direction, outlook and awareness of their own achievements and progress. Empowering learners to set their own performance targets, to collect evidence of their progress, to summarise the lesson, to self-evaluate and design their future learning aspirations would have a strong impact on the quality of teaching/learning.

2021–2022 external thematic assessment: the "inclusive school" lesson. The external assessment data show that schools' performance in the area of *leadership and management* (assessed according to eight indicators) scored higher than in the area of *teaching/learning and pupil experiences* (assessed according to three indicators) (see Figure 3.1.5).

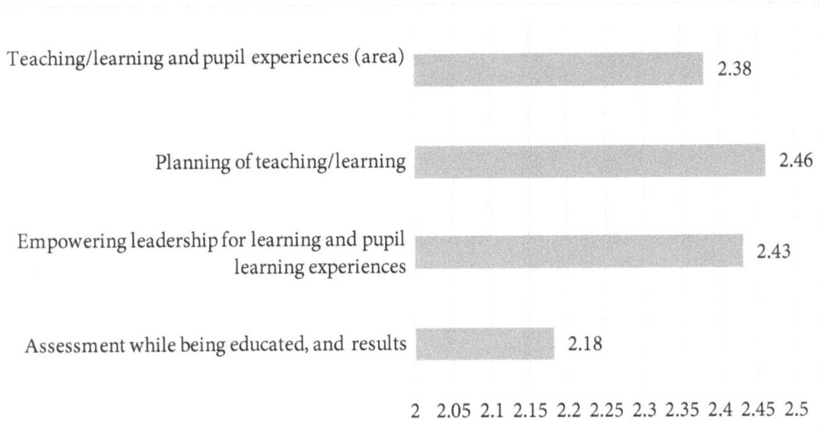

Figure 3.1.5: Mean scores for the indicators of teaching/learning and pupil experiences (number of schools N=61) (Data source: NAE, 2019)

The mean assessment score for schools' performance *in the area of leadership and management* was 2.90, with seven schools scoring 4 (very good). Looking at the individual indicators in this area, *school networking* was the most highly rated (eighteen schools rated at level 4 (very good) and forty-one schools at level 3 (good)). The more challenging activities were those related to *continuous professional development* and teacher *competence* (thirty-eight schools were assessed at level 3 (good), twenty-two schools at level 2 (satisfactory) and one school at level 4 (very good)).

The mean score for schools' performance in the area of learning *and student experiences* is significantly lower at 2.38 (Figure 3.1.5), with no school rated at level 4 (very good) in this area or in its individual indicators. In the individual indicators in this area, schools' performance was assessed more highly in the *planning of teaching/learning* (twenty-eight schools were assessed at level 3 (good), thirty-three schools at level 2 (satisfactory)), while the lowest scores were assessed for the indicator *assessment while being educated, and results* (eleven schools were assessed at level 3 (good), fifty schools at level 2 (satisfactory)).

In 2021–2022, when assessing the focus on inclusive education, *building an inclusive culture* was identified as a strength in more than half of the assessed schools, while in more than a third of the schools, *optimal resource allocation, school networking, shared vision and the roles of educational support specialists and teaching assistants* were identified as strengths (Statistics of the external assessment of the performance of general education schools. Results of the external risk assessment, 2021–2022, 2022).

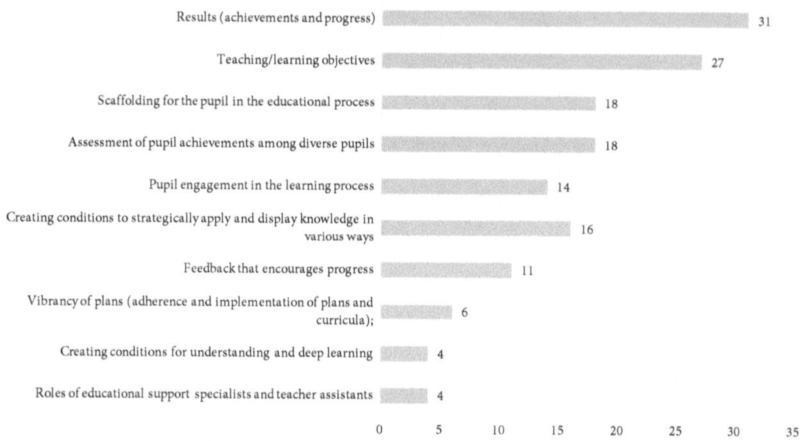

Figure 3.1.6: Aspects of performance to be improved in schools assessed in 2021–2022 (%, N=61) (Data source: NAE, 2022)

The aspects for school improvement identified by the assessors relate to the planning and organisation of the teaching/learning process (Figure 3.1.6). In almost half of the assessed schools, these included *results (achievement and progress)* and *learning objectives*, and in almost a third of the schools, they included *scaffolding for the pupil in the educational process, the assessment of pupil achievement among diverse pupils, and pupil engagement in the learning process.*

Planning and organising the teaching/learning process in the lesson. The assessment data show that although in most schools the assessors rated the planning activities performed by the educational support specialists and teachers and the support provided by the school to the pupil at level 3, one of the most frequently identified aspects for improvement in the lesson is the development and formulation of *the teaching/learning objectives* as well as the *scaffolding for the pupil in the educational process* (Figure 3.1.7).

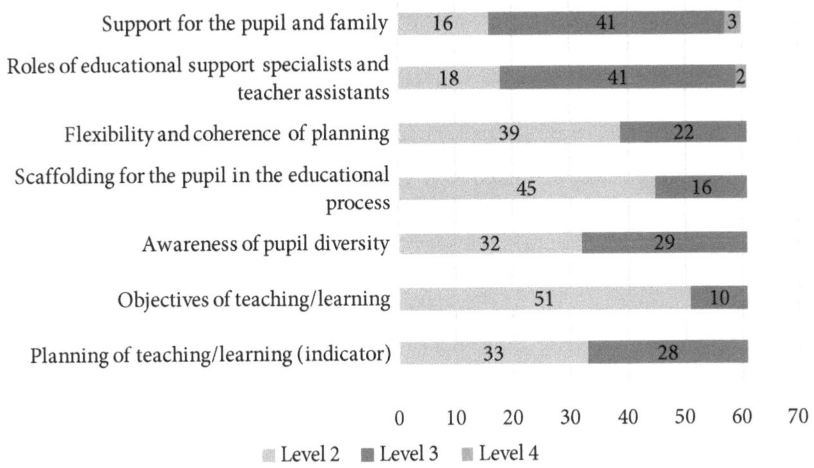

Figure 3.1.7: Distribution of schools by assessment level for planning of teaching/learning (number of schools N=61) (Data source: NAE, 2022)

Analysing the 2021 assessment of schools' awareness of pupil diversity and the envisaging of potential barriers to learning in lessons, it was observed that only in some of the observed lessons (between 7.5% and 30%) was the educational content of the lesson effectively planned and implemented on the basis of awareness of pupil diversity, in terms of the formulation of the lesson's objectives, the choice and application of teaching methods, the monitoring of pupil learning, the identification of barriers to learning, and the decision-making process for their resolution. For example, "in only 5 lessons observed by the assessors was the learning objective linked to the knowledge of the pupils, oriented towards their different learning experiences and identified as a strength"; "in only a part of the lessons observed (28.26%) did the teacher provide timely support to pupils, adapting and differentiating the educational content for children of different abilities, individualising with targeted guidance"; "awareness of pupil diversity was highlighted as a strength of the lesson in 15 lessons, i.e. 30% of the total number of lessons, which shows that only some teachers allow the selection of tasks that reflect the pupils' individual abilities in their lessons."

Teachers' decisions about planning specific lessons, setting goals and objectives, and providing scaffolding were mostly assessed at level 2 (satisfactory) (Figure 3.1.7). In a third of the observed lessons, the assessors identified strengths related to the planning of pupil teaching/learning and areas for improvement (Figure 3.1.8). In just over a tenth of the observed lessons, assessors highlighted as strong aspects the involvement of students in the discussion of the lesson's aim, objective and outcomes, the definition of the lesson's objective and its link to a learning outcome that is comprehensible to students: "The teaching/learning objectives are measurable, discussed with the pupils, and the expected results are known"; "The pupils know what each of them is aiming for in the lesson"; "The task is result-oriented, the children can achieve it"; the assessments of the quality of the lesson and the illustrations of the activities organised are taken from the lesson observation reports. In some of the lessons, the assessors recorded the relevance of the teaching objective and tasks to the different teaching/learning needs of the pupils: "Objectives and activities are focused on the pupil experience and the outcomes of the curriculum"; "The teacher takes into account the pupils' personal experience before setting the objectives of the lesson"; "The objective is linked to the pupil's personal experience". The strengths and areas for improvement in lesson planning are shown in Figure 3.1.8:

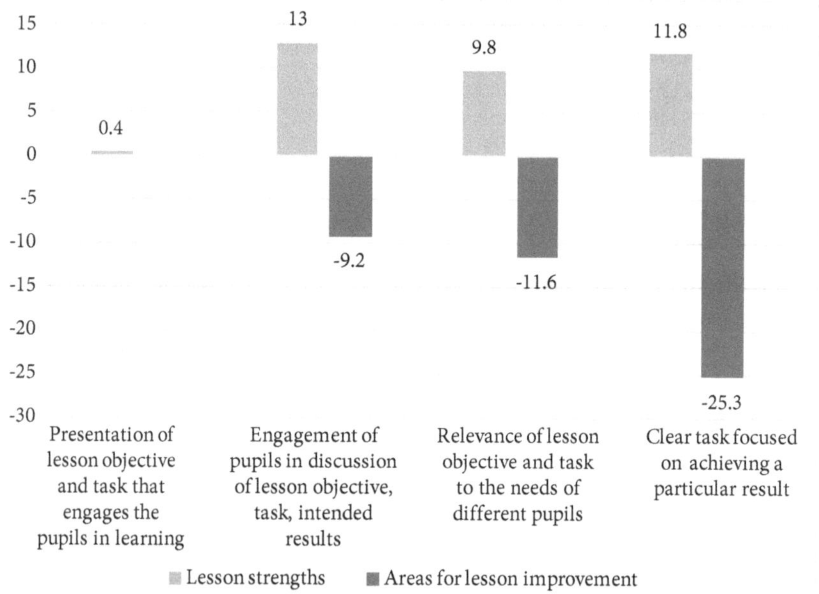

Figure 3.1.8: Strengths and areas for improvement in lesson planning (2021, % of lessons, number of lessons N=501) (Data source: NAE, 2022)

Only in relatively few lessons were the lesson's objective and tasks presented in an engaging way, allowing pupils to choose their tasks at the beginning of the lesson, providing guiding questions to achieve the objective and task, and actualising the task and linking it to practical activities and the pupils' experience.

The aspects of lesson planning identified as most in need of improvement relate to task formulation and lesson planning based on the teaching/learning needs of the pupils (Figure 3.1.8). In a fourth of the observed lessons, assessors pointed out that abstract objectives were set and presented to pupils, usually only identifying the activities: "The task […] is not measurable, the result is unclear"; "The lesson task is activity-oriented, so the result is unclear"; "The lesson task is not specific, the expected result is undefined". In almost one in ten lessons, the assessors identified the relevance of the learning task to the different teaching/learning needs of the pupils, the involvement of pupils in the planning of learning, the actualisation of their personal experience and responsibility in the lesson as the aspects of lesson planning that could be improved: "teaching/learning objectives are the same for all pupils, abstract"; "The task is not specific, not adapted to pupils of different abilities"; "The task is undifferentiated, no measurable criteria"; "The task and the expected result are not discussed with the pupils".

In the 2021 external thematic assessment reports, in seventeen out of thirty schools, the assessors noted that the majority of lessons (between 54.1% and 96%) included announcements or presentations of the lesson objectives to pupils. The analysis of external thematic assessment data for thirteen schools showed that in more than half of the observed lessons in these schools (from 52.2% to 68.5%), the teacher's announcement of the lesson objective to the pupils was focused on the activities, rather than on the outcome and the identification of the conditions for the activities: "improve agility and speed abilities"; "recall previously-seen members and match up similar members"; and "carry out measurements and calculations on a map". Teachers rarely discussed the lesson objective with pupils or encouraged them to set personal expectations for the lesson, to work towards them and to reflect on them.

Aspects of the practical expression of inclusive education in terms of planning for pupils' different learning experiences and abilities were noted by the assessors in only a fraction of the observed lessons: "The lesson objective was announced to pupils in 37 observed lessons, but in only one lesson (Lithuanian Language and Literature, class 7b) did pupils have the opportunity to set a personal learning task"; "teaching/learning objectives as a strong aspect of the lesson were highlighted […] in 9% of all observed lessons […]. Pupils are taught to set personal goals, the teacher's objectives and performance criteria are clear, and the educational objective is linked to the abilities, personal experiences, interests and inclusive and relevant context of the majority of pupils"; "In only 5 (7.5%) of lessons observed by the assessors was the learning objective linked to the pupils' knowledge, and set in a way that focused on the pupils' different learning experiences".

The strengths and areas for improvement identified by the assessors in the observed lessons in terms of scaffolding for the pupil in the educational process reflect the fact that lesson planning only partially provides for educational solutions and alternatives to activities that should help students to avoid barriers to learning and to ensure their learning success. The external thematic assessment of thirty schools in 2021 shows that scaffolding for pupils in lessons is mostly fragmented, often unplanned, linked to the teacher's response to pupils' learning difficulties that appear in the teaching/learning process, and does not provide an adequate system of learning support for pupils. We can only talk about separate elements of scaffolding for the pupil in the educational process and their expression in the lesson (Figure 3.1.9).

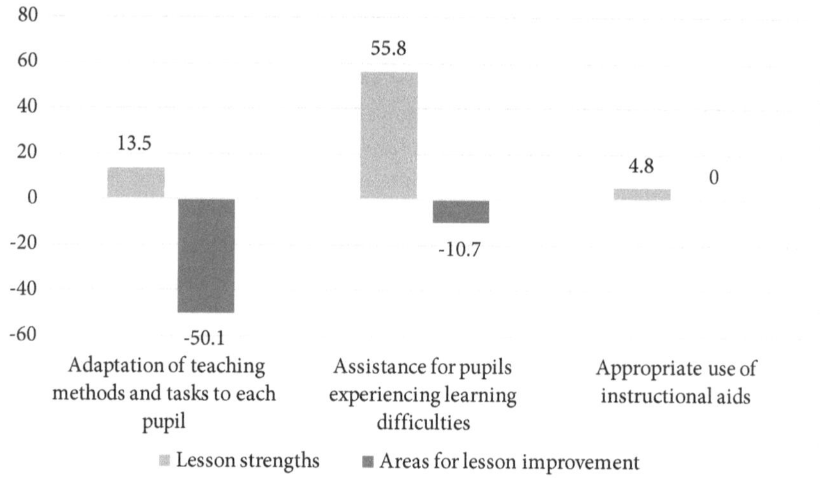

Figure 3.1.9: Strengths and areas for improvement in scaffolding for the pupil in the educational process (2021, % of lessons, number of lessons N=556) (Data source: NAE, 2021)

In more than half of the lessons, the assessors highlighted the provision of support to pupils who were encountering learning difficulties and to pupils with SEN as a strength of the lesson: "Systematically provides support, additional illustration of explanation"; "Support is provided to every pupil with learning difficulties"; "Almost all pupils receive help from the teacher, including SEN (works with an assistant)"; "The teacher helps some pupils to create text and express their thoughts" (Figure 3.1.9). The external thematic assessment reports reveal that pupils are supported with additional explanations, guiding questions, individual guidance, additional learning aids, peer support, and the ability to choose the tasks and the pace at which they are completed. However, in only some lessons (13.5%) did teachers plan and apply teaching methods and provide tasks based on pupils' learning needs and abilities ("The content of the education is adapted to the needs of different pupils"; "The tasks are chosen to avoid barriers to learning"; "The tasks are adapted to the SEN pupil's abilities"), and pupils were provided with a choice of learning aids during the activities (5%) ("Gives a choice of tools, monitors and helps to do the work well, gives advice"; "Supplementary tools enable achieving the lesson objective and making personal progress") (Figure 3.1.9).

The assessors noted that in half of the lessons, teachers applied the same teaching methods to all pupils, pupils used the same tools and the same tasks were assigned to the entire class: "Variety of methods needs to be improved, taking into account the abilities of the pupils"; "The tasks are all the same, the timing of the tasks is the same, and the different abilities of pupils are not taken into account"; and "There was a lack of adaptation of the educational content and the activities to pupils of different abilities".

The external thematic assessment reports note that in the majority of observed lessons, the educational content was not differentiated and individualised: "In 88.22% of the observed lessons, all pupils performed the same tasks, used the same teaching/learning tools, the same activities were organised for all pupils, and the work was done at the same pace"; "The tasks are mostly the same for all pupils, there are no tasks at different levels, there is a lack of differentiation and individualisation of tasks, and the more able pupils are not put to use, and there are no opportunities to choose a different way of learning. In addition, there is insufficient focus on pupils with SEN"; "Provided mostly the same tasks to the whole class or group, did not develop higher order thinking abilities, did not regroup pupils according to their learning needs" (External thematic assessment report on the performance of the Atgimimas School in Druskininkai, 2021, 14; External thematic assessment report on the performance of Anelė and Augustinas Kriauzai Primary School in Raudondvaris, Kaunas District, 2022, 10; External thematic assessment report on the performance of Šeškinė Primary School in Vilnius, 2021, 16). In one of the assessed schools, more than half of the observed lessons were organised without taking into account the needs of pupils with special educational needs (SEN): "In 69.44% of the lessons in which a pupil with SEN was present in the classroom, the same tasks were given to the pupil with SEN, or no tasks at all were given to the pupil with SEN" (External thematic assessment report on the performance of Alexander Pushkin Gymnasium in Vilnius, 2021, 15). In some lessons (11%), the provision of support to pupils was identified as an aspect of the teacher's work that needed to be improved, was ineffective or not targeted, and some pupils did not receive individual support: "Scaffolding is almost non-existent", "Sometimes help is given when it is not really needed"; "Some pupils did not receive help and support and did not manage to complete the *task*"; "Not all pupils receive individual support from the teacher".

In the external thematic assessment reports of four schools, the assessment teams reported successful scaffolding in only a few lessons: "In only 1 […] lesson (mathematics in class 3) did the assessors record successful scaffolding, with all pupils who had learning difficulties receiving appropriate interventions for overcoming the obstacles"; "In the lessons observed by the external assessors, scaffolding was highlighted in 3 of the 23 lessons as a strength of the educational process"; "Exceptional examples of scaffolding, using teacher-developed supplementary measures to overcome obstacles and suggesting that the pupil choose a different way of learning, were observed in the speech and language therapy exercises in class 2c (I)"; "Assessors highlighted pupils' cognition as a strong aspect of the lesson in […], i.e. in 9% of the lessons" (External thematic assessment report on the performance of the Sofija Kovalevskaja Pro-Gymnasium in Vilnius, 2022, 14; External thematic assessment report on the performance of Juventa Pro-Gymnasium in Šiauliai, 2021, 15; External thematic assessment report on the performance of Kaštonai Primary School in Biržai, 2021, 19).

Involving pupils in the learning process. The majority of schools score well (level 3) in creating an inclusive culture, where relationships between pupils, between pupils and teachers, and between teachers are based on encouraging positive behaviour, respect, trust, listening and hearing out, goodwill, caring, helping and sharing (Indicators for the external thematic assessment of the performance of general education schools in the period 2021–2022 on the theme "focus on inclusive education in general education schools", 2021). However, the aspects of the teaching/learning process, created by the teacher together with the pupils and related to the motivated engagement of each pupil in the learning process and the development of self-directed, deep learning, were rated as level 2 (satisfactory) (Figure 3.1.10).

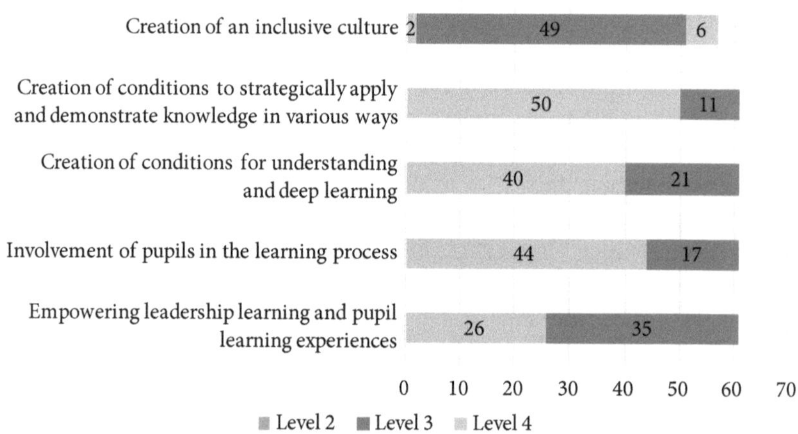

Figure 3.1.10: School assessment levels for empowering learning leadership and pupils' learning experiences (number of schools N=61) (Data source: NAE, 2022)

The strengths and areas for improvement identified by the assessors show that in a small proportion of the observed lessons, teachers were successful in creating opportunities for pupils to work together (11.7%). ("Cooperation among pupils is encouraged, mutual help is provided"; "Conditions are created for each pupil to engage in learning, to cooperate"; "Pupils are encouraged to communicate and cooperate in tasks"), the variety of teaching methods, tools and tasks used by teachers promoted pupils' engagement in the learning process (8.61% of the lessons). ("The methods used encourage pupils to engage in active learning"; "Interesting, engaging, age-appropriate tasks"; "The variety of tasks enabled pupils to engage in learning"), pupils were encouraged to learn on their own, i.e. to be involved in the planning of learning, to choose the way they learn, the tasks or the tools (5.14% of lessons) ("Some pupils are involved in the setting of the learning task"; "They are allowed to choose what and how many tasks to do"; "The way the task is done") (see Figure 3.1.11).

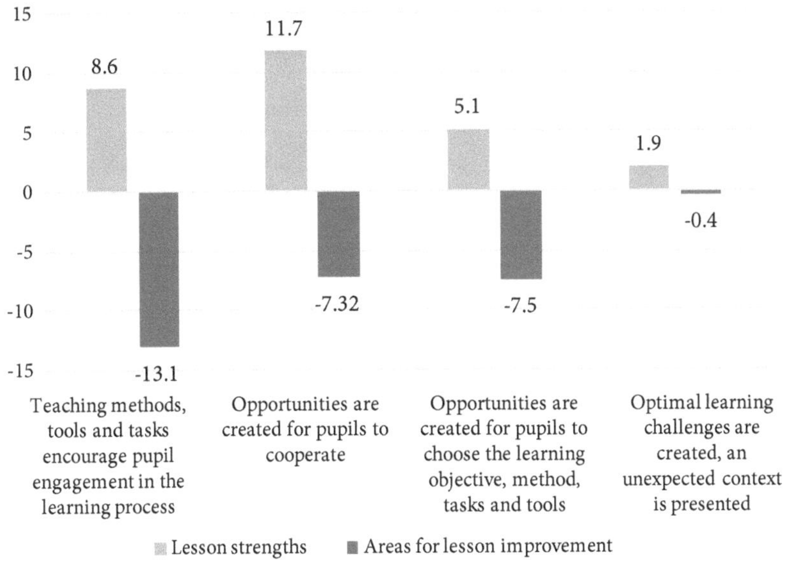

Figure 3.1.11: Strengths and areas for improvement in motivating all pupils to engage in the learning process (2021, % of lessons, number of lessons N=836) (Data source: NAE, 2021)

In lessons where the assessors identified strengths and areas for improvement related to creating conditions for pupils' deep learning, it was noted that in one-third of the lessons, teachers made good use of visualisation to present new material, made appropriate use of digital teaching tools, presented learning material in a variety of ways, and made connections between pupils' new knowledge and their existing knowledge: "The use of visual aids helps pupils to better understand the topic"; "The material is illustrated with different objects"; "The learning material is presented in different ways (sound, image, language, hands-on activities" (Figure 3.1.12).

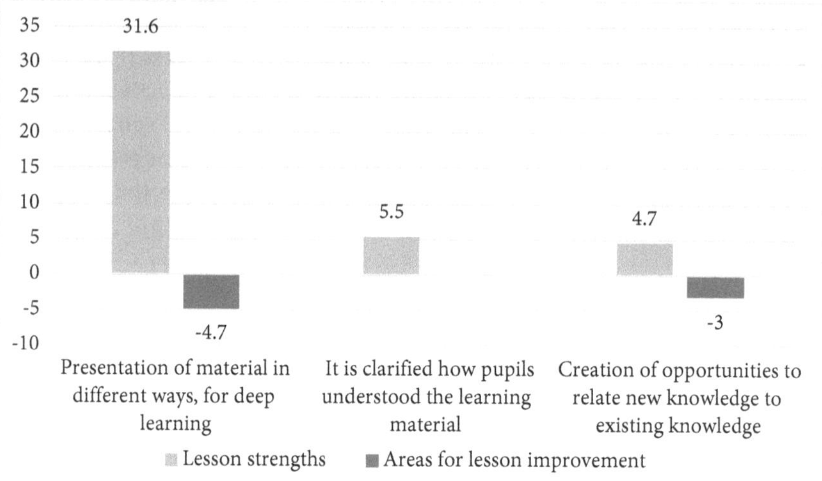

Figure 3.1.12: Strengths and areas for improvement in facilitating pupils' understanding and deep learning (2021, % of lessons, number of lessons N=508) (Data source: NAE, 2021)

This strengthened pupils' motivation to learn and increased opportunities for inclusion. However, in only a small number of lessons did teachers successfully check and clarify how pupils understood the new material ("The teacher makes sure that pupils have understood the words used"; "The teacher keeps checking that pupils understand"; "Pupils are encouraged to think more deeply about and grasp the essentials"), allowing them to make links between new and existing knowledge.

The analysis of the observed lessons shows that the majority of lessons rarely provided opportunities for each pupil to apply his or her knowledge by strategising, planning, designing, problem-solving, analysing, organising and relating it to his or her own experience. Analysis of the external thematic assessment reports shows that in seventeen out of thirty schools, adequate conditions for *strategic application and for demonstrating knowledge in a variety of ways* were provided in fewer than half of the observed lessons (between 10 and 45.1%): "In lessons, pupils demonstrated their knowledge through experiments, drawing diagrams, IT tasks, exercises, but the conditions for demonstrating knowledge, taking into account each pupil's abilities, differences and interests, were only partially provided";

"Good examples were observed in natural and human [...], mathematics [...], Lithuanian language [...], where pupils themselves explained the topic in various ways, raised problematic questions, were able to explain in their own words what they understood, and were encouraged to think critically".

In twenty out of thirty schools, *building an inclusive culture* was identified as a strength of the school's performance. In eight schools, building an inclusive culture was identified as a strength in the majority of lessons observed by the assessors (63.4% to 86%): "Good communication in the classroom, demonstration of trust in pupils, positive encouragement of desirable behaviour, adherence to agreed rules of work"; "Very good interpersonal relationships in the classroom, where the teacher's positive behaviour promotes trust and engagement of each pupil, and where interpersonal relationships are based on positive encouragement of behaviour"; "Good pupil-to-pupil relationships, teacher-pupil relationships, pupils' support for each other".

Assessment of pupils' achievements and progress and teaching/learning outcomes in the classroom. The external thematic assessment of schools shows that the lowest scores were assessed for the indicator *assessment while being educated, and results* (four schools were assessed at level 3 and twenty-six schools at level 2). In half of the assessed schools, *results (achievement and progress)* and *assessment of achievements among diverse pupils* were identified as aspects of school performance to be improved (see Figure 3.1.13).

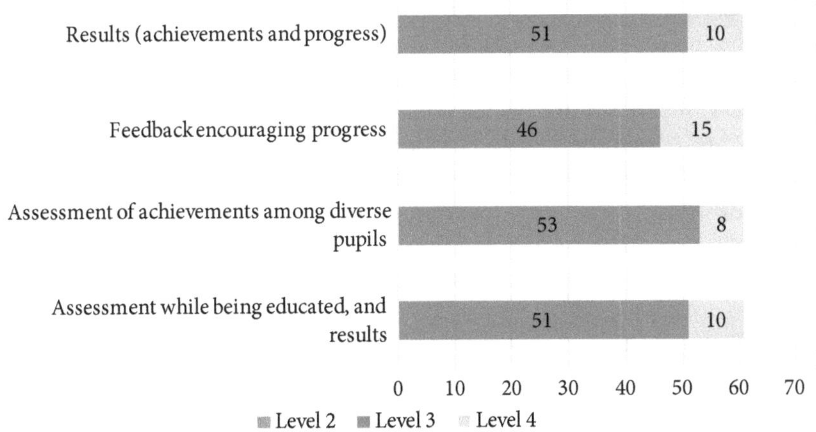

Figure 3.1.13: Mean scores for the indicators in the area of assessment while being educated, and results (number of schools N=61) (Data source: NAE, 2022)

The assessment of achievements among diverse pupils is unexceptional (assessed at level 2). External assessors' lesson observations noted the strengths of the lesson related to the assessment criteria (19.9%): they were presented to the pupils during the lesson, they were clear to the majority of pupils, and they were discussed with the pupils. In 47.7% of the observed lessons, the external assessors noted the assessment criteria as an aspect of the lesson that could be improved: lack of assessment criteria, lack of clarity regarding assessment criteria, lack of criteria for success, checking tasks without assessment criteria, etc. In 23.4% of the cases, formative assessment elements were noted as strengths of the lesson, facilitating pupils' motivation and personal progress, allowing pupils to make mistakes, consulting, and revisiting misunderstood content: "9 lessons (19.7%) made good use of formative and cumulative assessment, which enhanced pupils' motivation to learn and confidence in their work. Reflection allowed students to identify what they had learned, to assess their friends' answers, and to check their solutions"

Examples of activities noted during the external thematic assessment of schools show that a school often has agreed on assessment of each pupil's achievements and progress, but the assessment itself is not systematic ("The assessment of pupils' achievements and progress is regulated in the school's procedure for the assessment of pupils' achievement and progress"; "The learning progress and achievements in the learning process of pupils with special educational needs are assessed in accordance with the learning objectives of the pupil's individual education plan and the adapted curriculum, taking into account the pupil's potential"; "The learning outcomes of pupils with special educational needs who follow adapted general education curricula are assessed using the same point system as all pupils, with the same adapted assessment and reporting methods"); the assessment process is seen as an integral part of learning, fostering pupil confidence, reflection and direction ("Mistakes were identified as a natural part of each pupil's learning, fostering a drive for improvement, guiding the assessment of each pupil's performance, providing the right conditions for self-evaluation, and focusing on the impact of the activity on each pupil's performance"; "Teachers organised reflective activities with feedback, using purposeful tasks to encourage pupils to reflect on their performance"; "A variety of ways of assessing and self-evaluating pupils' performance in the classroom are used, and all pupils are clear about how they will be assessed and what the teacher expects of them"). The most frequently identified areas for improvement are the following: unclear or insufficiently clear assessment criteria, no opportunity for personalisation of assessment criteria, and poorly thought-out differentiated assessment of pupils. Large class sizes reduce teachers' ability to personalise, individualise and adapt the content for each learner. Only in a few lessons is *the assessment of achievements, in a context of pupil diversity* (see Figure 3.1.14), highlighted as a strength of the lesson: "Pupils and teachers were active, regular individual reflection helped each pupil to improve and work in a focused way, and continuous assessment of each pupil was a part of their learning"; "Individual teachers use a variety of assessment methods to plan, observe and adjust learning, including diagnostic, formative, summative, formal and non-formal assessment"; "In only 11 lessons (28.2% of the total number of lessons) was the lesson task linked to qualitative or quantitative criteria for assessing performance, and what would be considered good work was discussed with the pupils".

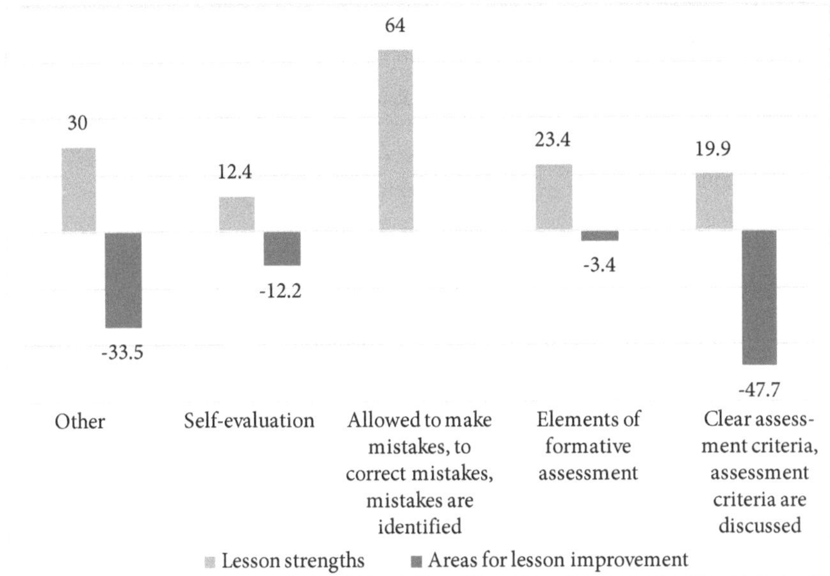

Figure 3.1.14: Strengths and areas for improvement in assessing achievements among diverse pupils (% of lessons, number of lessons N=189) (Data source: NAE, 2021)

The external assessment data shows that the *feedback encouraging progress* is unexceptional (assessed at level 2). When analysed in terms of individual aspects, the best-assessed aspect is the provision of feedback, which is timely and impactful (29.9%), with time for reflection (7.1%), based on a mutual dialogue about successes and failures (5.1%), information about learning is provided through consultation, timely and effective individual support, continuous encouragement, discussion of progress, monitoring, recording and reflection on learning, attention to each pupil, opportunities to make and record personal progress, and targeted and appropriate monitoring of learning enables pupils to make personal progress, builds confidence, and assessment helps and motivates personal progress (13.8%) (see Figure 3.1.15).

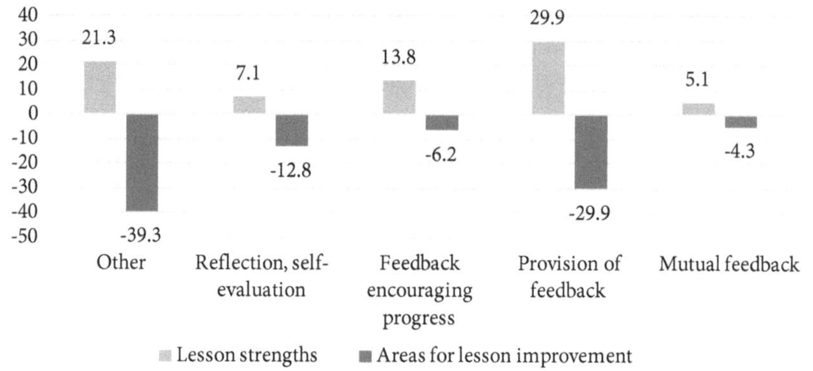

Figure 3.1.15: Strengths and areas for improvement in feedback encouraging progress (% of lessons, number of lessons N=169) (Data source: NAE, 2021)

During the external assessment, the assessors note that teachers, class teachers and educational support specialists often ensure that information about learning is provided to pupils and their parents/guardians on a regular basis, and that it is informative and personalised: “Most of the messages that teachers post in the e-journal are informative, help pupils to understand teaching/learning problems and how to solve them, and encourage pupils to strive for improvement”; “In most of the lessons (32 lessons, 82.0%), teachers gave good feedback individually and as a class, observed pupils’ mistakes, asked guiding questions and provided information about learning, but did not provide opportunities during the lesson for pupils to reflect on their own learning process and to make decisions based on that information”; “The provision of feedback in lessons is often a matter of pointing out mistakes, which does not strengthen pupils’ self-awareness, nor is it oriented towards learning success and better learning outcomes”; “The school provides a range of information and guidance on special education to all parents (guardians, caregivers) of pupils with special educational needs”. Feedback to encourage progress in the classroom is often one-way (teacher to pupil) and rarely reciprocal (dialogue), which would help teachers to choose appropriate teaching strategies and pupils to achieve optimal personal success, to close gaps in their learning, and to manage their own learning: "Providing feedback was identified as a successful activity in the lesson in only two lessons where the assessment was based on a dialogue between students and teachers, encouraging and helping to self-evaluate personal progress"; "Teachers and educational support specialists periodically provide pupils and their parents/guardians with information on learning, encouraging mutual feedback (dialogue) that helps teachers and educational support specialists to select appropriate teaching strategies and pupils to achieve personal success and to close gaps in their learning"; "Effective feedback in the educational process, helping pupils to make personal progress, was observed in some (26%) of the lessons, where teachers systematically observed and commented on pupils' performance, and helped them to find an appropriate solution in their learning". The aspects illustrating the indicator *assessment while being educated, and results were* often assessed at level 2 (86.7%), a situation caused by the formulation of learning objectives and tasks without assessment criteria, which hindered the pupils' ability to measure, identify and demonstrate their progress. In these lessons, pupils were left with unclear learning objectives and were not given the opportunity to plan, work towards and measure their progress and demonstrate their learning.

In most cases, assessment was not discussed at the beginning of the lesson, and the lesson objective did not include success criteria, so when the task was completed, the quality of its performance remained unmeasured and unclear. The analysis of the external thematic assessment data shows that teachers pay too little attention to feedback to encourage progress: formative assessment focuses more on observing pupils' learning, informal assessment of pupils through praise and encouragement, but too little on two-way feedback to help teachers choose appropriate teaching strategies and adjust teaching/learning, and to help pupils to reflect on their own learning and make optimum progress in their learning.

The external thematic assessment results showed that almost all pupils (including those with special educational needs) are assessed in the same way, using the same scoring system, and that scaffolding of pupils with special educational needs occurs by reducing the number of tasks and extending the time given to complete the tasks. Assessors advised using a wider range of tools and techniques for reflection in lessons, identifying mistakes for improvement, and involving pupils more actively in the assessment process (Figure 3.1.16).

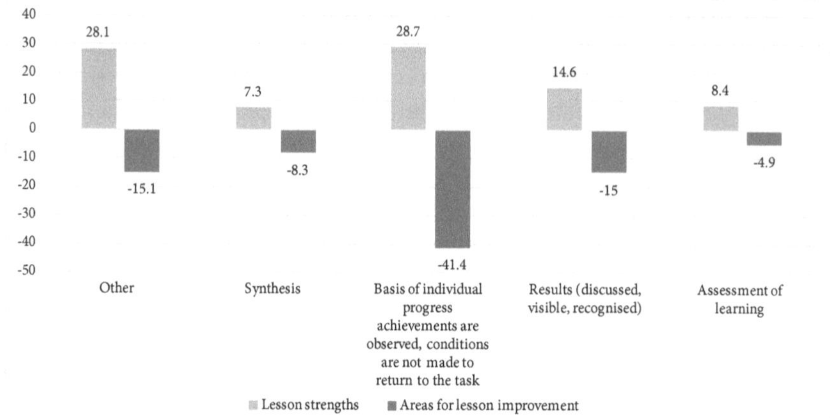

Figure 3.1.16: Strengths and areas for improvement (achievements and progress) (% of lessons, number of lessons N=186) (Data source: NAE, 2021)

After assessing all aspects of the school's performance, based on the data, the assessors rate the components of *the results (achievements and progress)* as strengths in 21.58% of the lessons, and in 78.42% of the lessons as areas for improvement. The most frequent strengths were: pupils' ability to self-evaluate, assignment of self-evaluation tasks, appropriate encouragement of pupils to self-evaluate, referring back to the lesson task, discussing the results and competences with pupils, discussing the effectiveness of support for learners (14.6%) ("The lesson task was revisited in 11 of the observed lessons (28.2%), in these lessons it was easier for pupils to measure individual achievements according to the teacher's planned result"; "Lessons do not systematically go back to the lesson task, to discuss with pupils how well the lesson task was achieved, what pupils' achievements were in relation to the task, and therefore do not allow pupils to self-evaluate their work in the lesson in order to synthesise what they have learnt and their learning outcomes and to plan the next steps in their learning"), lesson synthesis and pupil involvement in the process, recognition of progress (7.3%), recording, measuring, recognising, analysing, and reflecting on each pupil's progress, assigning targeted tasks to demonstrate progress, pupils' ability to monitor and self-evaluate their progress, teachers' ability to recognise and monitor learners' achievements, progress, and measuring individual progress (28.7%) ("Agreements on the measurement of individual progress are in place in the school, but in lessons the progress of all pupils and of each pupil is only partially effectively monitored, analysed and reflected upon in the classroom, taking into account the individual pupil's starting point, developmental potential and expected achievements"; "Effective assessment in the context of pupil development is observed in speech therapy exercises and in the special class lesson"), targeted learning for pupils, appropriate checking of mastery in a way that is acceptable to everyone (8.4%), attention to personality development, matching the developed abilities to the pupil needs, each pupil demonstrating his or her knowledge, recognising the work done by each learner, providing conditions to demonstrate his or her knowledge, and pupils being actively involved in lesson discussion (28.1%) ("The final summative assessment of a pupil recommended to follow an adapted general curriculum is performed at the end of the semester, assessing the pupil's progress, focusing on the characteristics of the pupils' levels of achievement as described in the general curriculum"; "The lesson is summarised in a superficial way, with discussion of emotions and activities, and the pupils not being included in the summing up; the pupils were not encouraged, on the basis of the learning outcomes, to plan their further learning, i.e. to set objectives for further learning, to plan achievements and progress") (Figure 3.1.16).

2022 external risk assessment: the lesson of schools "investing purposefully in the quality of education". Analysing the quality of the lessons observed in twenty-six schools according to different aspects of quality assessment shows that the *planning and organisation of each pupil's learning* was slightly better, with more than half of the lessons (55.3% of the observed lessons) being rated as either good or very good in this aspect. The mean scores for the *pupil support and motivation* and for the *assessment and self-evaluation of pupils* were slightly lower, but the *pupil support and motivation* aspect was rated as good or very good in 58.4% of the observed lessons. The lowest scores were given to the *orientation towards results* (53.5% of lessons with a satisfactory score and 8.9% with a poor score) (Figure 3.1.17).

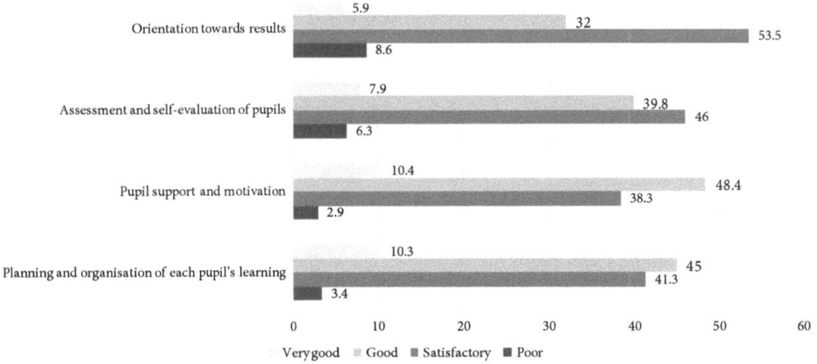

Figure 3.1.17: Percentage of lessons observed in 2022, by assessment level for each aspect of the lesson (number of lessons N=1 418) (Data source: NAE, 2022)

Planning and organising the teaching/learning process in the lesson. An analysis of the quality of the observed lessons in twenty-six schools, related to the planning and organisation of pupil teaching/learning, found that only some of the lessons had measurable learning tasks that reflected the different learning abilities of pupils. In almost half of the observed lessons, the assessors identified strengths and areas for improvement related to the planning of pupil teaching/learning (see Figure 3.1.18). In just over a tenth of the observed lessons, assessors identified as strengths *the relevance of the educational objectives to pupils' personal experience* and *the development of teaching/learning objectives that take account of pupils' different needs*: "The objectives take into account the pupils' personal experience, the school context", "The learning task responds to different needs, the teacher recognises the differences among the pupils, the weaker pupils are given fewer tasks, the stronger pupils are given more tasks", "The task is also given to a Ukrainian pupil", the assessments of the quality of the lesson and the illustrations of the organised activities are excerpted from the protocols of the lesson observations.

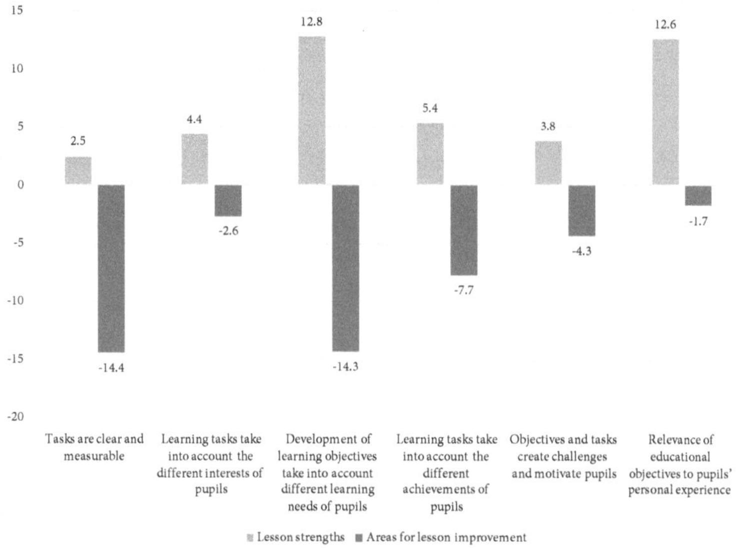

Figure 3.1.18: Strengths and areas for improvement in the planning of observed lessons in 2022 (% of lessons, number of lessons N=619) (Data source: NAE, 2022)

Aspects of lesson planning that could be improved relate to the *formulation of the task and the planning of the lesson, taking into account the teaching/learning needs of the pupils* (Figure 3.1.18). In 14% of the lessons, assessors pointed out that *abstract, unmeasurable tasks were set and presented to pupils, often only identifying activities or specific assignments*: “The task is not clear, there are no assessment criteria, so it is not clear how much needs to be done by whom”, “The lesson task is not oriented towards a particular learning outcome”, “The learning task focuses on what will be done in the test”. In a similar proportion of lessons, assessors identified the *relevance of the learning task to the different teaching/learning needs of the pupils* as an aspect of lesson planning that needs improvement: “The task is the same for everyone, does not take into account the different needs of the pupils”, “The learning task is not differentiated, does not take into account the different interests of the different pupils”, “It is oriented towards teaching all the pupils the same way”.

The strengths and areas for improvement identified by the assessors in the observed lessons in terms of *lesson organisation* show that in some of the observed lessons, teachers successfully organise activities that promote *collaborative learning* and the *actualisation of pupils’ experience in exploring new material* (see Figure 3.1.19). One of the strengths of lesson organisation most frequently identified by the assessors is the *linking of learning material to the pupil’s experience* (identified as a strength in 246 lessons) (“Pupils are encouraged to relate their knowledge to their experience”, “Pupils’ existing knowledge is built upon (professions, knowledge of a particular locality)”, “The educational material is effectively linked to what pupils have already learned in previous lessons”). It was observed that some lessons include questions and tasks that require pupils to recall and *use knowledge and abilities from other subjects* (Figure 3.1.19): “The educational material is related to mathematics and world studies”, “The content of the lesson is related to the geography of Lithuania (wildlife), Ventė Cape”, “When reading the information and representing it in graphs, mathematics knowledge is remembered”.

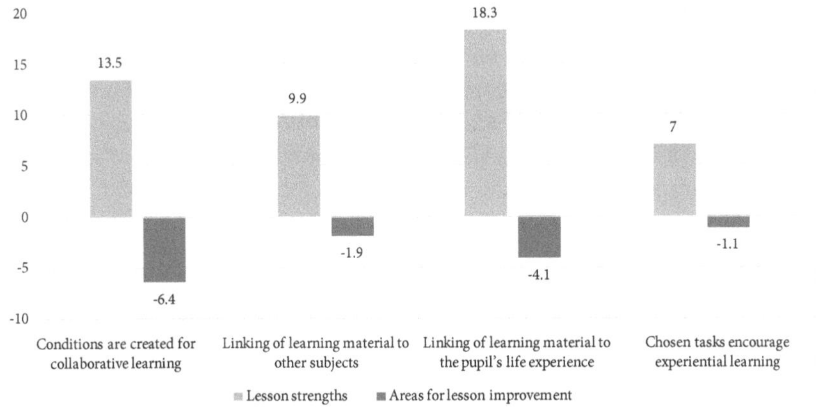

Figure 3.1.19: Strengths and areas for improvement in the organisation of lessons observed in 2022 (% of lessons, number of lessons N=1,343) (Data source: NAE, 2022)

Reviewing the external thematic assessment reports and lesson observation material, it was found that only in a few lessons did teachers provide opportunities or tasks that encouraged pupils to *visualise and explain their understanding and decisions*, and required them *to demonstrate their abilities or ways of doing things*. Of the 1,418 observed lessons, several dozen were identified as impactful in terms of teacher-organised activities that facilitated *deep learning*, where the pupil relates new knowledge to existing knowledge, systematises and reorganises the experience, and applies it to the learning task. In less than a tenth of the lessons, the assessors noted *effective experiential learning* ("Explanation of material is linked to pupils' experiences and actualised", "Recalling what is already known about the topic is encouraged in the moss identification task", "Pupils look at and analyse food labels"), but *exploratory, problem-solving learning* was observed in only relatively few lessons (it was highlighted as a strength in thirty-nine of the lessons).

Pupils' self-directed learning is becoming very important in today's context of pupil engagement in the learning process, in their activities and in the development of learning contexts to develop learners' competences. However, the lesson observation data show that students are not consistently and systematically taught how to learn in a self-directed way. In only 8.6% of the lessons did assessors observe a balance between the teacher's *guidance of pupils' learning* and the provision of opportunities to develop pupils' *self-directed learning* as a strong aspect of the lesson ("Explaining the lesson, constantly asks pupils questions", "Gives each pupil the opportunity to demonstrate and lead the exercise", "Teacher's explanation is coordinated with the pupils' independent work"). Activities organised to help pupils develop the essential *abilities of self-directed learning* (setting learning goals, choosing how to complete tasks, finding the right information and tools, discussing and evaluating their learning, planning and managing time, self-evaluating the effectiveness of their own learning) were episodic and sporadic in the observed lessons. It can be said that the assessors noted a slightly higher number of cases in which pupils were encouraged to choose the method of completing a task (32 lessons out of 1,418) or to find the necessary information and tools for completing a task (18 lessons out of 1,418).

Involving students in the learning process. External assessment data show that teachers encourage pupils' engagement in the learning process in their lessons. In 29.2% of the lessons, assessors highlighted *stimulating curiosity and enthusiasm* as a strong aspect of the lesson ("Targeted use of the tools (the smart board) to show the film stimulated pupils' interest", "The activities kept pupils interested and engaged"). In 9% of lessons, assessors reported that the teaching methods, tasks and support helped pupils *to experience learning success.*

The strengths and areas for improvement identified by the assessors show frequent focus on and support of pupils with learning difficulties and special educational needs. In 14% of the lessons, *the provision of support to weaker pupils* was identified as a strength of the lesson ("The teacher provides support to the weaker pupils by approaching them individually, giving hints, [...] questions as needed", "Individualised tasks for pupils with different needs, support from a special education teacher", "Support for the weaker pupils is timely, targeted"). In 10% of the observed lessons, the assessors noted well-organised activities that allowed each pupil to develop his or her abilities ("Extra, more difficult tasks are given to the more able pupils, and timely help is given to the weaker ones", "The teacher notices pupils' abilities in the classroom and gives them extra tasks in a timely manner"). However, *the development of pupils' higher-order thinking abilities, the use of various regrouping methods according to learning needs, and the provision of support in the self-evaluation process* were only observed in relatively few lessons. These data show that educators too rarely set out concrete steps that consistently and systematically help to organise the educational process according to the needs of pupils.

Assessment and self-evaluation of pupils' achievements and progress. In the observed lessons, aspects for improvement identified by the assessors included the assessment of pupils' achievements, pupil self-evaluation, and monitoring of progress. In half of the observed lessons, assessors pointed out problems related to the formulation of assessment criteria, creating conditions for students to experience learning success, and pupil self-evaluation of the learning process and the results achieved (see Figure 3.1.20). In a small number of the observed lessons, strong aspects of the teacher's practice were identified as engaging and purposeful *discussion of assessment criteria*, and purposeful and learning-enhancing responses to pupils' mistakes, personal achievements and progress ("Assessment is understandable to the pupils (example demonstrated of how the final result should appear"), "Assessment criteria are explained to pupils in an appropriate and engaging way", "Encourages pupils to ask questions and make observations", "Positive attitude, responds to pupils' mistakes in a sensitive way"). However, in ninety-five lessons observed by the assessors, the assessment of learning activities and pupils' achievements was organised without the assessment criteria being defined and communicated to the pupils ("Pupils are not made aware of the criteria for assessing good work", "Assessment criteria are not discussed, pupils are not aware of what will be assessed").

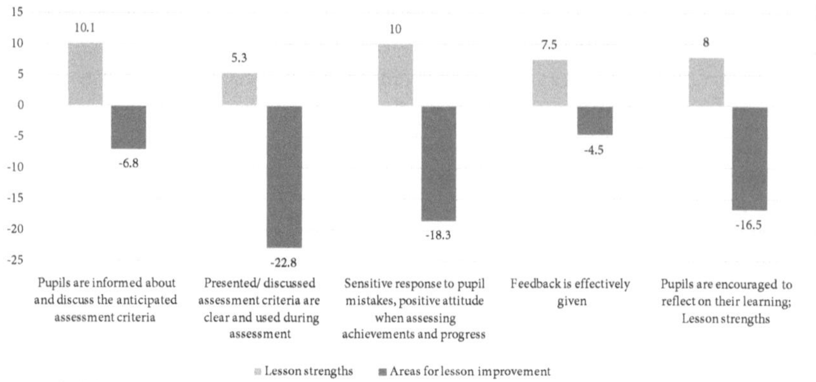

Figure 3.1.20: Strengths and areas for improvement in the assessment of pupils' achievements and progress in the observed lessons in 2022 (% of lessons, number of lessons N=1,392) (Data source: NAE, 2022)

In almost a fifth of the observed lessons, although the assessment criteria were presented to or discussed with the pupils, the criteria were vague and abstract, and in some of the lessons the assessment criteria were referred to as an assessment system. In the lessons, the assessors noted a lack of coherence between the assessment criteria presented to the pupils and the objectives set in the lesson. It was observed that the assessment criteria were discussed with the pupils at the beginning of the lesson, at the beginning of the activity, but were not revisited at the end of the activity or lesson. In some lessons, feedback to pupils on their learning and performance was not provided, and pupils were not encouraged or taught to reflect on their learning and progress (Figure 3.1.20).

Orientation towards results. The external assessment data shows that most of the lessons were planned to engage pupils in activities, to make the material more interesting and varied, but that the goal of creating new experiences for pupils and the focus on results were very often "forgotten" in the lessons, even though they were declared at the beginning of the lesson as the main goal of all the activities in the lesson.

Teaching pupils to monitor and self-evaluate their progress, to provide evidence of their progress, and to plan further learning activities based on this evidence was noted by the assessors as a sporadic occurrence in lessons. In some lessons, pupils were encouraged to explore new subjects, complete tasks and improve their performance, and partial and whole-lesson learning outcomes were discussed with pupils (see Figure 3.1.21). The strengths identified by the assessors indicate that some teachers' modelling of the teaching and learning process reflects an effort to focus on a particular outcome, to teach students how to plan their own personal learning and to set out what they should learn through a series of activities, within the constraints of time, experience, materials and other limitations. However, the relatively few instances of result-oriented teaching/learning reveal that it is not currently part of the planned and implemented teaching/learning content of the lesson.

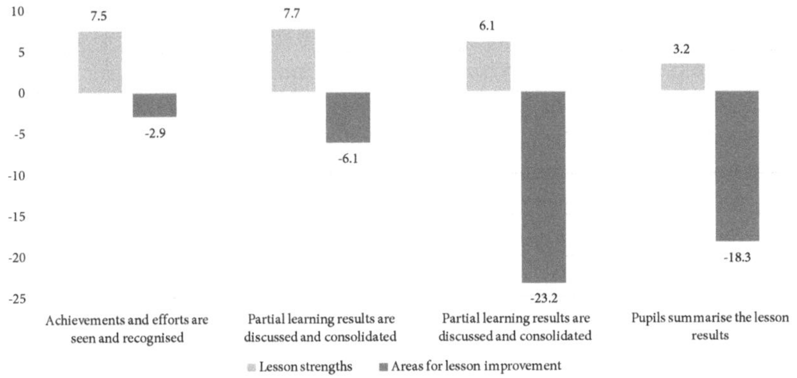

Figure 3.1.21: Strengths and areas for improvement in result-oriented teaching and learning in observed lessons in 2022 (% of lessons, number of lessons N=1,392) (Data source: NAE, 2022)

One fifth of the observed lessons ended without a purposeful summarisation ("Ineffective summarisation of the lesson, dominated by the teacher", "Lack of purposeful linking of the outcome to the task", "Did not revisit the task, used *Reflectus* application for self-evaluation"). In 18.3% of the observed lessons, pupils were not engaged in summarisation of the results or there was insufficient time, and it was therefore performed in a hurry (Figure 3.1.21). In relatively few lessons, the assessors noted that activities were performed together with the pupils in order to decide on follow-up activities.

The teacher and research activities at school. In order to encourage pupils to create and develop their own learning, it is essential for teachers to identify pupils' existing achievements, identify problematic areas of their learning, and design an action plan or educational support system to help each pupil succeed (Jegelevičienė & Prakapas, 2018; Čiužas, 2013). Therefore, the teacher's ability to observe and reflect on the appropriateness of the chosen educational content and its adaptability to each pupil's progress is becoming very important in the planning, and especially in the design of the implementation of the updated educational content. Teacher-performed research can contribute to problem-solving in particular situations through collaborative and ethically acceptable interactions between researchers and research participants in the research process (Adomaitienė & Zubrickienė, 2019). The teacher education regulation (2018) identifies the competence of professional action research as one of the special competences that must be acquired, developed and deepened throughout a teacher's active professional life. The description of the education and education studies group (2015), which defines the scope of the education and education studies group and the requirements for the training of professionals in these fields, provides that the first cycle of studies (professional bachelor's and bachelor's degree) includes the ability to perform research. The first cycle of studies (professional bachelor's and bachelor's degree) requires special competences to perform one's own action research, i.e. to collect data from several related contexts, compare them and look for causal links, and apply the results to improve one's professional practice. The second cycle of study (master's degree) includes the ability to perform complex and/or cross-subject educational research, to integrate, systematise and critically assess data and results; to make recommendations based on the results of research (including those at the systemic level) and findings to educational policy-makers, administrators, and the community, and to initiate discussion and change in education and educational practice. This cycle of study provides special competences to perform one's own action research of broader scope, to collect data from several related contexts of one's own practice, to collate and compare these data and look for causal relationships, to conceptualise the results, to apply them to improve one's own professional practice, to share them in a community of practitioners and to apply them to a broader context of professional practice, and to make recommendations to education policy-makers and administrators and to initiate change in education and educational practice.

Looking at the information provided by the assessors in the 2019 external risk assessment reports on the research performed in the schools, the most common types of research are on pupils' learning styles, pupils' non-formal education needs, and pupils' adaptation (see Figure 3.1.22). In some schools, assessors noted studies on pupils' motivation, their career paths, the prevalence of bullying and the impact of homework on learning.

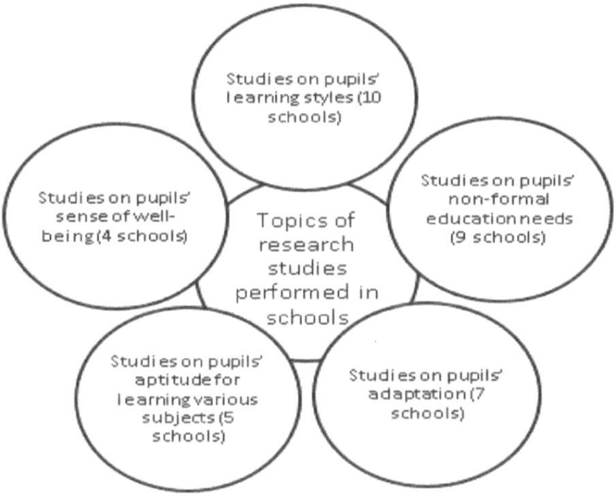

Figure 3.1.22: Topics most commonly covered in education research in schools (N=53)

The assessed schools tend to analyse the results of the National Pupils' Achievement Testing (in Lithuanian, NMPP) and the Basic Education Achievement Testing (in Lithuanian, PUPP), and to collect and analyse information on pupils' semester and school-year learning achievements and progress. Of the fifty-three assessed schools, the assessors observed that in twenty-six schools the results of the NMPP were presented, discussed and analysed, which were partially taken into account in the planning of the activities of the school, the methodological councils or groups. In nineteen schools, the results of the PUPP were analysed and compared from one year to the next, conclusions were drawn and suggestions for improvement were made. In ten schools, assessors identified analysing, comparing and discussing pupils' half-year and school-year learning outcomes as good practice, with a view to using this data for educational and lesson planning. The analysis of school assessment reports revealed that in the majority of the assessed schools, there is no systematic research and analysis of pupils' learning needs and abilities. In only four of the fifty-three assessed schools did the assessors identify adequate research, analysis and use of data on pupils' learning needs and abilities. It was noted that these schools had an overall mean performance score between 2.3 and 2.8 (maximum score of 4).

In answering the question *How do the assessed schools make use of the research data?*, there is a wide range of experiences (see Table 3.1.2). In some schools, the assessors noted that the results of the research (diagnostic assessment) are taken into account in planning each pupil's education (the offer of subjects and non-formal education activities, differentiation and/or individualisation of learning activities), the development and adjustment of pupils' individual education plans based on the results of the research, and the information is recorded in pupils' individual progress sheets. These experiences were observed in four schools. Of particular note is the "Success Pathway Model" developed in an assessed school, which includes monitoring personal growth and pupil learning achievements, assessment and self-evaluation, use of results, and informing of pupils' parents. The guidelines and tools developed for the implementation of the "Success Pathway Model" (a Success Pathway passport, tools for self-monitoring and reflection, inventories of achievements and progress, competency folders, analysis of pupils' expectations and results, techniques for reflection, etc.) help pupils and teachers to record, analyse and reflect on their own learning outcomes and to monitor the change in the number of social hours collected.

Nineteen school assessment reports conclude that the analysis and use of the data collected is unsystematic or insufficient. The results are presented, discussed and recorded, but no decisions are taken on how the situation and problems revealed by the research could be addressed to raise pupils' achievements and to promote an individual pupil's progress in a targeted way. In some schools, it was observed that teachers were left to decide whether or not to use the results of the research, and assessors did not observe discussion of or reflection on the use of planned, completed research: "[…] pupils' learning styles were studied. The findings were presented to the teachers at a meeting, but there was no agreement on how to apply the findings in the classroom, leaving it up to the teachers to decide whether to use the findings at all" (from the school's external risk assessment report).

Table 3.1.2: Experiences of using educational research results in school activities (n=53)

Aspects	Illustrations from external assessment reports
Fragmentary use of research results in school planning, taking into account pupils' individual needs and abilities (14)	*"In the gymnasium, there is not enough systematic research and analysis of pupils' teaching/learning needs and abilities, and the results of the research are not always taken into account when planning each pupil's teaching/learning".* *"The results of research (NMPP, PUPP) are partially taken into account in educational planning. The representatives of the methodological council stated that the results of the tests are discussed with the pupils who request it, parents are informed, and the results are discussed in the teachers' meetings".*

Aspects	Illustrations from external assessment reports
Presentation and discussion of research results to school community members, the methodological council, methodological groups, etc. (12)	*"The presentation of the results of the NMPP in the methodological groups and the teachers' council meetings is limited to stating the facts, without paying attention to the design of effective teaching/learning strategies, prioritising the tasks of improving the quality of education, and planning for the education of each pupil individually as well as all pupils collectively".* *"The reports are discussed in subject teachers' methodological groups and teachers' meetings, presented to the teachers' council, and discussed with pupils and their parents".*
Recording research results in teachers and class teachers' annual/long-term plans (6)	*"Class teachers' plans record research information on pupils' needs (physical and emotional health, behaviour, attendance, fulfilment of self-development and self-expression needs, academic performance, participation in non-formal education activities) and information on the assessment of each pupil's overall abilities and values".* *"An annual analysis of non-formal education needs is performed, and the results are used for further planning (e.g. if the analysis shows that one or another activity does not meet the needs of the pupils, the activity is dropped)".*
Using research results to solve problems, make recommendations and draw conclusions about pupil learning (4)	*"The learning styles of pupils in the gymnasium are studied and recommendations are made to teachers and pupils to ensure that teaching/learning is organised to meet the needs of pupils with different learning styles".*

As already mentioned, although in the assessed schools much attention is paid to the analysis and discussion of the results of the NMPP and PUPP, they are mostly analysed in quantitative terms and only the result is stated, for example: "Interviews with the methodological council, and analysis of the protocols of the teachers' council and the directorate's meetings suggest that the results of the diagnostic assessment and NMPP are not systematically taken into account: the results are analysed quantitatively, the outcome is stated, but no particular decisions are taken, no agreements are made on the planning of the education of each pupil as well as all pupils, no impact is analysed, no change, effectiveness or creation of value-added are examined" (*External risk assessment report on the performance of Miroslavas Gymnasium, Alytus District*, 2019, 15). "[…] formal monitoring of pupils' national tests of learning achievements, basic education achievement tests and matura (school-leaving) examinations, analysis of results in quantitative terms, limited to the statement of facts, and no attention to effective learning strategies, prioritisation of tasks for improving the quality of education, and the planning of the education of each pupil as well as all pupils, taking into account their abilities and needs (differences)" (External risk assessment report on the performance of Pivašiūnai Gymnasium, Alytus District, 2019, 12).

The external assessment data suggest that school communities should first agree on a systematic and coherent organisation of research activities in the school, which will only be successfully implemented and provide opportunities for improvement when the following questions have been answered: "how will the planned research help to clarify the pupils' learning needs and potential? How will the research contribute to the development of activities in lessons and activities organised at other times? How will the results of the research be used to improve the teaching/learning process? How will it help to self-evaluate the change in activities?". The research data and its targeted use would enable teachers to improve the educational process in a targeted and coherent way and to further plan for each pupil's achievements and progress, while parents would benefit from information on how they could/should support their children's learning, and how they could work with pupils to solve learning difficulties.

In summary, it can be said that the data from the 2019–2022 external assessment of Lithuanian general education schools reveals problems in the organisation of the educational process, which for several decades, and especially with the changing socio-economic context of the country, have become barriers to the development of an educational process that would meet the needs of learners, provide opportunities for pupils to be engaged in learning and to experience success. The data from the 2019 external assessment show that the teacher's research activities, such as organising research, analysing the obtained data, and relying on the data to plan and improve the educational process at the classroom and individual levels, are not part of the teacher's daily routine, which could help to solve the problems of adaptation of the educational content and learning difficulties.

3.2. Analysis of undergraduate theses on primary education in which action research was performed by subject and general competences area

First, we present data on the action research performed in primary grades in the area of Lithuanian language (see Table 3.2.1).

Table 3.2.1: Problem-solving by research subject, when learning Lithuanian language

Action research subject	Research method used to collect data	Solutions/results to pedagogical problems
Developing critical thinking through argumentation	Debates based on analysis of a literary work (N=1)	After the two debating activities and analysis of the data, it can be said that pupils enjoy debating, it encourages them to think, listen, express and substantiate their opinions. Pupils learn how to formulate a thesis and substantiate it.
	Discussion about reading works (N=1)	Many students are able to express an opinion in a sentence and substantiate it with arguments. Pupils are better at oral argumentation than written argumentation. Pupils are able to evaluate their own and their classmates' performance in a discussion.
	Written argumentation in the context of integrated education (N=3)	Pupils were able to express an opinion in a statement and substantiate it with at least one logical argument but struggled to explain the concept of argumentation and to identify argumentation.
Writing abilities	Dictations (N=3)	Pupils are able to discover mistakes themselves. After exchanging work with classmates, children analysed their work more carefully and corrected more mistakes. The way in which the pupil commented on the spelling when writing the dictation was the most successful way to write the text correctly. It is important when children are able to spot mistakes themselves and correct them.

(Continued)

Table 3.2.1: (Continued)

Action research subject	**Research method used to collect data**	**Solutions/results to pedagogical problems**
Creative writing abilities	Use of adjectives in creative writing (N=1)	Pupils use more adjectives after additional activities. Integral development of imaginative text production and vocabulary enrichment abilities. Children were particularly interested in presenting their activities using adjectives when creating a PowerPoint presentation.
	Mind map, comic creation, free writing (N=1)	The methods not only improved pupils' writing abilities, but also changed their attitudes, as they realised that creating through writing can be fun.
Reading competence	Building words with bricks using Lego didactics, linking words to pictures (N=1)	All children learn to recognise letters, combine sounds into syllables and some read independently (pre-school group).
	Ways to encourage active reading (N=3)	Teachers need to be aware of the individual needs and aptitudes of pupils. It is important to leave room for the pupil's choice of book and self-expression. The reading challenge and the workshop helped to interest in reading activities those first-year pupils who had low reading motivation before the activity.
	Comparison of the content of works of fiction + film analyses (N=3)	The visual material is analysed through performance of assignments. Pupils performed best in the integrated tasks involving text and film content. Pupils were able to identify and describe the main characters; identify similarities and differences between the works. The analysis of linguistic expression was more difficult. Pupils are able to describe the setting qualitatively.

Action research subject	Research method used to collect data	Solutions/results to pedagogical problems
	Reading abilities development (N=1)	Pupils' performance improved after the action research. All pupils performed well on four tasks, while only a few did so the first time. Finding implied information and characterisation of a character from several places in the text was more difficult.
	Text analysis working in pairs (N=1)	Pupils' results after the action research showed a significant change: as many as fifteen children's work met the criteria for the highest level, 7 for the basic level and 4 for the satisfactory level. The biggest increase was seen in the number of pupils reaching the highest level. The educational methods chosen, working in pairs and small groups, developed and improved pupils' reading abilities and their communication and cooperation abilities.
Speaking abilities	Storytelling using a series of pictures (N=1)	The method of sequencing the pictures in the correct order allowed the children to better understand the plot of the story and to retell the story coherently. The children's vocabulary was expanded and enriched on the basis of listening to and discussing the story and the sequence of correctly arranged pictures.
	Interview method (N=2)	The pupils participated willingly in the activity, behaved politely, were able to listen actively, take part in the communication situation, answered questions expressively, used complete sentences and shared their opinions.

In terms of the contemporary approach to the development of linguistic literacy in the primary classes, emphasis is placed on the relevance of educational content, the practical application of acquired linguistic abilities in everyday situations and the importance of developing pupils' internal motivation, which determines the quality of the development of these abilities (Maurer, 2001; Dumais, 2011; Wildová, 2014). We would like to highlight the area of speech development as one of the most integral areas, because speaking is not only about learning the language, but also about learning other subject content, which is analysed. Speaking abilities of primary school pupils have also been studied by other researchers (Dumais & Lafontaine, 2011; Dumais, 2015; Bianco, 2015; Hassan, 2012; Lafontaine, Dumais & Pharand, 2016). Researchers note that it is in this linguistic area that action research is well suited to studying these abilities, as they are short thoughts that are best analysed when they are written down or filmed. Oral language is essential for learning to read and write (Dumais, 2015; Bianco, 2015). In fact, a pupil who can communicate with peers and adults, draw conclusions and use appropriate oral narrative structure will find it easier to read and write and persevere while learning at school (Brown, 2014; Lefebvre, Bruneau & Desmarais, 2010; Romain & Roubaud, 2013; Lafontaine, Dumais & Pharand, 2016). In addition, schools continuously provide pupils with learning situations in which spoken and written language complement each other, from the very first activities in primary school. In short, speaking, reading and writing are at the heart of all learning at school (Dumais, 2015; Lafontaine, Dumais & Pharand, 2016). R. Nolin (2015) also shows that some of the most commonly used genres are conversation and discussion, i.e. genres where substantiation is key (Chartrand, Émery-Bruneau & Sénéchal, 2015), for example, to support one's assessment of a text read in a large group, or to support one's ideas or opinions on a particular topic. In fact, discussion and conversation are genres that children need to learn systematically from the first class. However, in educational practice, oral activities such as asking for permission, apologising, asking for information, asking for something or expressing a wish are the most common ones, i.e. speech activities that do not really require a deeper conversation or discussion and therefore do not develop argumentation abilities, because they do not require the substantiation of an opinion (Nolin, 2015).

Teaching problem-solving to primary school pupils can be combined with integrated abilities development in IT, technology and robotics. This is facilitated by the use of Lego didactics. Robotics is thoughtfully and purposefully integrated, allowing pupils to learn a wide range of subject content related not only to technology, but also to other subject abilities (such as Lithuanian language), cooperation and teamwork (Scaradozzi et al., 2015).

Analysing the results in Table 3.2.1, we can see that primary school pupils are able to perform quite complex activities: arguing an opinion, justifying a thought. They are able to change their approach to activities they do not like, such as writing abilities or creative writing, through action research, observation and analysis of their learning process. These results also show the importance of choosing the right approach that not only allows all students to learn with active participation, responsibility and commitment, but also motivates them to complete the activities from start to finish and, for more complex activities, encourages them to clarify and overcome difficulties. In addition to the analysis of readings, pupils are motivated by viewing and analysing the content of filmed extracts. Such environments allow for a different perspective on the readings (Haager, Klingner & Vaughn, 2007; Dion et al., 2010), a better understanding of the characters and empathy for their experiences (Brodeur et al., 2011). Our study is complementary to other studies conducted by D. Jakavonytė-Staškuvienė (2021). The complexity of students' arguments shows that they are able to interpret and evaluate the content of the text, express the main idea and discern the deeper meaning of the text (Jakavonytė-Staškuvienė, 2021). In addition, although active language learning activities require more effort from students to succeed in their work, children reported that these activities are fun and motivate them to learn and read. P. Thériault & N. Laurin (2016) explored the use of reading strategies in primary classrooms. The researchers found that teachers use more reading strategies before reading activities, when discussing the content of the upcoming text with the entire class, and during reading and analysis of the text they tend to use the reading strategies outlined in the textbooks. Hence, the availability of quality teaching materials is important for educational quality.

Summarising the experience of developing writing abilities, other researchers have carried out similar research. S. Rojas-Drummond et al. (2020) analysed the development of dialogic interaction and text production abilities in primary school pupils. The pupils worked together in a small group to learn how to produce texts through discussion. The findings of the study highlighted that dialogic interaction and collaborative learning helped primary school pupils learn to produce better-quality written texts, not only when working in small groups but also when working independently. Such experiences show that the right active-writing strategy, where pupils can discuss the idea of a piece of writing, vocabulary and sentence-writing together, can lead to better results and the learning of text production strategies. In addition, content analysis of conversations, where primary pupils work in groups to produce written narratives, shows that pupils are able to provide each other with the necessary information, to correct certain spelling errors related to particular aspects and contexts of the writing activity

(Herder et al, 2020). Thus, research in the area of writing abilities helps to understand how collaborative writing activities create contexts for sharing and discussing knowledge in peer-to-peer conversations, and it is worthwhile for education professionals to take this into account when designing collaborative writing activities, because they are likely to lead to better pupil performance. This is also evident from our research data (see Table 3.2.1). E. Duran & A. Karatas (2019) found in a study that repeated dictation and motivating children to read carefully what they write strengthens writing abilities. In addition, individual conversations with children, based on analysis of their work, are helpful.

We can see in Table 3.2.2. how the challenges of primary school pupils were addressed in the area of developing historical literacy abilities.

Table 3.2.2: Problem-solving by research subject, when learning history

Action research subject	**Research method used to collect data**	**Solutions/results to pedagogical problems**
Developing critical thinking through argumentation	Analysis of historical sources (N=3)	Pupils are able to identify an appropriate source to support a claim and to correctly identify the arguments given in the source; to substantiate when assessing past events; and to make credible arguments. Difficulties include using sources to make a suitable claim, supporting arguments with evidence (primary sources), assessing the credibility of a source, and selecting a credible primary source.
		Pupils have the most difficulty if they have not mastered reading techniques. Pupils formulated arguments on the basis of images in photographs. Pupils were able to identify appropriate key words for an object. They were able to search for general information in different historical sources.
		Third-year pupils are able to find relevant information, refer to sources, make arguments and substantiate their opinions. They are not always able to distinguish between reliable and unreliable sources.

Action research subject	Research method used to collect data	Solutions/results to pedagogical problems
Developing cognitive abilities in history	Constructive learning strategies (N=2)	Year 4 pupils are able to find facts in the direct content of a particular source. Pupils do not distinguish between the reliability of information as testimony and the reliability of a source as evidence. It is more difficult to find indirect information and present it as testimony to describe the context of that time. Pupils understood the meaning of the concept of primary source.
	Understanding historical context by analysing illustrations/pictures (N=2)	Pupils are able to identify changes over time in a particular thing or object; to place an event and object in a particular period; to identify the characteristics of a period in a general way; and to place historical events in chronological order. Difficulties include using concepts appropriate to a particular historical period, and particularly identifying a historical period in terms of its attributes.
Understanding the meaning of national symbols	Recognition by example, experience by reflection during an interview (N=1)	Through educational excursions and visual aids, primary school pupils develop an understanding of national symbols. Pupils know, recognise and distinguish the national symbols, but not all of them are able to explain their meaning and essence.

From the research conducted on the basis of the content of history, we can observe that the analysis of the content of history, if the appropriate methods are chosen, helps primary school pupils not only to become more familiar with historical events and objects, to see their development in the perspective of time, but also to understand the interaction and relationships between individual historical events and periods, to develop the ability to identify historical changes, to select information from historical sources and to argue for the interpretation of the past. The methods used in the activities enabled students to develop their thinking abilities, which are important components of historical literacy that help students learn to think "historically" about the past (Turner-Bisset, 2005; Nokes, 2019).

The importance of reflection, in a way similar to the context of understanding the meaning of Lithuanian national symbols, is emphasised by other researchers, such as D. Contreras & D. Aceituno (2017). They investigated the development of civics abilities when students actively participated in solving social problems. C. Cox, R. Jaramillo & F. Reimers (2005), D. Contreras & D. Aceituno (2017) present civics education as key to working with pupils on global issues such as poverty, inequality, racism, discrimination, access to justice, migration, etc.

The research analysed the problem area that prospective primary school teachers had chosen when analysing their practice in developing pupils' natural science abilities (see Table 3.2.3).

Table 3.2.3: Problem-solving by research subject, when learning natural science

Action research subject	**Research method used to collect data**	**Solutions/results to pedagogical problems**
Developing critical thinking through argumentation	Recognising local objects from a map or diagram (N=2)	Fourth-year pupils are better at drawing a route than third-year pupils, often using different signs to represent the route, sometimes drawing what was in the environment. Most pupils are able to substantiate their opinions and give different arguments when completing tasks. Most pupils understand and can represent the directions of countries around the world, although the fourth-year pupils performed slightly better than the third-year pupils on this task. None of the pupils could identify the actual perimeter of a site by looking at it. It is difficult for pupils of this age to determine distance by sight if this skill has not been developed, but after several similar activities, a much more accurate perception of distance and perimeter is noted. Fourth-year pupils are able to compare diagrams and maps, and to explain the difference between a diagram and a drawing. Third-year pupils tend to focus on only one aspect of the question, while fourth-year pupils are able to compare several aspects.

Action research subject	Research method used to collect data	Solutions/results to pedagogical problems
	Studying an aquarium (N=1)	Pupils were only able to substantiate if they were talking about content they had experienced themselves. They need to be taught to substantiate in a systematic way, analysing different natural science content.
Developing natural science abilities	Outdoor research (N=2)	Pupils are able to correctly identify the research objective, focusing on learning new information and on the research subject; when performing research and focusing on its steps, pupils quickly grasp the research process and are able to indicate the particular research step. During the activity, pupils found it difficult to identify the tools needed for the research: half of the third-year pupils and a quarter of the fourth-year pupils were unable to do so, but after the activity, as shown by the results of diagnostic test II, they were able to select the tools needed for the research and to substantiate why they were needed. The participants were able to weigh the research subject and to correctly record the results of the weighing, but not all informants were able to substantiate why the mass of the cones varied. Most students were able to identify which cones, fir or pine, would fit more per metre, but some pupils did not explain why the result was different. The summative task showed that pupils in year 3–4 are able to compare objects, perform experiments and write down the results, but they have difficulties in analysing the results and in substantiating their opinions.

(Continued)

Table 3.2.3: (Continued)

Action research subject	**Research method used to collect data**	**Solutions/results to pedagogical problems**
	Research in outdoor areas (N=2)	School outdoor areas provide formal and spontaneous learning opportunities as places for learning, playing, exploring and experiencing; they encourage children to explore themselves and their social environment. Pupils absorb information more quickly, learn to communicate and cooperate, and have a better grasp of natural science concepts.
Cognitive competence in natural science	Experiments (N=2)	Pupils used all their senses to experiment. Pupils can experiment both in the classroom and while learning beyond school boundaries. The activities are initiated from the pupils' perspective – pupils do everything themselves; teachers just advise and observe.
Abilities to explore nature and the environment	Green environment, outdoor spaces (N=2)	In the green environment, pupils learn to identify wild and domestic animals, birds, insects, trees, shrubs and other plants, and how to grow their own plants and understand the growth cycle. Pupils learn to use rulers, thermometers, scales, measuring cups, clocks; observe small bugs with a magnifying glass.

M. Demirel & B. Caymaz (2015) researched the motivation and internal disposition of prospective primary school teachers to work innovatively in natural science lessons. The researchers found that final-year students who have performed a wide variety of science inquiries themselves are motivated and willing to lead their learners, the primary school pupils, along an active learning path.

To summarise the science content activities, action research was implemented in such a way as to allow pupils to participate in active experimentation, exploring nature, the local environment or other green environments. All activities of this type not only allow the pupils to become familiar with their environment, to take an interest in what is going on there, to enrich their vocabulary, but also to master various measuring tools such as rulers, thermometers, scales, measuring cups, clocks, etc. The findings of the study by S. Camponovo & Z. Moody (2021) are similar to our study. They state that exploring the immediate environment allows children not only to learn more about nature, but also to be more independent and feel safe in their immediate environment. Environmental and sustainability issues as a necessary part of the competences of a future educator are highlighted by L.-A. Wolff et al. (2017). Teachers and pupils should be actively involved in programmes to make their homes greener, and experience how sustainability is incorporated in theory and practice in a variety of school subjects.

The following is an overview of the aspects of the content of mathematics learning that were analysed as part of action research (see Table 3.2.4).

Table 3.2.4: Problem-solving by research subject, when learning mathematics

Action research subject	**Research method used to collect data**	**Solutions/results to pedagogical problems**
Individual support for learning arithmetic, for the hard-of-hearing	Action research where individual support is applied to the explanation of tasks (key words illustrated with pictures, task conditions visually diagrammed) (N=1)	The use of visual aids to solve arithmetic problems facilitates the learning of mathematics for hard-of-hearing pupils. Visual aids for learning to count help pupils to find solutions to word problems, to relate quantities, to understand the condition of a problem, because their limited oral vocabulary allows them to independently solve only the simplest problems. Visual aids help them to understand what is given in a problem and what needs to be found. Because the relationships between the given and the sought quantities are not clear to hard-of-hearing pupils, the questions posed in the problem, the key words, especially *subtract, add,* greatly facilitate mathematics learning, because they themselves specify the mathematical action (addition or subtraction). As many as 50% of the problems given with key words were solved correctly by all pupils.

(Continued)

Table 3.2.4: (Continued)

Action research subject	Research method used to collect data	Solutions/results to pedagogical problems
Teaching reading and graphical representation of the conditions of a word problem	Interview, questionnaire with word problems (N=1)	Most of the pupils in the research understand the context of the conditions, the relationships between data, and the action to be taken, but some of the pupils are not able to select the data contained in the condition. Pupils were able to represent the condition graphically. Pupils use symbols, classify objects according to size, colour, shape.
Developing understanding of number relationships by solving equations in year 4	Analysis of pupils' work on equations, reflection, analysis of survey data (N=1)	Pupils can describe some aspects of the concept of an equation but cannot explain what an equation is. After activities involving solving equations in different ways (explanations, visual representations of data) and reflecting on the activities, most pupils understood the relationship between numbers in the equations they solved.
Opportunities for integrating ICT into mathematics lessons in primary schools	During action research, use of observation and written survey feedback (N=1)	ICT tools were used to develop mathematical abilities in the following areas: subtraction and addition, word problem-solving, geometric figure recognition, measuring and drawing segments, calculation of temperature and time. In addition, pupils worked independently and individually, at their own pace, to develop the abilities of using a computer or tablet for a particular purpose. Pupils enjoyed learning mathematics using ICT applications and were encouraged to take responsibility for their actions and results. The pupils worked in a good mood, relaxed and in good spirits, which is conducive to learning mathematics.

Action research subject	**Research method used to collect data**	**Solutions/results to pedagogical problems**
Developing internal motivation in primary school pupils through the Scratch learning environment	Action research using the Scratch learning environment in mathematics lessons, observation of activity and written reflection survey (N=1)	Pupils' internal motivation is high when the Scratch learning environment is used in the lesson. Girls were more motivated than boys to program the Lithuanian language subject content. Girls also liked to program the natural sciences content in the Scratch learning environment more than boys did.

Action research has been recommended by many researchers as a meaningful and useful science-based methodology for addressing content issues in mathematics education (Yorulmaz & Doğan, 2022; Paydar & Doğan, 2021; Vula, 2019; Feldman et al., 2018), because action research helps teachers reflect on how they teach mathematics and look for different ways to help children better understand mathematical concepts and actions. Teachers also learn from each other by sharing practical examples of their work. This is also evident in our research, because prospective primary school teachers who chose action research in mathematics were also looking for practical ways and strategies to help particular pupils understand mathematics better and to learn complex solutions, such as solving equations. It is important that teachers look for solutions for more effective pupil learning, and such attitudes and activities lead to improvements in pupils' mathematics learning and achievement (Vula, 2019). Teachers search for information, read up on the latest data on a particular problematic mathematical area, and then try out certain techniques in their classrooms. Moreover, E. Vula (2019) states that teachers find it easier to teach mathematics and perform action research when they can consult and confer with university teachers. Action research provides more opportunities for teachers to be responsible for improving their core content knowledge, and for teachers to refresh their didactic knowledge of research methods and their application in practice.

When analysing the action research projects with mathematics content, we can see that the most frequent choice was the path of particular examples, where elements of certain mathematics content are learned. Other researchers have performed similar studies using real-life situations and particular drawings, sketches or diagrams (Yorulmaz & Doğan, 2022; Yorulmaz, Uysal & Sidekli, 2021; Arsoetar & Sugiman, 2019; Uça & Saracaloğlu, 2017; Hatfield et al., 2016), stating that pupils' mathematical abilities improve, and the likelihood of mistakes decreases. S. Paydar &

A. Doğan (2021), during action research, while investigating a first-year pupil with difficulties in mathematics, noticed that musical interludes during counting, i.e. a noise-free environment to help the child concentrate, helped the pupil to learn, whereas research by B. Koc & I. Korkmaz (2019) showed that those with difficulties in maths due to dyscalculia benefit from one-to-one support, individual attention from the teacher and more time spent explaining number structure and an enriched environment.

E. Vula (2019) notes that the use of information technology in mathematics lessons can be an effective tool not only to engage pupils, but also to help them learn certain algorithms. The researcher notes that it is important for teachers who feel timid about ICT to dare to use it. We believe that some of the new ways of accessing ICT can be learned by pupils and teachers together, and sometimes pupils can also advise teachers. C. Rodríguez-Jiménez et al. (2023) & E. W. Kiru (2018) note that internal motivation and self-confidence of both students and teachers is enhanced by the targeted use of ICT in mathematics lessons, when more risks and responsibilities are taken. Such teachers use ICT in the educational process even when the curriculum does not require them to do so, and this results in higher pupil learning competence in mathematics by improving pupils' mathematical understanding, problem-solving abilities, and meaningful learning when mathematical abilities are applied to real life. Using ICT, pupils are more willing, engaged and attentive in the educational process. ICT also enables teachers to collaborate, share ideas and teach each other how to use certain applications. In this way, more children will receive mathematical content that is more interesting and better tailored to them (Kiru, 2018), helping to innovate in the educational process and change the culture of learning in the educational institution. Similar insights are supported by our research into the action research performed by prospective primary school teachers when ICT was used to teach mathematics. In both cases, the teachers note that the children were positive, willing to learn, motivated and achieved better results in the area of mathematical content. C. Rodríguez-Jiménez et al. (2023) state that although ICT is essential in the curriculum, there is very little research on the use of ICT in mathematics education, because the authors found only eleven scientific articles published over 12 years that analyse the didactics of ICT in mathematics education in the primary classroom. The researchers conclude that traditional methodologies still dominate educational practice and therefore there is a lack of more innovative approaches and research in mathematics didactics. The researchers found that the integration of robotics, digitised books, and touchscreens to help children with visual and hearing difficulties understand content, help children learn (Abiatal & Howard, 2020). Identified problems include the training of teachers to work with particular software and the adaptation of the software itself, for example, the integration of certain games (Anwar et al., 2020), the selection of educational content, etc. The analysis of the research checked whether technology helped to improve mathematics learning in primary classrooms, by increasing achievement, by enabling the exploration of different mathematical concepts and representations, and by providing interactive work. ICT has been shown to improve understanding of particular operations such as multiplication or division, to help develop meaningful learning, to enable the visualisation of abstract concepts, to aid subject mastery, to demonstrate the importance of procedures and to help overcome difficulties (Rodríguez-Jiménez et al., 2023; Lara Nieto-Márquez et al., 2020; Abiatal & Howard, 2020; Zaranis, 2018). The findings of these studies are similar to the results of the action research performed by our students, prospective primary school teachers, in that ICT was used to achieve progress in pupils' mathematics learning.

Action research has also been performed in the area of arts, for learning music, art and technology. Table 3.2.5 shows which problematic issues were addressed by the prospective primary school teachers in the area of arts.

Table 3.2.5: Problem-solving by research subject, when learning music, art and technology

Action research subject	Research method used to collect data	Solutions/results to pedagogical problems
Developing abilities of year 3 pupils, through the origami booklet method	Analysis and description of geometric shapes, through the origami booklet method and written survey (N=1)	The students struggled to make a simple folded piece according to a given diagram; pupils did not meet the precision parameters, lacked symmetry, and lacked the ability to make even folded lines. Pupils are able to make one geometric figure from another. There is often a lack of precision in folding and drawing, and children draw what they imagine rather than what they agreed on or see. There is a lack of words when communicating about drawings, and it is difficult to get deeper into the diagram and details of a drawing.

(Continued)

Table 3.2.5: (Continued)

Action research subject	Research method used to collect data	Solutions/results to pedagogical problems
Exploring the properties of contrast by creating three-dimensional spaces out of recycled materials	Action research, activity observation, discussion (N=1)	Pupils were able to construct a star according to the rules for composing different shapes and to notice contrasts, i.e. they were able to draw a contrast; they were able to construct elephants out of recycled materials and to notice the contrast in shape and size. During the discussion, they were able to give examples of contrasts.
Developing pupils' creativity through non-traditional art media	Using the creativity criteria assessment table, analyse the drawings of year 4 pupils, categorising the drawings according to the attributes of creative expression (N=2)	An appropriate learning environment (with musical background), free choice of the theme of the work, explanation of the art technique (pointillism), artistic means of expression (mixing of colours and hues, discussion of the composition), and painting with non-traditional means (blunt pencils, plastic knives and forks, fingers, cotton swabs) fostered the creativity of the pupils; the works of the pupils were unique, distinctive and original.
Developing the musical abilities of pre-school pupils using ICT	Action research using ICT in music activities; interviews with pupils (reflection on activities) (N=1)	The selection of appropriate ICT tools creates a supportive learning environment, making the activities more playful and imaginative; pupils are able to pay attention for longer, and several different musical abilities are developed simultaneously. Children were able to express the mood of the music through emotional expressions, to feel the rhythm, to intonate accurately. Each child's musical abilities increased with the use of ICT.
Developing a sense of musical rhythm in pre-school children	Action research with rhythm-sensing activities of varying complexity, with rhythm clapping and playing of different instruments, observation and recording of results (N=1)	After the activities, more than half of the pupils were found to have a medium level of musical rhythm-sensing, a third were found to have a high level and a fifth were found to have a low level. Rhythm awareness depends on the pupils' ability to concentrate, the ability to pay attention and their musical memory.

Action research subject	Research method used to collect data	Solutions/results to pedagogical problems
Developing pupils' graphic expression abilities in year 1	Action research, observation, analysis of drawings (line variety extension and ornamentation) (N=1)	Pupils are able to give examples of lines in the environment and in works of art, use more and different lines in their drawings, make compositions of lines, and make ornaments composed of lines. They produce the work in a more orderly manner and use lines and ornaments to fill in the background.

During the art action research, teachers analysed drawings or other artistic works produced by pupils. H. Uştu, T. Saito & A. Mentiş Taş (2022), R. Potočnik, T. Košir & I. Devetak (2022), T. Jokela (2019), A. Jordan-Douglass (2019), J. Turkka, O. Haatainen, & M. Aksela (2017), K. Ravanis (2017) state that the planning stage is particularly important in action research, where the ways in which a didactic problem is to be solved are chosen. These researchers identify the arts as one of the most integral areas that can be used in other subject areas, such as technology, engineering (Tetikci, Erim & Halaclar, 2021), STEAM or mathematics (Uştu, Saito & Mentiş Taş, 2022, Potočnik, Košir & Devetak, 2022, Jokela, 2019; Jordan-Douglass, 2019). It is important that the main work in such activities is in the field of art (Bramble, 2019), and abilities in other subjects such as natural sciences, languages or mathematics would be an additional part of the content (Byrd, 2019; Björklund & Ahlskog-Björkman, 2017). Indeed, the activity was organised in a similar way by the participant in our research, who taught the pupils how to fold origami, while at the same time the pupils were developing their geometric knowledge (constructing shapes, recognising shapes) in an integral way. However, researchers R. Potočnik, T. Košir & I. Devetak (2022), J. Pavlin & T. Čampa (2021) note that there are cases where teachers are irresponsible and careless in their planning of action research in the arts and leave the educational process to drift on its own, which often does not work well because the pupils do not have the necessary experience. In addition, there are cases where teachers themselves lack the knowledge of how to properly organise the educational process in the arts, and therefore recommendations describing guidelines for methodologies would be meaningful and purposeful, especially when it is recommended to integrate arts with natural sciences, because the curricular objectives and subject content of both subjects need to be aligned (Haidman et al., 2019).

Problem-solving as pupils come up with original product designs and decorative elements can be a part of the development of arts content, which also touches on other integral personal abilities such as critical thinking, problem-solving and creativity (Cutting & Kelly, 2015). This was the case for the participant in our research, whose activity involved using the frottage technique to develop her pupils' creativity. In addition, contemporary art forms, which are integrative in nature, are considered to be an appropriate means of introducing pupils to the exploration of the world around them and to the variety of ways in which they can use their knowledge of other subjects to create new and original works of art, reusing recycled materials. In addition, the results of the action research show that this approach to visual art teaching encourages cooperation and appreciation of art (Mills & Doyle, 2019) and contributes to the development of pupils' aesthetic awareness, where the visual image dominates all aspects of our lives (Blagoeva, 2019; Bautista et al., 2016). Our research involved action research where pupils used recycled materials to create contrasts. It is important that pupils reflect and share their insights on the artworks they have created, in this way children not only develop aesthetic taste and artistic cognitive abilities, but also enrich their vocabulary and expression of thought (Blagoeva, 2019; Blagoeva, Karppinen & Kairavuori, 2019).

In our research, two action research studies were performed in relation to the development of musical abilities, where children used ICT in a targeted way, rhythmically and instrumentally. In both cases, the pupils' musical abilities improved, although the authors of the study indicated that the results also depend on pupils' concentration, engagement, musical experience and memory. J. Laidlaw (2022) had very similar findings to those of our research on musical activity. J. Laidlaw (2022) states that during the action research, pupils successfully created original music with classroom instruments and demonstrated their understanding of creative experience, resulting in improved musical ability and musical understanding. In addition, the pupils expressed an interest in making music in the future, which shows that the methodology of the action research has proven its worth. As a negative factor, the author identified the absence of some of the pupils, which led to other children in the class having to change their initial idea of the music to be made. It is also important to mention that in every musical activity it is possible to see the development of the creativity of the pupils, because they fulfil certain elements in their own personal way, bringing in their own understanding and experience (Tan, 2019).

Researchers M. E. Culp & V. Wayman Davis (2023) state that music education is also linked to the teacher's ability to establish a relationship with the pupils and agree on the quality of the activity plan and its implementation. A. Mariguddi & T. Cain, (2022) propose to base music education practice on research that guides educators to develop action steps and put them into practice by working with pupils individually rather than collectively. For research-based practice to exist, it is necessary to describe the instructions in detail and to make them available to teachers so that they are able to put them into practice in their own activities.

We review the action research projects in which the authors of the bachelor's theses addressed more holistic problems involving general competences and their development, where practice is based on experiential activities (see Table 3.2.6).

Table 3.2.6: Problem-solving by research subject, when developing pupils' general competences related to experiential activities

Action research subject	Research method used to collect data	Solutions/results to pedagogical problems
Career education	Action research during educational sessions on different professions; interviews with pupils (reflection on activities) (N=1)	Pupils are educated about careers by exposing them to different professions; it is useful for children to learn about professions in a real-life setting, by interacting with people from different professions. Pupils most enjoyed trying out the actual steps involved in certain professions and the tools used in the working environment. Pupils took an interest in what abilities and characteristics are needed to do a certain job.
Developing cultural competences during trips	Organisation of educational trips, written survey of pupils, observation, interview (N=1) Organising experiential activities outside school (museum, library, natural outdoor environment) (N=1)	Pupils were interested in the national/ethnic culture, comparing and analysing the living conditions of today with those of the past; they understood the meaning of art and culture and the importance of preserving customs. Pupils' attitudes towards the educational trips and the trip activities are positive. The activities are organised according to Kolb's experiential learning cycle, with the following key stages: concrete learning, reflective observation, abstract conceptualisation, active experimentation. Through active participation in the experiential activities, pupils integrally develop subject and general competences, because they learned by doing.

(Continued)

Table 3.2.6: (Continued)

Action research subject	Research method used to collect data	Solutions/results to pedagogical problems
The project method in a Montessori primary school	Semi-structured interviews, analysis of documents (diagrams, drawings, written stories), written questionnaire (N=1)	The project-based approach enabled the development of pupils' individual abilities, because pupils consciously participated in the educational process and took responsibility for the results. Pupils deepened their knowledge through practical application, independent and creative problem-solving and cooperation; they managed their learning time independently. Pupils' abilities in moral, social, natural, technological and linguistic education increased. Teachers perceived the limitations of the project method to be the result of a lack of knowledge and mastery of this method. In Montessori educational practice, the project method helps to ensure that pupils are active, independent and that the learning content is related to life experiences.
Building relationships	Interviews, observation (N=1)	After the series of activities, the children were more open, more likely to express and substantiate their opinions about a story they had heard, and more likely to work in a friendly way with their friends. In addition, by analysing other people's stories, the children revealed that they themselves had experienced loneliness, not being able to get along with their friends, sadness, rejection; they reflected on how they would behave in similar situations next time. It is important to teach children how to maintain friendships, to listen to others' opinions, to resolve conflicts in a constructive way, and to use the necessary and appropriate vocabulary, to comfort, to ask or to reassure.
Developing social-emotional abilities	Action research, interviews, observation (N=1)	The development of social-emotional abilities takes place in a variety of lessons, through cognitive, practical activities, volunteering (through a service-learning approach). In these cases, children developed social-emotional abilities the most, while maintaining interpersonal relationships and helping others were developed the least.

The culture and pedagogy of contemporary schools aims to ensure that all pupils can learn successfully (Fullan, 2020, 2019; Fullan & Gallagher, 2020; Fullan & Quinn, 2020). Competence-based education relates to abilities that are applied in social life (Bakker et al., 2022; Nordin et al., 2021; Diesel & Scheepers, 2019; Fullan et al., 2018; Tepper et al., 2018). Our research focused on social-emotional competences, cultural literacy, interpersonal abilities, and teamwork abilities (participation in project activities). Competence-based educational practice is understood as assessing learners on what they do and know in practice (Brochu & Villemure, 2022; Jonnaert et al., 2020; Manalo, 2020; Ryan & Cox, 2017). In other words, learners are given the opportunity to demonstrate their abilities through a range of practical activities and assessments (based on pre-agreed criteria), so that pupils can demonstrate their competence in a particular area. Furthermore, this pedagogical approach implies that each learner should be given individual feedback and opportunities to improve his/her abilities in order to master the material to the highest possible extent. E. Moreno Sánchez, E. Castillo Viera & J. A. Rodríguez Mena (2017) emphasise that collaborative project activities help to develop pupils' practical life abilities, because they have to negotiate, learn to listen to one another, and perform activities in practice.

The action research aspects of monitoring pupils' self-evaluation and personal progress in our study are analysed in Table 3.2.7.

Table 3.2.7: Problem-solving by research subject, when developing pupils' general competences related to monitoring and self-evaluation of personal progress

Action research subject	**Research method used to collect data**	**Solutions/results to pedagogical problems**
Providing feedback for personal progress	Pupil survey, teacher interviews, completion of feedback forms, organisation of pupil reflection and recording of opinions (N=1)	Pupils appreciate the teacher's feedback and understand that it helps them to achieve better results, become more independent and responsible for their own learning process. Pupils feel that they need the most feedback in Lithuanian language, mathematics, natural sciences and history lessons. Oral feedback is the most useful, because it helps children to understand where they have made mistakes and how to correct them. Teachers find that feedback helps pupils to improve in the areas of academics, self-confidence and cooperation. It is important that feedback be positive, i.e. balanced. Providing feedback helps teachers to improve their teaching practice and to find new and more appropriate methods and approaches.

(Continued)

Table 3.2.7: (Continued)

Action research subject	Research method used to collect data	Solutions/results to pedagogical problems
Developing self-evaluation of learning achievements using the "break ticket" and "colours" methods	The action research was performed through observation, organisation of educational activities, analysis and interpretation of research data (N=1)	The "break ticket" and "colours" methods showed that pupils were able to self-evaluate their activities according to the given criteria, but it was difficult to comment and explain the results in more detail. It is important that the criteria and the process of self-evaluation to be used at the end of the activity were communicated to the pupils at the beginning of the activity; in this case, the children were better able to achieve and were more responsible and eager to improve their learning.
Assessment methods to monitor personal progress	Observation of activities, analysis of pupils' reflection notebooks (N=1)	Individual assessment and reflection techniques are useful because pupils learn in different ways, and the "incomplete sentences" method, the "learning diary", and the "break ticket" all proved to be successful; they allow pupils to reflect immediately after an activity on what they are already able to do, and they are given suggestions on what, how and why they could improve their work.

Competence-based education pedagogy focuses on the individual learning progress of each pupil, and on monitoring and supporting their learning (taking into account the individual needs of the learner) (Brochu & Villemure, 2022; Lasnier, 2014; Carrette & Rey, 2010). It starts with an assessment of the learner's abilities, from which content is selected to help the pupil make progress and experience success. E. Levine & S. Patrick (2019) linked the concepts of competency-based education to the monitoring and self-evaluation of personal progress in the following aspects:

1. Pupils are empowered every day to make important decisions about their learning experience, how they will construct their knowledge, and how they will demonstrate their mastery.
2. Assessment is a meaningful, positive and empowering learning experience for pupils that provides timely, relevant and appropriate evidence.
3. Pupils receive timely and differentiated support according to their individual learning needs.
4. Pupils make personal progress based on evidence of mastery.
5. Pupils learn actively, using a variety of methods and at various tempos.

6. Strategies to ensure equality for all pupils are embedded in the culture, structure and pedagogy of the school.
7. Learning objectives (knowledge, abilities and attitudes) are clear, identifiable and measurable.

We can say that our research followed the aspects identified by E. Levine & S. Patrick (2019), however, the most difficult elements to observe in practice were chosen, such as providing targeted and timely feedback in the educational process, trying out methods to monitor one's own performance and to analyse pupils' motivation, such as the "break ticket", "colours", "learning diary", and oral reflection on performance. We would like to point out that all the activities had positive results, because the children were able to appropriately assess and self-evaluate their achievements by analysing their work according to pre-agreed criteria. Teachers also noted that feedback is useful for the pupils, especially when they find out what has been done well and when they receive particular suggestions for improving their work.

3.3. Experiences of primary school teachers with advanced action research: analysis of the results of Focus Group 1

Context of the classes. All of the teachers who participated in the research work in public schools in three large cities (Vilnius, Klaipėda and Šiauliai). Most of the teachers were already working during their fourth year at university, so at the time of the research they had 3 or 4 years of work experience. Because the schools are located in large cities, classes have a large number of pupils (at least 24). In addition, there is a wide variety of cultural situations, with pupils who have come to Lithuania or have returned to Lithuania with experience in other countries. There are pupils with individual learning needs in the classes.

Cecile's class: The class has a large number of socially strong families and two children from at-risk families. The children are well provided for. There are children from different cultures, from different countries. There are children from Syria, from the war zone; there are also children from Turkey, from Istanbul, from Russia, and there are children from Italy. One girl speaks Italian fluently, and she also speaks Lithuanian fluently. There are six children who speak fluent Russian. The pupils are second-year pupils. The children are happy to be from different countries. They sang the national anthems of all the countries and studied the words of the anthems. They are curious; they are interested in why there is a war in Syria. They were interested in how wars are fought; they analyse how they could defend themselves.

Milana's class: There are a large number of children with different abilities. The pupils are in the fourth year. There is one Turkish pupil who not only speaks Turkish but is also learning Spanish. There are Russian-speaking children. There is a child who has learned Russian by playing in the yard with Russian-speaking children. There is a child with special educational needs. There is one girl with Asperger's syndrome. She finds it more difficult to express her opinion. There are also two girls who lived in the UK before starting to attend school here. One of them has adapted very well, while the other still has a lot of links with the UK even today, and she is struggling.

Clareta's class: The parents are simple, sincere, open, and respectful to me as a teacher. There is one boy from Japan whose parents speak Russian. The boy's father is Japanese. The child has already attended a pre-school group in Lithuania. The pupils in the class are first-year pupils. In some cases, the boy has difficulty understanding the Lithuanian language.

Zita's class: There are children in the class who have returned from emigration. One girl has returned from Ireland. She pronounces some sounds differently and is learning written letters. A few children returned a little earlier. There is a dark-skinned boy who has adapted very well, he is a leader in the class and has many friends. Most of the children are from middle-class families. The pupils are first-year pupils.

Oksana's class: There are twenty-six pupils, including a boy with autism spectrum disorder and a girl with an adapted programme. Because the school is in Samogitia, some children shorten words and pronounce and place the stress in many words incorrectly. They have problems pronouncing long and short vowels, so their pronunciation interferes with the correct pronunciation of words. There are no children from socially disadvantaged families. Almost half of the children have a good command of Russian, even though they are all Lithuanians; they have learned Russian from playing in the yard with Russian-speaking children and from the urban environment. The children are second-year pupils.

Ilona's class: The twenty-four pupils are second-year pupils: fourteen boys and ten girls. Three are Russian-speaking children; it is difficult for them to distinguish between the -e- and -ė- sounds. One girl has returned from Italy and has no learning problems. There are some children who learn very well, some who learn at an average level and some who learn very poorly. One child is socially neglected; he does not know certain elementary things. From the very beginning, the class was very diverse: some of the children were already excellent readers, and some of them could not even read or write their names. Some parents come from cultural work backgrounds: their parents were singers and actors. As a result, some parents allow themselves to be disrespectful to the teacher (the teacher mentioned one public conflict with one child's parent which arose due to the teacher's young age). Although the general context of the class is good, some children are spoilt and mischievous.

During the interview, Focus Group 1 participants were asked in which contexts they currently apply action research, and the lessons learned from their bachelor's thesis in their current teaching work. The teachers' views can be seen in Table 3.3.1.

Table 3.3.1: Views of Focus Group 1 participants on their experience of applying action research

Experience of applying action research	Examples of participant views	Researchers' comments
In the area of identifying/ testing pupils' abilities (N=2)	The text and film analysis action research that I did for my bachelor's thesis is more difficult to do with first- and second-year pupils. Therefore, I did not apply this particular approach. But I did apply the action research during reading, when I was teaching first-year pupils to read. I explained and taught them to pronounce correctly and to pay attention when they write words. For example, in a word the sound -e- is prolonged. I pointed out that if they the whisper the word correctly, then they do not make mistakes when writing. It can be said that I do small action research all the time, it happens naturally, and sometimes with a particular goal in mind. (Cecile) I applied action research to determine pupils' abilities when assigning tasks of varying complexity and analysing results, when pupils came back to school for year 2 after the summer holidays. It is a big month-long study, analyses, designing new tasks and all this work was done just to know what the class is like, where the children's strengths are and where we need to improve. […] In addition, I have an autistic pupil, a boy, so I am very responsible in observing and analysing what helps him, looking for ways to help him understand better, for example, counting up to 100. We searched with the assistant, with the special educator, using charts, objects, until we found that colours help him the most, which he marks himself, where the tens and ones are. When we found this way, his learning improved. I think every teacher uses action research, because every day we are dealing with different situations, different children, and it doesn't necessarily apply to the subject content.	From the thoughts expressed by the research participants, we can say that they conduct action research in a very focused and responsible way, because identifying pupils' abilities in a particular area shows what pupils already know as well as what pupils are not yet able to do, i.e. what is their problematic area that could be an area for further improvement.

(Continued)

Table 3.3.1: (Continued)

Experience of applying action research	Examples of participant views	Researchers' comments
	For example, there is a boy in my class who coughs when he is nervous, it interferes with his learning, and he starts coughing when he gets upset, when the teacher asks him a question he is not ready for. So, we looked for ways to help him. We have indeed found one – we just tell him quietly that we will ask him to read and comment on a certain task after he finishes it. And he feels good, the coughing fits are over. (Oksana)	
Monitoring personal progress (N=4)	We draw personal progress charts and graphs with the children. I noticed what it means to them when they do it. It is a desire to move up the steps, not to go lower on their chart. Whether it's a bar chart or whether it's a graph, they don't want to go down. That is what motivates them to make progress. (Cecile) Pupils have notebooks in which they write and set themselves goals to work towards and analyse how they have achieved them. They also complete personal progress charts. (Zita) My bachelor's thesis was about self-evaluation as self-awareness. As far as self-evaluation is concerned, this is an area that I am still learning to do well. The problem I face is the lack of time for quality self-evaluation. Sometimes I think up tasks for them to self-evaluate. It's important that in Lithuanian language, there is already a self-evaluation task after the activity. I also use Kahoot and Wordwall for the self-evaluation questions. (Ilona) Sometimes you don't even think it's research and you do it, and it comes naturally. The children are first-years, with very different reading abilities, so we did an action research, because some of the children don't do the agreed description of the books they have read, because some of the children haven't	As many as four research participants highlighted and gave different examples of how children learn to monitor their own progress, certain changes in activities and why it is important to monitor this area based on data. Teachers see that personal monitoring motivates pupils to move up the ladder, and revisiting and discussing certain issues in more detail helps motivate pupils to do activities that require more effort. Teachers also identified problems, such as a lack of time for more in-depth self-evaluation activities.

Experience of applying action research	**Examples of participant views**	**Researchers' comments**
	done this work. But when I explained to them again in detail how and why they needed to describe the book and I asked why the children don't describe them to me, maybe they didn't understand something? After this conversation, they started to describe the books. I can see that it is necessary to talk with them in great detail about what needs to be done and how. (Clareta)	
Integrated intercultural education activities (N=1)	The children did intercultural activities with their family. Each family that had come to Lithuania analysed how their values, attitudes towards certain things and, in a certain sense, their national identity have changed while living in Lithuania, because they need to know themselves even more in order to be able to know others. (Cecile)	Action research is also suitable for the pupil's deeper self-knowledge, for presenting himself or herself in a different environment, and the teacher's example shows that action research can be used in virtually all educational practice.
Giving pupils autonomy when working in groups (making Pillars of Gediminas in Minecraft) (N=2)	The pupils themselves took on their roles and decided who would be the leaders. They folded, glued, and worked together in a friendly way. The activity was long-term, but the important thing is that when asked what they remembered from the third year, most of them highlighted this activity. I think that activities challenging children but in a way they can cope with are very important and memorable for them. I divided students into groups. For example, playing the recorder (the woodwind instrument). The children were divided into groups of four and became assessors as they assessed each other's work according to the criteria. What	Teachers highlighted that in action research-based activities, children can be more independent and involved in the activities themselves, while the teacher can quietly observe the pupils' activities and provide support only when necessary. It is important that pupils' observations are taken into account and that they give feedback on how to improve certain activities. This is how modern educational practice is created.

(Continued)

Table 3.3.1: (Continued)

Experience of applying action research	Examples of participant views	Researchers' comments
	happened positively was that it took a long time to discuss the analysis of the work. What I noticed was that for some pupils it is more difficult to self-evaluate their own work objectively than to evaluate the work of classmates. (Milana) I organise free activities where I observe how children behave, who they are friends with and how they interact. […] Pupils constantly make observations and suggestions for improvement. There's also an agreement that pupils in all classes work this way, and we can see the data for each class on who has made what suggestions. (Zita)	
Visual aids, excursions (N=2)	During the excursion, the children became journalists, because they went to the Birds' Village, so they had to choose one bird, collect all the information about it, and when they came back, they had to prepare a presentation. Not only did they take photos during the trip, but they also asked questions of the guides, but they were also interested in the bird when they returned and gathered more information. (Milana) At this time, I have prepared additional visual aids for the pupils to try out in the educational process, i.e. a clock, multiplication-table window-shutters. (Ilona)	The tools mentioned by both teachers are targeted support to help students understand the content and to enable pupils to achieve the intended results on their own. It is important that learning beyond the school setting is applied in a purposeful, fun way, based on activities that children understand.

Organising action research based on the experience of children as researchers is another aspect highlighted by the interview participants, who said that this experience allows them not only to solve a certain problem, but also to achieve much deeper results on the basis of action research. If the activities are organised according to an action research framework, they start with targeted planning, implementation, observation (when data is collected) and deep reflection (Kurshumlia & Vula, 2021; Putra et al., 2022). This system of organising activities allows for the development of pupils' autonomy, activity and purposeful learning, in which the child takes responsibility for and monitors his or her own progress and abilities. *It is important to give children as much freedom as possible so that they themselves can make as many decisions as possible* (Milana).

The majority of participants in our research said that pupils are motivated by setting personal goals and monitoring their personal progress. In a classroom with children from many different cultures, the teacher used action research to enable them to gain a deeper understanding of themselves and to present their culture to their classmates. Something similar is stated by V. Balakrishnan & L. Claiborne (2017), who performed action research with a culturally diverse group of participants. The use of action research provides insights into opportunities and strategies that can be personalised according to the needs of the individual. The opportunity for participants to contribute to and shape the research process is an essential feature of action research (Bradbury, Lewis & Embury, 2019; Posch, 2019), and the results show that action research is more open to the participants shaping the process than could be expected from a purely theoretical perspective (Hopwood, 2024). This is confirmed by our research, in which more than one interview participant said that the only way to tailor the educational content to the individual needs of each pupil was through coherent planning, monitoring, reflection and consideration of particular needs.

Project activities based on action research help children develop psychomotor abilities and a better understanding of subject concepts (Sumarni, et al., 2016; Balakrishnan & Claiborne, 2017), for example, to better understand dance music production and the expression of creativity in music (Taryana et al., 2021). Participants in our research expressed similar ideas when they talked about a field trip, which can include project-based activities, where the pupil takes an interest in a chosen object and records information about it during the field trip, and collects additional material after the field trip. The various visual aids mentioned by another teacher in the research also help primary school pupils to learn more about concepts. When pupils themselves create, collect and record data, the better they are able to assimilate the learning material and apply it to life. (Sumarni et al., 2016). Teachers participating in our research also talked about the empowerment that comes from active learning in groups. School-based approaches have been found to be adaptable, implementable and often bring about significant changes in teaching practice, institutional collaboration and other important aspects of school education when action research is applied (Hopwood, 2024).

It is clear that the educational methods chosen in the action research help teachers to achieve significant changes in various aspects of education: from improving pupils' cognitive development, to better assimilation of educational content, to building classroom teams, to individual motivation. In addition, such activities provide teachers and children with a theoretically sound approach to changing educational practice. In this case, teachers alone act as agents of change, although, as our research has shown, they sometimes do not feel confident or even unconsciously perform action research to solve problems (Bradbury, Lewis & Embury, 2019; Hopwood, 2024). In addition, the flexibility of action research helps to address many of the issues involved in the successful implementation of educational content (Manfra, 2019; Wei, Lee & Chung, 2022), even though there is not as much time as the teacher would like to make deeper changes or to implement the action research even more consistently (Thorgeirsdottir, 2015).

It was asked what motivates the primary school teachers who participated in the research to perform action research in their classrooms. The range of teachers' views on this issue can be seen in Table 3.3.2.

Table 3.3.2: Examples of Focus Group 1 interview participants' motivations for performing action research in educational practice

Examples of motivations for performing action research	**Examples of views of research participants**	**Researchers' comments**
Pedagogical curiosity (N=3)	I keep thinking, what if … and I think it's interesting to see what change will happen if we change a certain element. I am driven by curiosity and the desire to see for myself what will happen, what will be the change – whether it works or not. […] And curiosity arises from a certain situation. I myself tried digital exercises and there was a gap, trying to find out how they learn. When I tried to teach them digital abilities, I analysed what kind of support helps them and what they have learned on their own, so that they can do it. (Cecile)	The teachers' answers show that they are enthusiastic, questioning and looking for solutions. It is also positive that the teachers identified themselves as curious, flexible, analytical, willing to make decisions after a good analysis of the situation. This shows that they are ready to work and highly motivated.

Examples of motivations for performing action research	Examples of views of research participants	Researchers' comments
	I like seeing where we are and then thinking about what we want, where we want to go. Then you try to make an effort, see what the children need so that I can help – that's what motivates me the most. (Clareta) It's intriguing to see how much can be done and what interesting activities you can come up with. I ask myself what to do with children of average ability, because we tend to focus on the very gifted and those with very high individual needs. And the question arises, how to motivate everyone to want to do their best and to be able to say that they have done their best to achieve this or that goal, so that they can be proud of themselves and set their own internal goals in order to achieve success. (Milana)	
Having a purpose (N=2)	You always have a purpose, even if you don't think of it as research: either to check what the children have learned or to teach them something. For example, when I organise group work, I don't organise it just any which way, but I have a certain system and from that I can see what the children have developed, what they have learned. This way I organise more interesting activities where children's emotions are expressed. (Zita) We want to maintain the whole format of the activity – from start to finish. The self-evaluation is how the end of the activity is framed. (Ilona)	These educators identified the starting point for action research, because, when you analyse a problematic situation, you set a goal towards which you will work in order to make and see a change. Another important aspect is seeing the steps from start to finish.

(Continued)

Table 3.3.2: (Continued)

Examples of motivations for performing action research	**Examples of views of research participants**	**Researchers' comments**
Getting to know the individual pupil and contextualising the educational content (N=1)	The situation is very different if you compare it with your studies, when you have your own class, particular children, where you are always trying to do better, because there is always room for improvement, we have to get to know the children, to change the methodology, to change the ways we do things. I think it is only through action research that we can get to know our pupils and enable them to move upwards at their own pace, to move and grow. (Oksana)	Teacher Oksana identified the essence of contemporary education, saying that action research needs to be performed on a continuous basis, addressing various aspects.

Developing the learning-to-learn cycle in the educational process aims to strengthen sustainability by embedding action research-based practices (Hopwood, 2024). However, often performing action research, long-term evidence that changes are sustainable or that they will have a lasting impact is often outside the scope of the research (Postholm, Klemp & Nordbotn, 2023; Hopwood, 2024). However, the essence of action research is to get to know each learner and adapt the content to their context, discovering what the problematic issues are and envisaging how to solve them. In this case, action research-based practice needs to be continuous and systematic, because educational situations are constantly changing, and so are the particular problems that need to be addressed. But as Oksana, a participant in our research, said, *the teacher performing action research can get to know his or her pupils and enable them to move upwards at their own pace, to move and grow.*

U. Bergmark (2022) notes that action research is related to teachers' social roles and the development of positive emotions. If teachers feel emotionally and socially secure, they will work harder to achieve their goals and evidence-based pupil progress. In fact, these aspects were also identified by the teachers in our research, who stated that they were willing to put action research into practice in a good-willed way, driven by their own pedagogical curiosity. Teachers are keen to improve the educational process, i.e. they see opportunities to learn from their colleagues (Appova & Arbaugh, 2018). What we have identified as pedagogical curiosity has been called by other researchers (Bergmark, 2022; Appova & Arbaugh, 2018) altruistic motivation, and is linked to a desire to help pupils achieve their goals and individual progress. Achieving progress in line with set goals leads to an even higher dimension – the greater good of society (Bergmark, 2022; Appova & Arbaugh, 2018). In addition, teachers also noted that pupils found the activities in the action research to be interesting and socially engaging. By organising the educational process according to the stages of action research, teachers are more effective because they think more deeply about their educational practice (Childress, 2019). It is also important to focus on problem-solving, in which educators engage students together. Such activities motivate all participants in the educational process, who are willingly involved in resolving situations. Teachers become more reflective, seeing the essence and meaning of action research (Gilbert, Voelkel & Johnson, 2018; Childress, 2019). When teachers take into account the individual needs of pupils, positive results are achieved by all pupils, especially when all the teachers working with a particular child begin to consult and work together regarding that child (Donohoo, 2017).

It was asked how research participants prepare for action research. Their answers can be seen in Table 3.3.3.

Table 3.3.3: Answers of Focus Group 1 interview participants on how they prepare for action research

Examples of preparation for action research	**Examples of views of research participants**	**Researchers' comments**
Envisaging all the stages of an activity, preparing particular tools for particular children (N=6)	I clarify the purpose of the activity and anticipate all the steps of the activity. […] Because I have a pupil, a non-Lithuanian boy, I have to prepare additional materials for him, because he does not understand some of the content. I create specific checklists for the children. (Clareta) I'm teaching first-year pupils this year to self-evaluate their work. This also involves correcting work and checking and correcting the work of the students themselves. They self-evaluate according to the criteria and, when they are able to self-evaluate properly, then they can help a friend. Children are very keen to help a friend and therefore try to learn to self-evaluate properly. They also learn to find information themselves. I use a number line. (Zita)	It is important that each research participant mentioned the stages of the action research. In addition, they gave examples related to their particular classroom contexts. This situation shows that writing a bachelor's thesis

(Continued)

Table 3.3.3: (Continued)

Examples of preparation for action research	Examples of views of research participants	Researchers' comments
	We have laminated checklists that children know about and can use. For example, when it comes to remembering diphthongs, vowels, some children get confused, forget them and find it difficult to do the tasks. They know where to find the handouts and they can use these tools. There are a lot of laminated materials in my classroom. There are all sorts of rules laminated for an autistic boy, which the other children also use when they need them. (Oksana) I always teach my children to make a plan. We signed the work plan on the board. We worked out each stage and the children had something to go on. I always give the children materials to refer to, which can be questions, with clarifications, with examples. […] I showed them how to make slides, and later they started to make the slides for themselves. […] I have tried to involve the children themselves as much as possible, so that they become participants, and I am a mentor, a counsellor, so that I can help them if they need help or to find information. (Milana) In the case of hybrid education, where some of the pupils were learning from home, I had to think about how to present the material in a way that everybody could understand and do the tasks. So that both the children sitting at the computer and the children sitting in the classroom could see everything. (Ilona) I anticipate right away how the children themselves will be able to monitor and self-evaluate their own stages and changes. […] I also give pupils the opportunity to choose the strategy for performing their activities. For example, when solving mathematical problems, children can choose whether to visualise the solution by hand or by using a certain app. And after the activity, they can discuss with each other which strategy was more useful. (Cecile)	from the field of action research has developed the ability to plan, implement, monitor and reflect on the process of action research based on the educational situation of particular pupils in a particular classroom.

Examples of preparation for action research	Examples of views of research participants	Researchers' comments
Parental involvement (N=1)	The most important thing I do is to communicate with the parents and explain the importance of this activity, describing in as much detail as possible what will be important about it. I anticipate how the children themselves will be able to observe and self-evaluate their own stages and changes. […] When I introduce new tools to parents, I explain why they are worth using, how they are useful and how they will help the children in our classroom, what will change when we do an activity differently, how they will improve our work. For example, if we organise a class event, I explain to the parents how it will benefit the child and what self-awareness competences the event will develop in the children. We began to participate in the Apple's Friends programme, and I explained to parents why it was important, how it was more useful than our weekly one-hour classroom talk; why it was useful for us to talk about emotions, not only about experiences where the children had been, but why we needed to connect it with emotions. […] Parents then also share responsibility for these activities. (Cecile)	One teacher mentioned that parents also help in her classroom, as they can observe the pupils, see what they are doing, what they are doing and how they are doing, and what results they have achieved. We think this is a positive aspect that helps to extend the field of action research beyond the classroom.
Anticipated work in groups (N=2)	We do a lot of group work, even though the children are only first-years. I like this way of organising work. It helps to motivate the pupils, because there is a clear system, they are involved and help each other. […] When working in groups, I divide the children into groups of three or four, so that their individuality can come through. Another point is that children have roles to play when working in groups. They are able to distribute the roles because they have done it more than once. (Clareta) There are lots of activities based on action research when children work in groups. I also	Teachers Clareta and Zita identified group work as a common approach to action research in their classrooms. Group work is a contemporary educational method that can help to engage

(Continued)

Table 3.3.3: (Continued)

Examples of preparation for action research	Examples of views of research participants	Researchers' comments
	put a lot of thought into it and even who is going to work with whom, because there are some children who just can't work together, so there is no randomness in grouping in my classroom. I think about everything very carefully. Sometimes I bring in children who get along a bit less well, but then they have a counterbalance. Indeed, I notice from the classroom when there is already too much group work. (Zita)	pupils in the educational process and enable them to achieve higher results.
Children's conscious learning (N=1)	It was very important to me that the children understand that we can make mistakes and that it is perfectly normal to make mistakes. We learn in such a way that when we make a mistake, we have to analyse it, why the mistake was made, how we can change and how we manage to correct it. There are a lot of children in my class who are very withdrawn and afraid to give answers. When asked, they get lost and don't know what to say. We are trying to get out of this, we have already talked about the fact that we can be wrong maybe a thousand times. After these conversations, you realise that the children receive it in different ways, that some of them find it difficult to get over themselves. It is important that they learn to accept failure, but in a safe environment. […] We are working very hard on this. The important thing is that they are already raising their hands (wanting to answer), and those children were the ones who had been withdrawn. (Oksana)	Teacher Oksana's thoughts show that the aim is to create a deep awareness among learners. Analysing mistakes, finding answers to why the activity was successful or not is part of action research, which students are taught to do.

Teachers can improve through action research because they have to raise issues and find solutions (Spencer et al., 2020), understanding that only through reflection can they see both the problems and the progress of the educational process (Vaughan & Mertler, 2020). In addition, in this case, educators are also aware that the situation is constantly changing. This was confirmed by all the participants in our research, who gave particular examples from their classroom contexts. Moreover, by explaining that making mistakes and learning from them is a perfectly natural process. From the situations presented by the teachers, we can conclude that each teacher's teaching is distinctive, although they all have a good knowledge of action research methodology. That the teachers are deep, reflective thinkers is also shown by statements in their interview, such as: *I anticipate right away how the children themselves will be able to monitor and self-evaluate their own stages and changes.* (Cecile). [...] I clarify the purpose of the activity and anticipate all the steps of the activity. (Clareta). [...] I always teach my children to make a plan. (Milana). [...] I also put a lot of thought into it [...] I think about everything very carefully. (Zita). [...] We are working very hard on this. (Oksana). From these statements we can see that teachers naturally engage in the process of questioning and problem-solving (Henriksen, Richardson, & Mehta, 2017; Mertler, 2021), to create positive educational change for their pupils. Moreover, the situational analysis shows that the teachers also see it as a positive thing that they discover in their classrooms, because they emphasise that it is specific to their classroom, because it takes into account the pupils, etc. In addition, Clareta and Zita identified group work as an advanced method of active learning pedagogy, on the basis of which they conduct action research. Other studies have shown that group work encourages pupils to learn actively, take responsibility and solve problems in order to progress (Jakavonytė-Staškuvienė, 2021a, 2021b; Jakavonytė-Staškuvienė, Žemgulienė & Sakadolskis, 2021).

The responses of the teachers who participated in our research suggest that they could develop action research not only in their own classrooms, but also in the schools where they work. They could then build a community of learning teachers and not only perform action research themselves, but also mentor colleagues. Such experiences motivate everyone in the school and give meaning to everyone's activities, demonstrating that there is meaning at every step in educational practice. In addition, each step is important for the further development of those involved in the educational process (Thorgeirsdottir, 2015; Mertler, 2021).

It was asked how often research participants integrate inquiry-based activities into the educational process, relating them to action research, and what forms such activities take. We asked what percentage of all activities are action research-based activities. The teachers' particular thoughts and forms of activity can be seen in Table 3.3.4.

Table 3.3.4: Answers of Focus Group 1 interview participants on how often action research is applied in the educational process and in what forms

Forms of activity	Examples of views of research participants	Researchers' comments
Applying the elements of action research on an ongoing basis to improve both the process and the content in line with the needs of the pupils in the class (N=4)	I have never thought before what the extent might be, but I think it might be 60%, maybe 70%. If you look at it in general terms, in terms of every activity being improved. I have only been working for three years, so I have touched the activities, but they still aren't set in stone, and the methodology is tangible, but there is always a desire to improve, to add something of my own. That's why I think that every activity I do has an action research component, because I adapt to the classroom where I work. This is why the percentages are not exact. I apply elements of action research to up to 90% of my activities; and targeted action research was certainly present in at least 30% of my activities. (Cecile) If you look at a lesson, or a child's experience, or an action research that is already being done in a targeted way, with a hypothesis. A real action research with a goal and a hypothesis, less than half of my work is like that. But if we are talking about the whole of the lessons and the experience of the pupils, then it would be more than half. (Clareta) When we prepare for each lesson, we ask ourselves questions like what we can do more of, what can we do better, because the textbooks have similar methods, even though the topics change, but we have to reach all the pupils with the same information.	It is important to note that four focus group participants mentioned that every activity has elements of action research. This situation shows that teachers have mastered action research-based practice and do it continuously. Importantly, they ask questions to which they seek answers; they anticipate particular results, even if at first these results may be less tangible.

Forms of activity	Examples of views of research participants	Researchers' comments
	So, I think we do the minimum action research every day. But since we are delivering the content for the first time, we have to spend a lot of time figuring it out ourselves. I look for new facts that are not in the textbooks, so I think we do that every day. (Oksana) Sometimes I see a topic and I analyse and explore what my pupils are supposed to take away and learn from the content of that topic. Then I also try different approaches in the lesson, i.e. I explore. Other times, you plan a lot of content, but it becomes boring or doesn't go as I planned. And an element thought up on the spot helps to give meaning to a certain lesson. I find it difficult to prepare for world studies lessons because I really want to know all the answers to what the pupils might ask, but now I'm no longer afraid to tell the pupils that I don't know it all, but that we can work it out together, even with the second-years. (Ilona)	
Ack of assessment/ cognition of pupils' abilities (N=2)	I think it's quite difficult to determine how long. Especially when I'm still a relatively new teacher. Every day I find myself doing everything for the first time. Every day I ask myself if my first-year pupils will really do the activity well, because it is my first time working with first-year pupils. Even though I have doubts about whether they will do it, they just step up and do it, those children. Every time I ask again and again if they can do it, and we try and we do it. In reality, where I actually do the whole action research which I think through very well, I do for 20–30% of the whole educational process, but cases, activities that I sometimes do unconsciously, applying action research, it certainly is a higher percentage. (Zita)	Two of the research participants said that, because they are still in the beginning years in a certain classroom, they do a lot of research and analysis because they still do not have experience and cannot expect certain abilities from the pupils because they do not know the children that well. So, it can be said that action research helps them to get to know the pupils.

(Continued)

Table 3.3.4: (Continued)

Forms of activity	Examples of views of research participants	Researchers' comments
	As for the more serious action research, we monitor our classroom situation, analyse it, see if there are problems. And we certainly don't wait for the problem, if there is a problem, to resolve itself, because it certainly won't resolve itself if we don't do anything. I think every class is different, has different problems. (Oksana)	
Systematic and meaningful education (N=2)	I just think that some of my lessons are less dynamic, and I'm just trying to introduce some kind of system so that the children have a routine. For example, the children know the flow of the mathematics lesson, that somebody is going to do the problems, somebody is going to do the assessment, they already know one step ahead. Every world studies lesson is like a separate exploration, with lots of material, lots of inquiry, lots of experiments, searching for information, learning to find it. The process is different in different lessons. (Milana) Children collect coupons in return for certain activities, which can be exchanged for activities or tasks, or even to lead a lesson. There are already four pupils who have given lessons and explained calculations. And they even use phrases learned from the teacher in their explanations, for example, the first child, after doing their task, says that he has already done it, and the second child, who is in the role of the teacher, says to him that now you should check it and wait a little bit for the rest of the classmates. Children already know certain roles. (Ilona)	Importantly, action research also contributes to the systematic and meaningful nature of education; teachers and pupils are taught to think several steps ahead, thus planning activities. It also allows those children who are ready to take on the role of teacher, and to be teacher's assistants.

The research participants relate action research to getting to know pupils and empowering pupils to be active. Researcher H. Thorgeirsdottir (2015) has similar findings, relating action research to paying attention to pupils' opinion, when children are not only active participants in the educational process, but also creators in that process. One area of action research could be the monitoring and analysis of pupils' learning, looking at what and why pupils are doing well, what they think about it, and how they themselves anticipate goals and steps towards change in order to make even more progress in a particular area (Thorgeirsdottir, 2015). The research participants have confidence in their pupils and recognise their potential, for example, Ilona mentions as an incentive the fact that four pupils have already taught a lesson or part of a lesson. Indeed, primary school pupils are capable of setting educational goals, monitoring their progress and effort according to criteria, as shown in other similar studies (Hattie & Donoghue, 2016; Escorcia & Fenouillet, 2018; Ponomarioviené & Jakavonyté-Staškuviené, 2024). Primary school pupils are able to analyse their work, plan further goals and the steps/tasks needed to achieve them (as a change), if teachers devote time and attention to this in the educational process, motivate pupils to do so, and provide feedback to the children on the monitoring of the set goals (Ponomarioviené & Jakavonyté-Staškuviené, 2024).

It was asked with whom the teachers can consult and share insights in their educational institution when the teachers plan and perform action research. Research participants' views on this question can be seen in Table 3.3.5.

The majority of the research participants emphasised that they have one or more colleagues with whom they share experiences and solve problems, and with whom they talk about their educational practices. This is a very important aspect, because for the development of teachers it is necessary to share one's own experience, to be critical, to have several alternative solutions for any action in the educational process. In order to develop, an educator needs to have a person, also known as a *critical friend*, who is able/willing to give honest advice (Kemmis, McTaggart & Nixon, 2015). As we can see from the research participants, these friends are sometimes family members or former course mates who are contacted by phone, because the school environment lacks a friendly community and colleagues who are not only able and willing to give advice, but also to improve themselves. If change is to be achieved, the team involved in the action research, both teachers and advisers/facilitators, need to be known to each other, of good will, familiar, so that all colleagues can trust each other (Kemmis, McTaggart & Nixon, 2015). Milana, a research participant, also identified this element as a significant barrier to progress if the community is not welcoming, because everyone involved in action research needs to be willing to learn, to be able to recognise and find ways to solve problems.

Table 3.3.5: Views of Focus Group 1 interview participants on the forms of teacher consultation

Forms of consultation used in the school	Examples of views of research participants	Researchers' comments
Collaboration with teachers in parallel (same year) classes and other colleagues (N=5)	We now have a close relationship with parallel second-year teachers in the school. We discuss with each other what works and what doesn't. We have as many as six parallel classes. And there is a large group of second-years: there are two teachers who have been working for 16 years and four teachers with 2–3 years of experience. We can smoothly share experiences and discuss performance. Nobody has asked for this to be included in any kind of report. (Cecile) I share the successes of activities with my colleagues. I'm lucky to have my course mate Oksana nearby and we talk all the time. […] The problem is that my current classroom space is very distant from the other primary classes, at the end of a completely different corridor, mixed in with the older classes, so if I want to talk with somebody about something, I have to walk down the corridor for 4–5 minutes, which is why my colleagues say they rarely see me. But that's really because I don't have enough time to walk down and back. (Clareta) Teachers of parallel classes meet twice a year to discuss their classroom contexts, to talk about who and which children are doing very well, what problems pupils are having and how we are trying to solve them. (Zita) The deputy headteacher (vice-principal) encourages us to share our thoughts and experiences with our colleagues and to present our activities to them for up to 10 to 15 minutes during the teacher	Most of the teachers who participated in the research have close relationships in the immediate school environment, either working in parallel classrooms or interacting with colleagues from different classes, but in close proximity, on the same floor. This shows that young teachers have already established an environment in which they can share examples of their work and discuss key issues of concern to them. In addition, the teachers expressed the idea that successes are also shared on their school's website.

Forms of consultation used in the school	Examples of views of research participants	Researchers' comments
	meetings. We can prepare presentations: what we did, how we did it, what worked, what didn't work. If something goes really well for the teachers, the school shares this information on Facebook. We are very cooperative with the teachers in the other classes near our classroom and we talk all the time. We can always ask the administration about any difficulties or problems, because the administration is always willing to help us, they don't leave us alone and we find a solution together. There is a community, but perhaps we ourselves need to be more vocal and participate more actively in the community, to join in, not to feel so modest that we are inexperienced, though sometimes we really do lack the courage and confidence in ourselves. […] It is difficult at first for a new, young teacher, when you are standing in a large group of teachers, and you don't know anyone. Of course, there are colleagues who come up to you and ask how you are doing, where you are from, but it takes time to get used to it. (Oksana) The deputy headteacher (vice-principal) brought me to the teacher of a parallel class and asked her to help me. She always helps. She advises me on how to present this or that material, we work together on the quizzes and tests, I can compare the results of the classes, discuss what all the children did well and which were the most difficult tasks. We have weekly meetings. […] There is another teacher in whose class I used to work as a teaching assistant, and she helps me a lot. If I go to her with questions, she always gives me advice and material. (Ilona)	

(Continued)

Table 3.3.5: (Continued)

Forms of consultation used in the school	**Examples of views of research participants**	**Researchers' comments**
Online self-reflection questionnaire, social group on e-platform (N=3)	At school, we have an online self-reflection questionnaire where we fill in what worked well and what needs improvement. (Clareta) Last year, we wrote reflections on activities monthly, based on a set goal. This year, we're exploring new programmes. (Zita) We have a group where we share worksheets, slides, educational programmes. (Ilona)	Half of the research participants reported that the school uses self-reflection questionnaires, various forms of reflection, which they analyse and use to support teachers.
Organising activities for teachers working in pairs (N=1)	Sometimes we organise activities together, in pairs, with some other teacher. We then plan together and agree on everything. (Zita)	Zita also mentioned another form, pair work. This form is progressive, especially when teachers trust each other and there is a practice of mutual development.
Reflecting with family members (N=2)	I am in an environment with colleagues who are in the last year or two of their career, and they already know that, and there is no motivation there. In my environment, I was told that there is nothing to share, we are all perfect and know how to work. Even in the strategy, no areas for improvement have been identified. […] I see at work that the real values of education are no longer a concern in my school. I reflect every day with my own family members, because there is no conversation about this at school. (Milana) At home, I do reflection every day. My husband knows about my pupils and every evening listens to my stories about them. (Ilona)	Two teachers also talked about reflecting on classroom contexts and school work with family members. Milana described a particularly difficult situation, where the school community is inactive, unwilling to improve and does not see a reason to change, because most teachers do not see their own future in their work.

In summary, the focus group interview findings suggest that action research-based practices provide a framework for collaboration and inclusion, emphasising the value, individuality and needs of each learner (Hopwood, 2024; Winberg, Garraway & Wright, 2023). This practice is often at odds with neoliberal managerialism or even capitalist forces that favour competition, selection and differentiation, so it is important to keep the moral-ideological aspects at the centre of action research (Engeström et al., 2023; Engeström & Sannino, 2021; Winberg, Garraway & Wright, 2023; Hopwood, 2024). Similar sentiments were expressed by the research participants, that there are times when they feel insecure at school or hesitate to speak up (Ilona, Milana and Oksana), because the teaching community either does not want change, or views young, relatively inexperienced teachers with suspicion or distrust. In fact, such an environment of suspicion and lack of collegiality among community members hinders the performance of high-quality action research. Similar aspects have been noted by A. Feldman (2023), who emphasises criticism and epistemic fairness as related aspects of action research in educational practice.

3.4. Motivation of primary school teachers for action research and forms of organisation of the educational process: analysis of the results of Focus Group 2

First, we would like to present the socio-cultural context of the classes with which the teachers in Focus Group 2 work.

Elzė's class context: The context is really diverse, with children from large families and bilingual families. The pupils are third-years. There are two children from abroad: a girl from Germany and a boy from Russia. Although the boy can read and write well in Lithuanian, he writes in Russian when he makes notes for himself. The teacher also says that the child has mastered excellent writing abilities, because he writes in Russian in Cyrillic (Russian letters) without mistakes, and the child behaves in such a way that he doesn't want to forget the Russian he has learned. Reading is always a sensitive subject for first-year pupils, because we have to learn not only the technique of reading, but also how to love a book, how to create traditions. Because, for example, if a family has not had them before, what we can offer at school so that the child brings home books and involves the whole family in the reading process, brother and sister, too. This has really worked for some things, in large families, brothers and sisters also want to read together. I consider this to be a success of action research and I continue to apply it successfully, because reading abilities improve and the motivation to read increases.

Violeta's class context: The teacher works with deaf pupils who are second-year pupils. Three of the children are completely deaf, one is hard-of-hearing and uses ordinary hearing aids, and one has a cochlear implant, a major operation had to be performed, and the hearing aid was connected to the auditory nerve. One pupil lives only with his mother, who is Russian-speaking. The parents of another child have hearing and are Russian-speaking. The child's Lithuanian language abilities are not very good, because he hears Russian at home with his hearing impairment and learns Lithuanian at school. The children from deaf families are Lithuanian and use sign language at home. It is very difficult to work with deaf people, because they have a very different way of thinking, and communication is very different. They have sign language, and they can communicate. But as far as the Lithuanian language is concerned, this is a huge problem, and we are struggling now in schools with the fact that pupils don't want to learn the Lithuanian language. A very large number of deaf parents themselves do not know Lithuanian and do not see any need to teach and explain it to their children.

Ana's class context: It is a diverse class in terms of ability. 75% of the children in the class come from bilingual families, with a predominance of Russian and Polish, and therefore have difficulties with the placement of stress in Lithuanian words. There are some children who speak Russian as their first language and only later started to learn Lithuanian. These children express their thoughts in Lithuanian more slowly, with pauses, and take longer to think because they are thinking in another language. There are many families who take great care of their children, and consider their main duty is to learn, and this is evident in the children's achievements. The teacher notes that some parents may not pay enough attention to monitoring their child's learning, to family conversations about school activities. The children come from different social contexts. The classroom culture is based on common human values and the development of respectful behaviour towards each other.

Johanas's class context: The pupils are third-year pupils in a private school, there are eleven children in the class, 3 of them from bilingual families, two families speak English and Lithuanian, and a third family speaks Russian and Lithuanian. From the parents' perspective, they compare their children's education with their own learning practices when they were at school. The school works from content created by the teachers and does not rely on one textbook, so parents keep asking why there is not a single textbook.

Elė's class context: The children are fourth-year pupils. Most of the pupils are Lithuanian, and two of the children's families speak Lithuanian and Russian. There are some children who speak in dialect because their parents came to Vilnius from different regions of Lithuania, such as Panevėžys and Marijampolė. The children talk with their grandparents, too, whose dialects are different, so some of the children confuse the Lithuanian sounds e-ė and pronounce some words incorrectly. There are children with special educational needs: a girl with a stutter, others with attention disorders and dyslexia, but the classroom is a safe environment, all children are encouraged to speak, and they learn to express their thoughts clearly in oral language. There are two large families: children grow up in families with three and four children. But there are some who grow up as the only child or with one brother or sister. There is also a family that has adopted a girl, which is why this topic is relevant in the classroom. Mother's and Father's Day is an important topic because there are divorced families, some of them have started new families or the child(ren) live with their mother.

Liza's class context: It is a Polish-speaking school, where the language of instruction is Polish. Third-year class. Many large families. It is a rural school, there are families with 5 or 6 children. All the children have both parents, but most of the parents show little interest in the educational process. It would be better if parents were more interested in the life of the school. Parents are not interested in their children's education and do not motivate them to learn within the family. The teacher even gets the feeling that parents want the school to contact them as little as possible. Some of the parents receive social benefits.

During the interview, the research participants were asked in which contexts they currently apply action research in their pedagogical work. Teachers' views can be seen in Table 3.4.1.

Table 3.4.1: Views of Focus Group 2 participants on their experience of applying action research

Reasons for performing action research	Examples of participant views	Researchers' comments
Activity assessment (N=3)	I am personally interested in action research, and I apply it, and I have an inclination for it in my classroom. [...] I mostly apply research for my own performance self-evaluation, for a leap forward, and I mostly like to collect information about my pupils when I interact with them. (Ana) We introduced reflection notebooks in my classroom and the children filled them in at the end of each lesson, and my conclusions were that not everybody was comfortable with this kind of reflection. Then I tried to adjust – some stayed with the same style of reflection, I looked for other ways for the rest of the pupils, like conversation, and now the online Kahoot quizzes, which are very popular. I apply it, I use it, and I am glad that I had this experience and now I can use it. (Johanas)	It is important that teachers highlight the action research by emphasising the monitoring of each pupil's individual abilities and personal growth, and the instruments used, such as a reflection notebook, a discussion or questions at the end of the activity.

(Continued)

Table 3.4.1: (Continued)

Reasons for performing action research	Examples of participant views	Researchers' comments
	To encourage children's reading abilities, during discussions, the children promote, almost advertise, the books they are reading, ask each other questions, give advice and give compliments. So, the book presentation becomes another way of discussing books. And very often they talk about them in their free time. And I think that's good, because I hadn't noticed that before in the classroom. (Elė)	
Better understanding the pupil in a different context (N=1)	The informal environment is also very helpful. Because I also have a club, […] and it's just like research material, because you see the pupil in another environment. I'm very much focused on that personal knowledge, because it's very important to me. (Ana)	Getting to know the pupil in different contexts.
Continuity of action research activities (N=2)	My bachelor's thesis was a good topic and situation for doing the research in my classroom (the classroom where the participant works). And I had to read a lot of sources on the use of active reading techniques. And those techniques, when they were introduced during the action research, are still being applied in the same classroom. It's just that now it involves all pupils. In the action research, I focused on two situations – two individual pupils. When I was able to successfully apply the two approaches I had chosen, that's what we now apply all together. (Elzė) I did the research in the third-year class, now they are in the fourth-year class, so they themselves are comparing the text and the film – and we did Pippi Longstocking and Carlson there. And when they read their books, they look for whether the book is based on the film or vice versa. I am glad that they are applying it and remembering it. And to continue to build those understandings of the text alongside the films, I haven't had to do that. (Elė)	Pupils recall the lessons learned from the action research and base their own further activities on them, even in the following year's learning. This demonstrates the sustainability of the learning gained during the action research.

Reasons for performing action research	Examples of participant views	Researchers' comments
Mastered action research techniques (N=3)	When we were studying pedagogical action research, we paid attention to all the stages, now maybe I'm skipping some stages or paying less attention. But I try to follow the steps. We have reading diaries in the classroom now, so automatically my colleague and I also set out why we had them, what we wanted to achieve, then we formulated a hypothesis, then we anticipated those activities. And we kept looking, succeeding, failing, that timing. I'm still applying this; I'm going to continue with the research that I did in my bachelor's thesis. (Johanas) I think I am applying the steps of action research, but maybe I am just not calling it that. (Elė) My bachelor's thesis was on the application of ICT, so for me, now that I'm working remotely, I'd say it's a plus. I use it every lesson. Of course, I didn't do my research with my own class, I did it with another class, and now I work a bit differently. (Liza)	During the discussion, Johanas also reflects on his experience as a teacher-researcher, what he has already mastered and how he learned it. This reflection also shows that an educator has a deep knowledge of action research methodology, understands its significance and naturally uses this tool as a basis for his or her practice.
Personalising activities according to the child's individual needs (N=1)	I work more with one of my pupils who has special needs, but it's the use of ICT in the classroom with this boy that really helps me a lot, because it's actually much better for him and it's more stimulating for him. [...] And when we use different apps, different websites, he works much better, and progress is visible. (Liza)	The methodology tested in the action research during the bachelor's thesis helps to adapt the process to the individual child.
Not used further (N=1)	Well, I've actually written about experiential learning, purposeful activities, learning in non-traditional spaces. It was fun to write the thesis and to work with my class, because I had never applied experiential learning before and I didn't really understand what it was at first. And it was interesting to experience and to get my hands on it and to look deeper. But the most important thing is that I *work with deaf pupils,* and we need to recognise that reality, to accept the truth that we don't really know a lot and we have a lot of gaps in our knowledge.	It is important that the teacher identified the reason why she is bases her practice less often on action research, although it is likely that it could be done more often even in this area.

(Continued)

Table 3.4.1: (Continued)

Reasons for performing action research	Examples of participant views	Researchers' comments
	[...] I've put my research and experiential learning aside for the time being, it's spring now, the weather is getting nicer, so when the weather is nice, I plan to go back to experiential learning. (Violeta)	

From the data in Table 3.4.1, we can see that it was meaningful to base the bachelor's thesis on action research, because most of the teachers use action research as skilled practitioners in their work (only one of them does it very rarely because of the particular group of pupils, children who are hard-of-hearing). It is important to note that most of the focus group participants demonstrated a deep understanding of action research through examples of their own practice and their reasons for using certain aspects in their teaching. In addition, some aspects were transferred by the teachers to other activities, and some action research projects were so relevant to the children that they carry the experience with them to a different classroom, in a different context (the application of the strategy of comparing the content of a book with a film in the educational process, presented by the teacher Elė). The result of our research, related to the continuity and sustainability of action research, is fundamentally related to insights of Latvian researcher I. Salite (2008), I. Salite et al. (2016), that it is important to prepare teachers in conditions of action research by providing environments for teachers to reflect on what they do, how they do it and why they do it, and to decide what needs to be continued and what needs to be abandoned. Our research data shows that action research helps some educators to gain a deeper understanding of pupils' personal qualities, to tailor the educational content to individual pupil needs and abilities, and to self-evaluate the educational process and outcome. This shows that students who have developed their abilities at the university are able to develop high-quality didactics that are in line with the paradigm of contemporary education, which is linked to the child's perspective, takes into account the child's needs and capabilities and thus solves the problems that arise. A practice based on action research is open to systematic collective thinking, an environment that can contribute to the development of continuing education and to sustainable development (Salite et al., 2016). It is important to emphasise that action research-based practice, from the point of view of our teachers, helps them to achieve better educational outcomes with their pupils and, at the same time, helps teachers to develop themselves in the development of educational content.

In our research, a teacher also mentioned that action research helped to personalise education according to the child's needs. A very similar claim is made by A. Burns & N. Kurtoğlu-Hooton (2016), because they were better able to connect with pupils during the action research. Feedback methods also improved, and researchers had a better understanding of their pupils' needs and knew how to meet those needs. A participant in our research said that action research allows her to get to know her pupils better in other educational contexts. L. H. Al-Obaydi, Nashruddin, F. F. Rahman & L. O. A. Suherman (2021) emphasised that action research has a particular impact in a social context, because both pupils and teachers take more responsibility and seek solutions to problems by talking to colleagues. It is important that educators have complete freedom to choose any topic, strategy, activity and teaching material.

In addition, the research participants were asked what motivates them to develop action research in their teaching practice. Table 3.4.2 shows examples of activities and the educational process reported by the teachers.

Table 3.4.2: Examples mentioned by Focus Group 2 participants on what motivates them to develop action research in their teaching practice

Examples of motivations for choosing action research	**Examples of participant views**	**Researchers' comments**
Practice-based planning, performance and monitoring of practical activities, in consultation with pupils (N=3)	Once the data was collected and the particular methods were selected, I found it very useful to have the children involved, not only as mere participants in the research, but also because they helped to organise it. We all planned together that if this is a reading challenge, how will I implement it. And reflecting on what we have been doing lately with the children, it is really a fact that I am adapting their own participation in organising and planning certain activities. (Elzė) So in the same way we made a plan, we made a plan together with them about how I would have to plant a plant, what I would have to do, what measures I would have to take, how I would observe, what I would learn by observing, so that I could measure	Drawing on pupils' experience and initiative was expressed as one of the most important factors for organising action research and thus solving various problems in the pedagogical process. It is also important that pupils are involved not only in the educational process, but even in the planning

(Continued)

Table 3.4.2: (Continued)

Examples of motivations for choosing action research	Examples of participant views	Researchers' comments
	the length of my seedling, what sprouted, why it sprouted, how much I had to water it, and we even divided into certain groups to see what happened, for those who were watering every day, what happened, for those who were watering every second day. It's how we organise action research with the children so that they are not just participants, so that everything is not planned and done for them, but so that they make a real effort and understand for themselves what we are trying to achieve with these activities. (Elė) I would say any such research, even momentary … I was like, during Zoom, we came up with a lesson where they weren't going to read the text expressively, there had been no homework, but we just spontaneously thought of taking the text and each of us reading a piece of it. It was a subject text with dates, numbers and in fact one pupil read it perfectly. We even talked about it with the pupils, maybe you were getting ready for this? No, so what do you do in your free time," I asked her. "I read encyclopaedias." Then I thought – how do you read them? Silently or aloud? Out loud. That's the whole research for you. 5 minutes of work. And it revealed what has an effect. My motivation for this is just to help the student to have the tools and to improve their learning. And most importantly to notice personal progress. (Ana)	stage, when they can suggest ideas for the organisation of education. During the activity, as Ana says, the circumstances and reasons for a particular situation are brought to light, and this leads to a deeper understanding of the educational process and of the pupils.
Meaningfulness of activities, encouragement of pupil-initiated activities that improve pupils' achievement (N=6)	I ask what the meaning of the activity for the child is and for me as an educator. First of all, for me to make sure that what you are doing is really meaningful and useful, because very often teachers tend to do a lot, do a lot, and not pause. Why do I try with children? So that I can develop	All the teachers who participated in the research see action research as a way of ensuring the **MEANING-FULNESS** of

Examples of motivations for choosing action research	Examples of participant views	Researchers' comments
	research-based practice, I encourage different activities when the children themselves are engaged in those activities. (Johanas) Pupils are engaged in a very different way when they can learn on their own, when they can plan and initiate activities; it's not the same when I just plan and ask them to do things. Children's engagement is completely different during action research. (Elzė) For me personally, it is always very important, too, how I feel and why. […] I always wonder, too, if it's worth it, what will be the benefit, what can I myself achieve, from myself? What can I expect from the children? For the children, I try very hard to involve them. And I want them to be more independent; […] when the children do better, you feel better, too. (Violeta, Liza) Children's feelings and emotions, how they enjoyed doing the activity and the results they get, are what motivates, and I would very much agree about the meaning. The children themselves say that it is important to them that every activity has meaning, and since I have been teaching this class since the first year, and they are now in the fourth year, I can share that I can really see how much work was put into the first year with the conversations because there was a lot of discussion, talking, sharing, and how independent they really are now. (Elė) The main motive is pupil achievement. I am very interested in what improves achievement. The topic of my bachelor's thesis is the interview method for developing speaking and listening abilities. I did this activity in year 1–2 and now we are in year 3, with a textbook where	the educational process. In our opinion, these research results show that educators have mastered and understood the benefits and the essence of an action research-based educational culture.

(Continued)

Table 3.4.2: (Continued)

Examples of motivations for choosing action research	Examples of participant views	Researchers' comments
	we came across that interview method, my pupils, they feel like kings, they know everything, it's nothing new to them. We are participating in a project to improve the promotion of reading, so we also have to create tasks there. We, the teachers, have to create the tasks. And I'm very good at using exactly that action research-based interview method that I have analysed. And let's say before I did the action research (before I did the bachelor's thesis), I didn't even understand how it should be applied. And now I can feel the benefits of it. The motivation would be to help the student, to show his/her personal progress, to show that he/she is improving, and specifically what is improving his/her learning. (Ana)	

K. S. Yoon et al. (2007) state that if teachers improve, look for ways to improve pupils' achievements, are open to new experiences and themselves learn, then pupils' results will improve, too. It can be said that this idea is shared by the teachers who participated in the focus group. Teachers find that action research helps to initiate pupil learning, autonomy, planning of educational content and choice of pathway for activities. And these assumptions make the educational process more flexible and more effective, because the educational process uses the most reflective and high-quality methods to help master the content that is being learned. In this way, teachers adapt to the educational process, becoming more flexible, more reflective and more deeply reflective, and committed to changing and improving their teaching practices (Granziera, Collie & Martin, 2019).

The culture of consultation, of cooperation with pupils, identified by the participants in our research, is close to the ideas discussed by M. Fullan et al. (2023) and UNESCO (2023), emphasising the development of social intelligence: the individual and collective development of ideas and activities based on what we call the "human paradigm", the ability to communicate, collaborate and co-create with others. Particularly in the age of technology, these scholars advise most of all to rely on pupils, to consult and confer with them, to involve them in the search for solutions. Today's primary school pupils were born into a technological world. It is important to educate them as changemakers in society and as creators for society. Artificial intelligence may prove to be the most powerful force ever known, which can dramatically increase people's ability to work together (Fullan et al., 2023). But to do this, the structure of the school needs to change, and the educational process and time management need to be much more flexible.

To see how well pupils are progressing, teachers need to be interested in what children are doing outside of school, and what they are interested in outside of school. This point was emphasised by research participant Ana, who discussed an example of a girl reading aloud and analysing encyclopaedias at home. Such examples from children not only show their own knowledge, but also motivate other pupils in the class to behave and learn in a similar way, because pupils can also be role models and authorities to their peers. Peer mentoring can be formal, with a particular role and pupil structure assigned to a particular mentor, or informal, which happens naturally as pupils meet more experienced peers who mentor them (Benjamin, 2020; Collier, 2015; Colvin & Ashman, 2010). It is important that pupils feel comfortable, free and uninhibited when learning, because this environment encourages and motivates pupils to take an interest in activities. Calmness, concentration and smiling indicate that the pupils' emotional and physical environment is appropriate (Read, 2015; Robinson, Mourão & Kang, 2015), and in such an environment, higher levels of learning achievement are possible (see Table 3.4.3).

Table 3.4.3: Aspects mentioned by Focus Group 2 participants, which teachers consider before action research

Aspects considered before performing action research	**Examples of participant views**	**Researchers' comments**
Empowering pupils to work independently (N=1)	I put more emphasis on autonomy, on independent learning. […] What I encourage children to do most of all is to think and to use at least the tools on offer, so that they can see the tools. […] When I see mistakes in a piece of writing, I show the learning tools, colour certain key words a different colour and recommend talking to a classmate about the spelling. The children then discover the mistakes themselves. (Ana)	Action research creates the conditions for pupils to work independently and individually, with timely support, which is in line with contemporary pedagogy.

(Continued)

Table 3.4.3: (Continued)

Aspects considered before performing action research	**Examples of participant views**	**Researchers' comments**
Applying schemas (N=3)	Schemas, basically, schemas. There are a lot of schemas in the textbook. We are learning how to use the different schemas, how to read them, because for some of the children it is new; there are children of different abilities in the class; you could say three levels of pupils. […] Schematic support is specific. Such as sentence formation. If I see that they are having trouble making sentences, then we make schemas and try to put them on the board, asking questions, all together. (Ana) The biggest help is me, the teacher, if we analyse different schemas, examples, then I show the pictures according to a certain schema and the children create a written story. If they forget the spelling of certain words, they are very good at finding a table or a schema and looking up the right answer. There are posters in the classroom and various charts. (Violeta) I would very much agree with all the examples, the most important are the rules, the schemas, and I try to present the information through several senses: the word, the image, so that they can hear and see, because children's abilities are very different. (Elė)	Three teachers mentioned tools that they think about before an activity, because it is only tools that are purposeful, freely accessible and mastered by the children that enable independent learning.
Improving motivation through experiential learning (N=2)	Motivation can even come from putting a sticker instead of a stamp on an envelope. Immediately, a debate arises: what's the big deal? Who needs that? Sometimes the examples of the immediate environment in the classroom confuse some people. So, if we don't introduce experiential learning, they probably won't understand what to do. (Ana) It is really necessary for everyone to feel good, to feel safe and to be able to engage fully in the activity without worrying or being scared that it is unexpected. Another thing is that there certainly are children in the classroom who are more engaged and who	Teachers emphasised both the physical and psychological environment, external and internal motivation, all of which affect learning.

Aspects considered before performing action research	Examples of participant views	Researchers' comments
	are less engaged, especially when working in groups. […] To avoid this, we try to choose a role for everyone when the children are in groups, so that they know in advance. If, for example, we were making yoghurt. Each group had three children. Each person had their own responsibility and at a certain point they could fulfil themselves and feel needed. […] These seem like simple steps, but the distribution of these steps also helps. For those who are perhaps less active, less brave, it helps them to be included and not left out. (Elzė)	
Taking into account individual pupil needs (N=3)	There is one student in my class who gets very agitated if there is an inquiry-based activity or if something changes in the daily routine. This week we were making yoghurt with the children, so we prepared the recipe and the entire yoghurt-making plan for this child in advance, we explained the whole process and during the activity the child felt good and actively participated. (Elzė) I always help especially weak pupils, while others are able to find help themselves in the classroom environment. (Violeta) For example, in the first-year class, one had a number chart, another counted on his fingers, and a third knew how to count by heart. They were simply introduced to different ways of learning, and each person chose the one that best suited him or her personally. […] I try to create associations for the children, I remind them of certain things in different contexts, for example, we were talking about Sigismund Augustus during a history lesson, and a month ago, we had read the love story of Sigismund Augustus and Barbora Radvilaitė; so, I first asked them what they remembered from the love story, and the children said Sigismund Augustus right away. That is how I relate the content. (Elė)	Adapting the material to the needs of the pupil is one of the tools to achieve both a high-quality process and a high-quality result. All this needs to be thought about before the educational process and, in some cases, needs additional preparation.

(Continued)

Table 3.4.3: (Continued)

Aspects considered before performing action research	Examples of participant views	Researchers' comments
Activity objective, and criteria (N=3)	I first anticipate what we are going to do and the criteria for what we want to learn, so that it is not only fun but also useful. I share the criteria with the pupils so that they also know what is expected of them. My class likes to do different projects, so I make an example of what the title should look like. We have agreed that the title should be clearly written, distinct from the rest of the text. (Johanas) It's important to think about what the children will be doing and the tasks you will be giving them. (Violeta) All the time, we start by presenting and discussing the full plan for the day, what we will do and how we will do it. This is usually in the form of drawings. (Liza)	The general didactic tools that are important in the educational process are mentioned.
Visual handouts needed to complete the work (N=2)	I also make sure that the environment is full of tips and visual material. For example, we are now talking about space, so there is a book about space in the classroom, and I have also printed out some sheets of paper which are on the shelf by the board, but in the classroom the children have to find them themselves and can use them to find the answers to the questions they have. I have noticed that they sometimes are a bit lazy when it comes to looking for information themselves. (Johanas) We use visual material in almost all our lessons. Because we are a bilingual school, we write the words in both languages and add a picture, so that it is easier for the child to remember the word and pronounce it correctly. In addition, we draw a plan of the text. We read a few sentences and draw what we have understood. We also draw the characters and the events in an activity. (Liza)	For contemporary children, visuality, an accurate representation of what will be learned, is essential. Of course, the environment itself is also important, with all the necessary materials available to children.

Aspects considered before performing action research	Examples of participant views	Researchers' comments
Discussion, self-evaluation (pupils' own reflection on their work) (N=1)	At the end of the activity, we make presentations of the work. After presenting the work, we hang all the work on a board and each child rates all the work according to the criteria by sticking a coloured slip of paper on the board to indicate which work meets all the criteria and which does not meet them. Usually there are a lot of slips on one work and fewer on another. Then we discuss the reason. And when the children analyse the work with a lot of slips, they see that it meets all the criteria. And the other work, which has far fewer slips of paper, when they analyse it, they see that only two out of four criteria are met. (Johanas)	Reflection creates the conditions to reflect on what the pupil has done and experienced; what they have achieved, why they have achieved it and what they need to improve. One of the group members mentioned this aspect, of envisaging it before the activity.

Helping students to learn when they have mastered certain abilities, using strategies, is a prerequisite for contemporary education and didactics. This was confirmed by the participants in our research when they talked about the targeted use of different schemas for learning content in different subjects (see Table 3.4.3). The use of strategies is highlighted by M. J. Eady & L. Lockyer (2013), stating that once they have mastered the use of strategies, learners will be able to absorb any information at any time in their lives. Even schemas help to both personalise and differentiate the educational process, because they can be presented in a wide variety of ways: images, keywords, complex statements, problem questions, etc.

During the preparation stage, it is very important to consider and self-evaluate what and how the educator will work with the pupils. In order to select the right approach or strategy and the right ways to support learning, it is important to consider objectively and deeply both the process and the outcome, which is why assessment plays an important role in action research (Efron & Ravid, 2013). Such activities contribute to a more holistic understanding of pupil learning and growth, which includes both the didactic aspects of access and the necessary tools. The members of the working group to prepare the Lithuanian document *Description of the procedures for assessing the learning achievements of pupils in general education curricula and for using assessment results* (2023) placed the greatest emphasis on assessment in the educational process, understood as comprehensive support for the learner.

During the research, it was asked how often and in what ways research participants integrate inquiry-based activities into the educational process, linking them to action research. Ana said that up to 20% of activities per month are inquiry-based activities, but in the future would like to devote at least half of the total time of the educational process to inquiry-based activities, i.e. 50%. Ana also mentioned that it is likely that some of the content, although she organises it on the basis of inquiry-based activities, is not perceived or identified as inquiry-based activities. This may be a lack of deeper reflection abilities on the part of a young teacher. Elzė said that she spends at least 20% of her time on this, because she organises inquiry-based activities at least once a week. Johanas said that he allocates up to 40% to inquiry-based activities. Violeta was embarrassed by this question during the research and said that "I'm actually ashamed to say it, but our pupils don't even reach maybe 1% for these activities, but [...] I myself reflect on all my activities up to 40%, and there is always one or another inquiry-based aspect to them" (1:01:04–1:02:06). Elé expressed the idea, agreeing with Ana, that she usually applies these activities intuitively, without thinking that they are action research-based activities. "I would tend to agree with the idea that I don't call it that, maybe it's my bad, that it's the activity, that it's the research, that maybe it's just a minute's conversation, but it's still research that we consider or we find out about the emotional well-being of the child because I'm very much focused on the personal conversations [...] But I don't know how to say to myself yet that I've explored this, maybe I still need to learn it." (1:02:11–1:03:10). The thoughts of our research participants are very close to the insights of researcher C. A. Mertler (2021), who states that teachers find it difficult to identify and label classroom activities as research. In addition, teachers often think they are incompetent to perform real, serious research. Moreover, C. A. Mertler (2021) emphasises that only a teacher who reflects deeply and intuitively can perform action research. Liza said that she certainly does spend 20% of her time per month on experiential activities, but did not mention particular forms. Particular forms of activity mentioned by the teachers can be seen in Table 3.4.4.

Table 3.4.4: Views of Focus Group 2 participants on the forms in which action research is applied in the educational process

Forms of activity	Examples of participant views	Researchers' comments
Project activity (N=1)	Weekly activities are usually focused on a particular topic. For example, if this week's topic is Healthy Eating, then at least one project per week, and sometimes it is possible to develop the same project for two weeks, and I think it works. (Elzė)	The project usually addresses a certain problem or generates a product, so the approach described is appropriate.

Forms of activity	Examples of participant views	Researchers' comments
Children's independent activity according to criteria (N=2)	I try to get the children to investigate things for themselves, so there are certain criteria, so they can draw their own conclusions after the inquiry. (Johanas) We were learning about the Rasos Cemetery, and they had to find the information themselves, so they could get a general idea from the images, and they had to talk about it themselves. (Violeta)	Action research is related to problem-solving and empowering learners to act, so authentic, autonomous activities reflect the essence of such education.
Personal conversations (N=1)	I pay a lot of attention to personal conversations, and sometimes there is a sensitive situation in the classroom and a child calls me over for a personal chat. It's a real thing. (Elė)	Personal conversations are associated with personalised educational practices that take into account the individual needs of the learner. It is also linked to action research in a particular class.

In a way similar to our research, D. Esparza, R. L. Lynch-Arroyo & J. T. Olimpo (2022) worked with STEAM teachers, analysing deep practices based on action research, and found that professional development through action research methods increases the inclination of educators to apply evidence-based practice and make data-driven decisions. In addition, teachers who have mastered action research also teach their pupils to analyse and reflect more deeply on data-driven activities when learners work independently. Of course, for this to happen smoothly, more time and resources are needed for the activities. M. Abraczinskas & N. Zarrett (2020), K. S. Williams (2024) confirm that action research-based practice empowers learners to act independently and responsibly, taking greater responsibility for their own learning. In addition, action research helps to resolve social inequalities among learners, because children have the opportunity to interact and collaborate in groups of different abilities, and because teachers can provide one-to-one guidance and personalised advice to pupils. This is a practice that was also expressed by participants in our research. E. Crocetti, R. Erentaitė, & R. Žukauskienė (2014) state that independent work, where the individual takes responsibility, enhances positive personal development. A. Malorni et al. (2022) emphasise project-based activities as a form of education suitable for developing action research practices.

During the research, summarising the ideas expressed in the interview, it was sought to identify what problems the participants take into account and what situations they are currently dealing with that could be considered as action research for the future. The ideas expressed by the research participants in relation to the educational process or pupils' leisure time at school are summarised in Table 3.4.5.

Table 3.4.5: Views of Focus Group 2 participants on what problems determine how they organise pupil activities

Problems, when it is sought to change the situation	Examples of participant views	Researchers' comments
Reduced learning motivation among pupils (N=2)	I'm looking for ways to increase pupils' motivation, because motivation has fallen for some pupils, so I need to look for ways to improve it. (Ana) I think that at the same time, I should think again about how to motivate and encourage children even more to do their homework. (Liza)	Teachers know the pupils in the class well, because they see a drop in motivation among some pupils.
Lack of leisure activities (N=1)	I am not satisfied with the time spent during breaks because the children do not find activities for themselves. This was not a problem with last year's pupils, because they played board games, and we had a tradition of reading breaks. And now I also have to teach the children what they could and would like to choose for themselves. For the time being, though, it's me directing them to do this or that activity. (Elzė)	It is important that the teacher cares not only about what the children do during the educational process, but also about their leisure time. She points out that pupils should be able to organise their leisure time independently but have not yet developed this ability.
Ability to check completed work (N=1)	In our classroom, there is currently a problem with checking the completed activities, because the children immediately put the work down without even reading it through again. The aim is to get them to read it and find and correct the mistakes themselves, if there are any. So, we will have to find ways to do that. (Johanas)	It is important that the teacher pays attention to a detail of the educational process, such as checking the result of the activity, which is important because after checking the result it is possible to correct mistakes, but for primary school pupils it takes an effort to perform this activity, and it is something that needs to be learned.

Problems, when it is sought to change the situation	Examples of participant views	Researchers' comments
Insufficient recognition of a child's existing abilities (N=1)	For some children, I still wonder if they really cannot learn and do not understand, or if there is no conversation in the family about the importance of Lithuanian language abilities that the child will need. Maybe I don't pay enough attention to what the child can do. Maybe I should still look for ways to develop memory. (Violeta)	Because the teacher teaches special children who are deaf or hard-of-hearing, exploring their abilities or potential is a challenge that requires a lot of effort and a search for certain techniques.
Lack of respectful communication (N=1)	In my classroom, I need to find ways of promoting respectful behaviour so that everyone communicates and behaves in a respectful way. Balancing adolescence. I also need to find ways, as a teacher myself, not to get drawn into their emotional outbursts, how to react appropriately myself. How to respond to their expressions and choices. I asked the special educator to give me advice, to suggest some ways. (Elė)	Mutual understanding and courteous interaction are a challenge that needs to be learned and continuously revisited. It is important that the teacher notices it and tries to address the situation.
Homework preparation (N=1)	What else should I do to make sure my children don't forget to do their homework and send it to me? (Liza)	Forgetting to do homework can be just an excuse for it not being done, so it is necessary to consult with pupils and motivate them to do it, and to find out the reasons why homework is not being done.

N. Salihović & A. Dizdarević (2020), G. Codina & D. Robinson (2024) state that action research-based practices help meet the individual needs of each child and provide the support they need. This is especially true when all the professionals needed to meet the child's needs work together in partnership. H. Connett (2020) seconds the idea that action research-based practices help to identify children's special educational needs and increase their positive integration in educational practice.

Taking Ana, Liza, Elzė and Johanas's ideas into account, we can see that all of these teachers are looking for ways to enable children to learn willingly, to have high-quality leisure time at school and to take responsibility for their own learning. That this is important is recognised by researchers (Darling-Hammond et al., 2019), stating that teachers' tried-and-tested strategies for maintaining relationships and learning opportunities needed to promote children's well-being, healthy development and transferable learning prove useful in educational practice. When children have developed the capacity for self-regulation, teachers can respond to individual differences among learners, address difficulties, and schools can create the conditions for all children to find a positive path to learning.

The pursuit of more accurate feedback, identified by research participant Johanas as a high-quality aspect of improving educational practice, is also mentioned by S. Boss (2020). It is important for both the teacher and the pupils themselves to identify how they are doing and to look for ways to improve their educational practice. Fostering a culture of inquiry and sharing experiences with colleagues increases the quality of learning (Boss, 2020). The fact that this culture is fostered by the participants in our research can be seen in the particular problematic situations that were raised. C. A. Mertler (2021) highlights that effective education depends on the teacher's ability to identify classroom problems. Teachers are responsible for identifying the scope and scale of the problem and making informed decisions based on the collected and analysed data (Henriksen et al., 2017; Dana & Yendol-Hoppey, 2019; Mertler & Hartley, 2017; Mertler, 2018, 2020, 2021).

During the research, it was asked with whom teachers can discuss, ask for help and seek advice on activities in the school, because this is important for the planning and implementation of action research in the educational institution. The responses of the research participants regarding the forms of collegial consultation used in the school are presented in Table 3.4.6.

Table 3.4.6: Views of Focus Group 2 participants on what forms of collegial consultation are used

Forms of consultation used in the school	Examples of participant views	Researchers' comments
Mentor or educational supervisor appointed by the school (N=4)	I work in the same school where I did my practice placement. I'm very happy about that, because I did my practice placement in the same school where my child was learning, with his primary school teacher. The school invited me to work there and appointed a mentor. (Ana)	We can see that in school, teachers can consult and confer either with the mentor-teacher or with a senior administrator.

Forms of consultation used in the school	Examples of participant views	Researchers' comments
	We have an education manager who is an idea generator. She not only comes up with ideas, but also advises on how to implement them. We can share with her what we did, how we did it, whether it worked or not. (Johanas) It is also possible to consult with the deputy headteacher (vice-principal), who has checklists for certain situations and can advise on the best way to deal with a certain issue in a particular case. (Liza) You can always go to the school administration for help and not be afraid of not being listened to or not being understood. The school has only ninety students, so the whole school community is like one big family, where experiences are shared, both the hard things and the good things. (Violeta)	
Experienced teachers (N=2)	I can always ask for help and share my insights with teachers who have experience. (Ana) I've been working at the school for five years, starting as a teaching assistant. The staff is very good, and there are two deaf teachers with whom we discuss various situations when necessary. (Violeta)	It was pointed out that educators with more experience or better knowledge of a specific area, such as the education of deaf children, also provide advice.
Experience days (in-service days, inset days) (N=4)	The school has experience days (in-service days, inset days), and on these days we present the methods we use: what works, what we use. (Ana) We have methodological meetings twice a month. They are held either in-person or online. There are topics for the methodological meetings, for what we will talk about. The purpose of the meetings is to share what we are doing, how we are doing it, what we could do differently. The last topic was about assessment, we talked about how each teacher assesses. We adopted common agreements in the school, what all teachers will have to follow, what will be told to parents. At the	A targeted form of experience sharing and development in the form of experience days was mentioned. It is important to emphasise that these are planned meetings for which teachers prepare in advance, try out certain methods and activities together,

(Continued)

Table 3.4.6: (Continued)

Forms of consultation used in the school	Examples of participant views	Researchers' comments
	same time, I presented my bachelor's thesis, because it was about assessment, and I told them about the theoretical material I had collected. (Johanas) It's a very large urban school with three branches. Meetings are organised during seasonal week-long holidays to talk and discuss. […] Even though we work in different branches, we know each other and keep in touch. […] There are people you can share your thoughts with and ask for advice. (Elė) We meet once a month in the methodology group. We discuss children's learning and methods. Because there are relatively few pupils in the school, a lot of attention is paid to the individual child, even discussing how brothers or sisters are learning, and how to communicate better with the parents of that child. (Liza)	and share both positive results and aspects that have failed or been less successful, as well as make decisions on how to improve further activities. Indeed, a lot of elements of action research in practice are embedded in the content of this form.
Observing a colleague's lessons (N=4)	We can observe our colleagues' lessons. (Ana) Observing each other's lessons and visiting each other's lessons is encouraged. Observation of other teachers who work with the same class is encouraged, because there are English and sports teachers, too. By observing each other's lessons, we can share tips on how to help one child or another. In my classroom, there are no problems with certain children, but in the lessons of other subjects with the same children, other teachers have problems. Therefore, the administration encourages sharing experiences with colleagues, even on classroom management issues. […] When you go to lessons on a different subject taught by another teacher, you see that even sports activities can be applied to mathematics or Lithuanian language lessons. (Johanas) We also observe each other's lessons and can learn techniques from each other. We discuss how the same method could be used in other ways. (Liza)	In order for action research to be carried out not only by one teacher but by the whole school community, observation of colleagues' activities and a culture of consultation are important, as most of the focus group participants mentioned. This aspect is significant in highlighting the fact that teachers discuss after the observed activities and thus reflect more deeply on

Forms of consultation used in the school	Examples of participant views	Researchers' comments
	Observing colleagues' lessons is encouraged. After the observation, there are a lot of discussions, not only with the teachers but also with the school administration, because we make certain agreements on the way forward. We discuss the most important points, what we can change. (Violeta)	both the observed and organised practices.
Sharing with a colleague when working in pairs (N=2)	Most of the time, I share my experiences with a colleague because we work in the same class. In fact, she is the only one I can share with, because we work in a gymnasium that as of now does not have any more primary classes. […] The way we talk and share as a pair has worked, because we can share the responsibility as a pair. Even when working with parents, it helps a lot when we are together, when we can support, advise and assist each other. We are good at it. (Elzė) In our school, there are second teachers, who start out as teaching assistants and after a certain period of time themselves become main classroom teachers. (Elė)	An innovative model of organising the pedagogical process is mentioned, which is used by few schools in Lithuania, where two teachers work in the same class. They then share areas of activity and often consult on what content and how to implement it.
Social group on an online platform (N=1)	We have a teachers' group where we post if we need a quick answer to a certain question, we send links, and we share methodological material such as slides. (Elė)	This too is an innovative form, but it was only mentioned by one research participant. It allows for a quick exchange of information and receiving the necessary feedback.

S. P. Gordon & R. D. Solis (2018), D. Nguyen & D. Ng (2020) confirm that communication and collaboration among teachers, administrators and others responsible for education, a culture of consultation and data collection, and the ability to plan, are essential for performing school-wide action research. Researchers emphasise that often even members of the administration need to be taught how to conduct action research. It is also important that the entire school community is willing to do it, that they are positive and that teachers feel supported by school leadership. The headteacher (principal, director) may not actively participate in the activities, but it is important that teachers feel his/her support and continuity (Gordon & Solis, 2018). Johan, a research participant, expressed similar thoughts, mentioning that the school's education manager is positive, always helping, advising, supporting and generating ideas. In addition, the voluntary and active participation and cooperation create positive relationships among teachers and among teachers and administrators.

Data collection and analysis must be integrated into the full cycle of action research: first, to help the team decide on a focus area, set objectives and develop an action plan; then to gather feedback on progress in the area being developed and stakeholders' concerns about the activities being performed; and then to identify results and develop plans for continuity (Gordon & Solis, 2018; Nguyen & Ng, 2020). In addition, it appears that several data sources and methods of data collection and activity organisation (Ari & Çiftçi, 2022) best serve the team implementing the action research, because they continuously manage and update the flow of data-driven decisions throughout the process. Moreover, even teachers themselves, although they may be sceptical at first, realise after several successful attempts that education can be organised in a different way, applying different teaching methods than they were used to before (Ari & Çiftçi, 2022). Very similar models were identified by focus group participants (Ana, Johanas, Elė, Liza), speaking about experience days (in-service days, inset days), where they mentioned that they meet once or several times a month in a targeted way, collecting data on the use of a particular method or activity prior to such meetings. And during the meeting, discussions are held on the basis of the data, on what has worked, what the reasons were for this or that result, and what, how and why to develop further. In this way, the continuity of the activities is ensured, and the competences of the educators are further developed.

The ability to observe, the willingness to make adjustments and to take the necessary decisions in a given situation where adjustments need to be made are also highlighted (Gordon & Solis, 2018). Similar insights were expressed by participants in our research (Ana, Johanas, Liza, Violeta), when they spoke of observing colleagues' activities and discussing them actively and reflectively. The continuity of activities, with certain minor adjustments, helps to improve educational practice, adapting content to the particular context of the classroom according to the needs of the pupils, which is the hallmark of action research-based practice

(Nguyen & Ng, 2020). This is important to note when planning long-term, even multi-year, action research (Gordon & Solis, 2018).

In summary, it can be said that the variety of forms of collaboration mentioned by the research participants, as applied in schools, enables teachers to develop their personal and collective competences (Ari & Çiftçi, 2022), which is essential for every teacher, for teacher-leaders who are able to design, implement and reflect on educational practice. Teacher-initiated collaboration is recognised in schools as a form of professional development that fosters a culture of sharing and development (Nguyen & Ng, 2020). A culture of data-driven decision-making in every school should be the vision for the future of teaching.

Discussion

Our empirical study shows that active learning approaches can improve the achievement of many primary school pupils when children are encouraged to participate actively. The targeted use of action research in education can also address the needs of pupils with difficulties. Often, improvements in overall performance tend to narrow the achievement gaps associated with socio-economic inequalities. However, this pattern has not been confirmed in all countries; in some countries where overall performance in mathematics (e.g. Singapore and Iran) and science (e.g. Lithuania) has improved substantially over the past 20 years in TIMSS, the achievement gaps between high- and low-socio-economic status pupils have also widened more sharply (Broer et al., 2019; Mullis, Martin & Loveless, 2016; Mullis & Martin, 2017; Karakolidis et al., 2021). In these countries, student achievement has improved only for certain population groups, namely, students from socio-economically disadvantaged backgrounds have not improved and have even worsened. We believe that action research, where pupils are not only active but also collaborative, will help to improve the achievement of all pupils, including those living in socially at-risk environments.

Action research allows students to participate actively in the educational process: sharing experiences, expressing their opinions, arguing, discussing content in different scientific fields. The right conditions must be in place for such an educational process: creating a safe, attractive classroom environment, linking the development of language abilities to other subjects, learning about cultures, and developing critical thinking abilities. It is important to base the educational process on the concept of the dialogic space (pair or small group discussions) (Pitsia, Karakolidis & Lehane, 2021). It is useful to apply technology in a targeted way: to record pupils' reflections, conversations, presentations and to analyse this content by listening to audio recordings or watching video recordings (Wagner, Skaftun & McTigue, 2020; Håland et al., 2021; Monteiro, Mata & Nóbrega Santos, 2021).

Using action research in education will help us to achieve inclusive education. Inclusive education means that all children, no matter who they are, can learn together in the same school. This means reaching all learners and removing any barriers that may limit their participation and achievement (UNESCO, 2021).

1. **Key aspects that are evident from ANALYSIS OF EXTERNAL ASSESSMENT DATA ON THE PERFORMANCE OF GENERAL EDUCATION SCHOOLS: Planning the educational process, taking into account the diversity of pupils, providing feedback, focusing on the results of the organised**

teaching/learning, and assessing pupils' achievements and progress, can be identified as challenges in the implementation of the educational content, which have not been sufficiently addressed in the recent past at classroom and individual level. Lesson observation data show that teachers have difficulties in planning a teaching process that allows them to organise activities with a diversity of learners, taking into account the needs and abilities of each learner. Researchers stress that in addition to clarifying and knowing pupils' levels of achievement, their needs, their learning characteristics and any expectations or interests they may have, it is important to systematically collect information about pupils' learning during the planning of the education process. Another important, if perhaps now-traditional, aspect of any activity is reflection on the effectiveness of teaching and learning (Ralabate, 2016; McConnell, Conrad & Uhrmacher, 2020). This can help to get to know pupils better, monitor their progress and adjust or change planning models. Data from external school assessments and their analysis reveals other issues related to the educational process and the experiences that pupils have during the process. In the classroom, insufficient attention is paid to agreements regarding the expected outcomes, the definition of assessment criteria, pupils' self-directed learning, reciprocal feedback, and the discussion and self-evaluation of learning outcomes. Research shows that pupils are more motivated to learn when they understand the link between particular tasks and achievements, when they feel able to do what is expected of them, when they have clear goals and are more persistent in their learning when they are able to make choices, to manage the resources available to them and to cope effectively with the obstacles that arise (Dumont, Istance & Benavides, 2010; Dubosas, 2016). In the lessons observed by the assessors, pupils were mostly taught to set learning objectives, set criteria for assessing their learning outcomes, choose learning methods, work collaboratively with other learners, and self-evaluate whether they had achieved the (teacher's/their own) learning objectives. However, researchers emphasise that, in order to develop self-directed learning abilities in a coherent and systematic way, the teacher's organised activities need to integrate the planning, implementation, monitoring, management and assessment of learning into a coherent whole. It is emphasised that at the beginning of learning, at the planning stage, the ability to self-evaluate what the learning needs of the learner are, what knowledge and abilities he or she already has when faced with a new task, topic or problem, becomes crucial (Dubosas, 2016; Van Deur, 2018; Bishara, 2021; Morris & Rohs, 2023). However, the analysis showed that these aspects of self-directed learning receive very little attention in the lessons observed by the assessors.

The aspects of the educational process identified above are directly related to the teacher's competences to identify the problematic areas of the pupils' teaching/learning and to design a plan of action or a system of educational support to help each pupil to achieve the desired results. It is worth noting that the above-mentioned aspects of lesson organisation in need of improvement are not just a result of recently identified problems in the organisation of the educational process: *teaching/learning planning, self-direction of pupil learning, results in the lesson, assessment/self-evaluation of progress and achievements* (Art lesson: what needs to change, 2012; History lesson: teach or learn? 2012; Another look at the educational process, 2014; Quality of performance of general education schools, 2015; Lithuania. Education in the country and regions, 2016; Quality of performance of general education schools, 2018; Kazragytė & Kudinovienė, 2018). Assessing the results of National Education Strategy 2013–2022 (2012), it is said that it is difficult today to talk about the orientation of inclusive education in general education schools. The organisation of learning based on the involvement of pupils in the planning of their own learning, the flexible design of learning content, and the scaffolding and adaptation of teaching/learning for the success of all pupils, is today more an aspiration than one of the features of the teaching/learning process being developed in Lithuanian schools (Implementation of the National Education Strategy 2013–2022. Material for discussion, 2024).

2. **Key aspects that are evident from ANALYSIS OF ACTION RESEARCH-BASED BACHELOR'S THESES:**
   2.1. **Speaking, listening, reading and writing are integral areas of language education in primary classes, which are not only the foundation of the language subject, but also the foundation for learning other subjects. Action research helps to identify the most appropriate educational approaches to develop abilities in the area of language. In addition, it is possible to try out innovative approaches such as discussion or debates as well as text and film analysis; Lego didactics developing writing abilities.** The importance of learning environments is also highlighted by other researchers (Darling-Hammond, et al., 2020; El Islami & Nuangchalerm, 2020; Nuangchalerm, El Islami & Prasertsang, 2022; Mesci, Schwartz & Pleasants, 2020; Songsee & Nuangchalerm, 2022; Tortorella et al., 2021), identifying harmony between the online environment, the classroom environment and the real learning situation as an integrated approach that helps students learn in different contexts. By developing subject-specific abilities, the activities can also help pupils to develop gratitude, rationality, empathy, and the ability to apply scientific knowledge to society and to

life in the immediate environment, taking into account societal, socio-cultural factors (Gandolfi, 2021; Häyrynen, Keinonen & Kärkkäinen, 2021; Jumriani et al., 2021; McComas & Clough, 2020; Varghese & Crawford, 2021). In order to be sustainable, pupils should develop a language-based sense of awareness, the ability to preserve the culture of their local community, to learn about customs, traditions and history (Hillen, 2020; Mesci et al., 2021; Nuangchalerm et al., 2022; Tengö et al., 2021; Wheeler & Root-Bernstein, 2020). The impact of film analysis on the development of linguistic abilities is confirmed by other researchers (Phuntsho & Dorji, 2023). In addition, analysing films in the classroom increases pupils' motivation to learn languages, because watching a film allows children to understand more of the meanings of words and to analyse the contexts in which those words are used. Maintaining motivation in language learning is difficult, especially if the pupil is motivated only by external factors and does not have sufficient linguistic ability to express his/her thoughts orally (Daar, 2020). Language learning through action research is supported by songs and artistic activities, adapting memorisation strategies based on activity-based learning (Yuan, 2023). It is important that when learning languages, children have the opportunity to revise, to have a calm and pleasant learning environment, to go back and reflect on what they have learned. During reflection, it is important to emphasise and reinforce the elements of the activity that the children have done well, so that they can recognise that they have already learned them (Yuan, 2023). During the action research, the teacher not only orally praised the pupils when she noticed positive signs of language learning, but also gave them cards with the words "You did it!". This resulted in a positive response and feedback from the pupils, an increase in the number of pupils who started to speak the language they were learning, and some of them also handed in their work to show that they were able to express themselves independently as requested in the assignment (Yuan, 2023). The action research found that a positive learning atmosphere in the classroom is facilitated by circumstances such as effective time management, clear instructions and expectations, and taking into account individual pupils' learning needs.

2.2. **Historical literacy abilities were developed by primary school pupils on the basis of action research, by learning to analyse historical sources through argumentation, applying learning strategies, identifying historical periods from the surroundings and developing an understanding of the significance of national symbols during educational field trips.** In Lithuania, for many years, the learning of history was dominated by learning "dry" facts, especially dates, without paying much attention to the context. From the above-mentioned approaches chosen during the action research, we can see that primary school pupils learned to analyse historical sources, to know the historical context of their own country, and to express their thoughts through argumentation. All this is important for the development of critical thinking in pupils. The research of N. Palacios Mena et al. (2020) showed that working with historical sources, identifying change and continuity and constructing narratives, helps primary school pupils to learn and understand the past in a progressive way. J. Domínguez (2015) discerns and encourages the identification of change and continuity in history lessons, which allows a look into the past, not only to understand and explain what happened and how the current situation was reached, but also to reflect on how these changes took place (speed, events, circumstances or direction), and to assess their significance and relevance for today. Such abilities cannot be developed without deep critical thinking, which is essential for trying to make sense of a certain historical context and the circumstances surrounding it. Children's attitudes and understanding are influenced by the context of their present life, socio-cultural aspects, and life experiences (Palacios Mena et al., 2020), therefore, the experiences and abilities of children living in different environments may differ due to environmental influences. In addition, researchers (Palacios Mena et al., 2020) have found that pupils' historical literacy abilities are better developed by teachers who have a good knowledge of action research methodology and can apply it in practice. In addition, the activities motivated pupils to learn about and deepen their understanding of historical phenomena, and the importance of motivation in both teacher and student activities has been emphasised by other researchers in history didactics (Becher & Gläser, 2018; Cooper, 2014a, 2014b; Palacios Mena et al., 2020). Researchers advise looking for ways to motivate pupils to take an interest in history and learn about it. This idea is consistent with the results of our research, because the active strategies applied in the action research, such as analysing historical sources, searching for historical objects in the immediate environment, and getting to know history better during excursions, have had positive results. A. Becher & E. Gläser (2018) state that very little research exists on how primary school pupils develop historical literacy abilities. Moreover, history didactics are still in the early stages of moving from the mechanical memorisation of dates and facts to the importance of sources and contextual interpretation in learning to reconstruct the past. Since primary school pupils are able to analyse and argue from sources, they can be taught history from the first year (Becher & Gläser, 2018). This was taken into account in Lithuania's update of the content of history education in 2022 (Curriculum for pre-school, primary, basic and secondary education, 2022).

2.3. **In order to develop natural science literacy in primary school pupils, action research was performed in the field of natural science, investigating plants and animals in nature, observing the life of an aquarium, experimenting and creating green environments, and recognising objects from a diagram.** The activities show that natural science education abilities were developed in pupils through active participation. K. G. Tsoumanis, G. Stylos & K. T. Kotsis (2024) state that in Greece, girls' achievements in natural sciences education are statistically higher than boys', although all children show positive attitudes towards the content of natural sciences education. In addition, urban pupils perform better than those living in less-populated areas (villages or towns). The same trend is also observed in Lithuania, where the best results are found among pupils from large cities (OECD, 2019; TIMSS 2019, 2021). M. Z. Kamarudin & M. S. A. Mat Noor (2023), having analysed thirty-three action research studies in natural sciences education for primary school pupils, found that the majority of action research improved pupils' learning outcomes. In addition, teachers who have tried action research endorse the method as an effective way to promote the educational process and outcomes. Through action research, pupils themselves learn the procedures of scientific activities (from planning, implementation, observation and reflection) (Cairns, Dickson & McMinn, 2021; Díez-Palomar et al., 2022; Kamarudin & Mat Noor, 2023). It is research-based teaching and learning, involving a series of systematic procedures of scientific activity. The use of action research projects in primary science education has improved children's reasoning abilities (Harper, 2017; Syawaludin, Gunarhadi & Rintayati, 2019; Kamarudin & Mat Noor, 2023) and environmental abilities (Tekbiyik & Çelik, 2019). In addition, children's independence is enhanced through natural science investigations (Blanchet-Cohen & Di Mambro, 2015; Díez-Palomar et al., 2022), as are analytical critical thinking abilities (Buslón et al., 2020; Díez-Palomar et al., 2022; Hawamdeh, 2020; Mulyanto, Sadono & Koeswanti, 2020; Phoopanna & Nuangchalerm, 2022). In summary, it can be said that the ability to understand scientific knowledge, to learn about the world around us, is directly linked to citizen participation in democratic societies (Díez-Palomar et al., 2022). Promoting scientific literacy from an early age should therefore be a key priority in democratic societies. Dialogic debates on scientific issues develop pupils' scientific literacy, especially instrumental learning, analytical and critical thinking in the use and mastery of subject concepts, and social abilities. It is important to underline that the pupils debated the natural sciences content in a way that interested them, and that the expression and assessment of their ideas was based on arguments. Therefore, natural science explorations based on action research draw attention to the need to design and implement educational practices based on scientific evidence, which create spaces where children can share their arguments based on evidence.

2.4. **Performing action research in mathematics content education focused on solving equations, graphical representation of word problems and the purposeful use of ICT tools for solving mathematical tasks, and the development of pupils' internal motivation through the use of the Scratch learning environment.** As can be seen from the content elements, more complex, problematic cases such as solving equations, solving word problems and innovative elements such as programming in the Scratch learning environment were chosen for primary school pupils to stimulate their interest in mathematics. Pupils' mathematical literacy is developed by differentiated activities (Aguhayon, Tingson, & Pentang, 2023; Cannon, 2017) or by activities when support is provided for a deeper understanding and comprehension of the content. This not only improves pupils' mathematics achievements, but also their confidence in their ability to learn the subject. In the case of our research, this was done by the pupils graphically representing the condition of the word problem. In this way, the children read the condition several times and got better and better at reading it. Primary pupils need to master a large number of mathematical concepts in order to be able to solve mathematical problems fluently and to perform mathematical reasoning and solutions (Sun, Li & Zhu, 2016). However, when moving from specific visual thinking to abstract logical thinking, pupils find it difficult to understand abstract mathematical concepts. Based on the theory of action research, five elements of mathematical content visualisation activities were proposed: situation, reflection, interaction, monitoring and assessment (Sun, Li & Zhu, 2016). Organising education around these elements aims to develop not only pupils' mathematical thinking, but also their independent learning, cooperative inquiry, acquisition and transformation of mathematical knowledge, and problem-raising and problem-solving abilities. The results of the research showed that visual learning in mathematics can improve the mathematical learning abilities of primary school pupils (Sun, Li & Zhu, 2016). Slightly different steps in action research for learning mathematics are suggested by other researchers (Syarifuddin & Atweh, 2022). First, they suggest mapping the mathematical concepts that will be needed to analyse a certain topic and solve problems. The mind-mapping activity encouraged pupils to prepare in advance for the topics to be discussed in class (Syarifuddin & Atweh, 2022). In addition, classroom discussions were organised after solving the tasks, which provided a social context in which pupils could work together to solve mathematical problems, present their solutions to each other, and substantiate why they solved the problems the way they did. Finally, as part of their homework, pupils practised solving mathematical problems and wrote reflections, i.e. they reflected in writing on how they had solved the problems (Syarifuddin & Atweh, 2022). Indeed, this entire learning cycle is based on a framework of action research. We can say that action research offers a systematic and deliberate approach to changing teaching (Manfra, 2019), especially when children fail to learn certain content. Working as part of a community of practice, action research practitioners engage in continuous professional learning activities. They address problems in everyday practice and seek change (Manfra, 2019), all of which enable pupils to achieve better results.

2.5. **In music, art and technology content lessons, pupils were encouraged to develop their creative abilities by applying certain techniques, folding booklets using origami techniques; using recycled materials to construct three-dimensional spaces, drawing with non-traditional art tools or drawing with graphic tools, developing rhythmic sensitivity and other musical abilities with the help of ICT.** Music and art education is an important learning subject that can give pupils the opportunity to express themselves creatively. This is an area that is receiving increasing attention in the twenty-first century. Moreover, creativity is essential to support pupils' musical learning and development (Tan, 2019). J. Laidlaw (2022) in Canada used action research to develop pupils' creativity, with children creating original music, which improved their musical abilities and understanding of music. The researcher also identified problems that arose during the research, such as pupils' absenteeism, which hindered consistent participation in the process. It is important to note that all the pupils in the research produced original music. They had a choice of instruments: they could either make music from instruments available in the school or bring their own instruments (Laidlaw, 2022). Most of the pupils reported that making music with instruments was an enjoyable activity and expressed an interest in making music again in the future. These findings are similar to those of our research, because in our research each pupil was able to make individual progress in musical and artistic literacy development. J. Julia et al. (2020), during the action research, first trained music teachers to master the Scratch learning environment. The researchers found that teachers can easily use and master Scratch in music production with media tools. In our research, too, the teachers first mastered the ICT applications in music production and only then taught it to the pupils. Furthermore, it was observed that the targeted use of ICT tools increases pupils' interest in music, and teachers experience success in teaching music. It is important for teachers to have mastered the tools, to know their potential for creating music or otherwise developing musical abilities, and then to be open and willing to innovate and apply ICT in a targeted way in the music education process (Austin et al., 2010; Julia et al., 2020). In the field of art, F. Morin (2022) states that it is possible to use communication tools in the process of the activity and to record one's thoughts and reflections that arise during the creative process or, when in nature, to record images of nature (taking photographs and/or making recordings) that can be later applied to the creative work. Reflection is an important area of art throughout the entire process, so action research allows for the exploration of ways to reflect in a way that is as acceptable as possible to the creator (Morin, 2022).

2.6. **During the action research performed to develop pupils' general competences related to experiential activities, activities were chosen to promote cultural competence development during the field trips, i.e. pupils learned about future professions, developed positive interpersonal relationships, social-emotional abilities and experiential abilities during visits to museums, libraries and natural outdoor environments.** In terms of the content of the general competence's education, we see that it was linked to the subject content and that pupils developed certain areas of the general competences by learning in nature, in the library or in the museum, while developing natural scientific, linguistic and historical literacy. The same can be said for areas such as interpersonal relationships or socio-emotional abilities, which are integral and developed throughout the entire educational process. The development of socio-emotional abilities in the field of collaborative learning has been explored by other researchers (Jakavonytė-Staškuvienė, 2021b; Jakavonytė-Staškuvienė, Žemgulienė & Sakadolskis, 2021; Nokes-Malach et al., 2019; Simion & Stan, 2020). Collaborative learning helps develop abilities such as mutual understanding and social-emotional abilities throughout the school year. Giving children the opportunity to negotiate and to organise their own activities, with constant supervision and guidance from the teacher, can help to develop their understanding of general life abilities, such as distribution of work, responsibility, commitment, timeliness, etc. Changing children's roles in a group is good for both the child and the group, as well as giving a perspective on the different roles children can play and discovering what works well for them in school life (Simion & Stan, 2020). It is important to emphasise that most children enjoy collaborative learning because they understand the benefits of a consultative culture and learn to listen to each other and to substantiate their opinion (Jakavonytė-Staškuvienė, 2021b). Collaborative learning should focus on topics relevant to pupils' lives, so that solutions can be found and properly applied (Simion & Stan, 2020). In addition, we would like to emphasise that activities to develop emotional and social competences should be regular, continuously supported and promote children's active involvement (Storey-Hurtubise et al., 2022). Developing the social and emotional abilities of primary school pupils is a key factor in creating a collaborative classroom atmosphere and reducing destructive or aggressive behaviour between pupils (Santamaría-Villar et al., 2021). Primary school pupils already understand, recognise and respect their own cultural background, and are open and willing to learn about other cultures (Smith, 2019). Pupils gather cultural information from their classmates and use these experiences in different ways. By learning that not everyone has the same cultural make-up, pupils are able to be respectful towards each other, especially when they have been learning together from an early age. Primary school pupils have already developed cultural awareness and respect for the person next to them (Smith, 2019). Respect creates a positive atmosphere in the classroom environment that fosters a sense of belonging. Culturally sensitive education can be a catalyst for cultural understanding and develop pupils' tolerance, acceptance and support for diversity. This must be brought to pupils' attention and attitudes must be fostered throughout the entire educational process, and these are long-term goals (Dixon, 2023; Robinson, 2022), achieved through experience and its application in other situations. For this to happen smoothly, there should be a single national language, agreements are respected, the teacher should be able to recognise and manage pupils' psychological trauma, parents are made aware of and encouraged to follow classroom agreements, cultural awareness is developed in an integral way with socio-emotional abilities, and positive behaviour is encouraged rather than punishment (Robinson, 2022). Cultural competence and understanding of each other can be developed through pair work, where pupils from different cultures work together as each other's assistants and advisers (Dixon, 2023). Working together also made pupils more motivated to complete their tasks. Working in pairs allows pupils to analyse culturally sensitive texts.

2.7. **Our study included action research to develop pupils' general competences related to monitoring and self-evaluating their personal progress. The pupils' self-evaluation system proved to be successful in the use of the "learning diary", "unfinished sentences", "break ticket" and "colours methods", which are related to particular lesson agreements and the development of a culture of adherence to these agreements, where the work is assessed according to pre-agreed criteria. At the same time, these methods include elements of reflection on the educational process and the result. In addition, the frequency and type of feedback that pupils receive in lessons was analysed in relation to the monitoring of personal progress.** The research data of D. Vasileiadou & K. Karadimitriou (2021) are close to those of our research, because the authors found that rubric-based self-evaluation (particular agreements) helped primary school pupils. It improved their overall performance in all three subjects and made children more attentive to the analysis of their work. Pupils analyse not only the results, but also the learning strategies used (Kniffin & Baert, 2015). Assessment of one's own performance can be a valuable part of teaching, because it helps pupils to achieve better learning outcomes (Andrade, 2010; Kniffin & Baert, 2015; Vasileiadou & Karadimitriou, 2021). In addition, the self-evaluation of pupils' performance improves teachers' performance by providing them with useful information about how pupils think, i.e. the teacher learns what and how the child thinks, whether his/her opinion is correct in relation to the subject content, etc. The pupil also learns about the quality of the work by carefully assessing his/her own work against the criteria, because he/she is able to identify strengths and areas for improvement. In addition, the pupil knows what the teachers expect and at the same time understands that their assessment of his/her own performance is related to their efforts to revise and improve their own work (Andrade, 2010). For such educational practice to be successful, teachers need to have a positive attitude towards this innovative approach and to be aware of the benefits of its use and, of course, to be trained in how to use it, for example, to be able to develop their own particular criteria in the context of the content in each subject (Vasileiadou & Karadimitriou, 2021). Assessment of a pupil's own work is most useful, both in terms of achievements and self-regulation, when it is used in a formative way and is based on teaching and learning (Andrade, 2019). In addition, the accuracy of one's own performance assessment process can be improved by having already gained experience (Harris & Brown, 2018; Yan, 2022; Yan et al., 2023). In order to find out what pupils think about self-evaluation and how they do it, it is useful to formulate open-ended questions related to the particular educational content that will be assessed. Using open-ended questions allows pupils to reflect more deeply and freely on the assessment of their own work, without being constrained by standardised answers (Wong, 2017). Factors such as individual aspirations and/or expectations and elements of the curriculum influence the self-evaluation of primary school pupils' performance (Yan et al., 2023), influencing the implementation of pupil self-evaluation and the monitoring of personal progress.

Analysis of bachelor's theses using action research in primary classrooms showed that it is meaningful to apply it to the development of critical thinking through argumentation (Jakavonyte-Staskuviene, Jašinauskas & Kudinoviene, 2022). This approach can be developed in a variety of subjects, allowing pupils to formulate hypotheses and arguments based on the content they are analysing, for example, through reading texts, historical sources or exploring an aquarium. Our research showed that primary school pupils are able to formulate a hypothesis and arguments on the basis of analysed material and are able to substantiate their opinions (Jakavonyte-Staskuviene, Jašinauskas & Kudinoviene, 2022). It is recommended that similar activities be performed more frequently and systematically so that pupils learn to substantiate various aspects of the subject content. The proper conditions must be in place for such an educational process: a safe, attractive classroom environment, the development of language abilities linked to other subjects, cultural awareness and critical thinking. It is important to base the educational process on the concept of a dialogic space (discussion in pairs or small groups) (Pitsia, Karakolidis & Lehane, 2021). It is useful to use technology in a targeted way: to record pupils' reflections, conversations, presentations and to analyse this content by listening to audio recordings or watching videos (Wagner, Skaftun & McTigue, 2020; Monteiro, Mata & Nóbrega Santos, 2021).

3. **Key elements for developing action research-based practice that are evident from TEACHER FOCUS GROUP INTERVIEWS:**
   3.1. **Focus group participants, who have already mastered the action research methodology, demonstrated a positive attitude towards action research and an understanding that action research must be performed continuously, to identify pupil abilities and to resolve various problematic areas of educational content assimilation.** This is evidenced by the following statements made by the focus group participants: I do small action research all the time, it happens naturally, and sometimes with a particular goal in mind. [...] Looking generally at how every activity is improved. I have only been working for three years, so I have touched the activities, but they still aren't set in stone, and the methodology is tangible, but there is always a desire to improve, to add something of my own. That's why I think that every activity I do has an action research component, because I adapt to the classroom where I work. I keep thinking, what if ... and I think it's interesting to see what change will happen if we change a certain element. I am driven by curiosity and the desire to see for myself what will happen, what will be the change – whether it works or not. (Cecile) I applied action research to determine pupils' abilities when assigning tasks of varying complexity and analysing results, when pupils came back to school for year 2 after the summer holidays. It is a big month-long study, analyses, designing new tasks and all this work was done just to know what the class is like, where the children's strengths are and where we need to improve. [...] I think it is only through action research that we can get to know our pupils and enable them to move upwards at their own pace, to move and grow. (Oksana) *Every day I find myself doing everything for the first time. Every day I ask myself if my first-year pupils will really do the activity well, because it is my first time working with first-year pupils. Even though I have doubts about whether they will do it, they just step up and do it, those children. Every time I ask again and again if they can do it, and we try and we do it.* (Zita) I am personally interested in action research, and I apply it, and I have an inclination for it in my classroom. [...] I mostly apply research for my own performance self-evaluation, for a leap forward, and I mostly like to collect information about my pupils when I interact with them. (Ana) Our research results coincide with the research data of P. W. Taruc (2016), in which it is stated that teachers have positive beliefs and a positive attitude towards action research. Teachers also express positive views about being involved in action research. The participants in our research were teachers who are familiar with action research methodology and are already advanced practitioners

of the methodology. The importance of teachers' expertise and their knowledge of action research is directly related to their attitude towards action research, as stated by other researchers (Oestar & Marzo, 2022; Soverano & Laguador, 2022). In addition, a positive attitude towards action research allows teachers to gain useful experience in this area (Soverano & Laguador, 2022). Research performed by J. R. SR. Soverano & J. M. Laguador (2022) showed that primary school teachers have a very high level of positive attitudes towards action research, which is related to the criterion of usefulness. Moreover, the idea of these researchers to base the pedagogical studies of primary school teachers on action research is directly related to the field we are developing and applying in practice in Lithuania.

3.2. **Teachers in the focus groups emphasised the importance of continuity of action research and application of mastered methodologies, when educational practice proves its value and produces positive pupil learning outcomes.** All of this shows the depth of practice and thought of teachers who understand the importance of consistency and a systematic approach in training primary school teachers. It is also the thinking of educators who are already advanced in action research and who are willing and able to base their practice on research. Teachers' responses highlighted the value of the bachelor's thesis applying action research: *My bachelor's thesis was a good topic and situation for doing the research in my classroom* (the classroom where the research participant works). And I had to read a lot of sources on the use of active reading techniques. And those techniques, when they were introduced during the action research, are still being applied in the same classroom. It's just that now it involves all pupils. In the action research, I focused on two situations – two individual pupils. When I was able to successfully apply the two approaches I had chosen, that's what we now apply all together. […] We all planned together that if this is a reading challenge, how will I implement it. And reflecting on what we have been doing lately with the children, it is really a fact that I am adapting their own participation in organising and planning certain activities. (Elzė) *When we were studying pedagogical action research, we paid attention to all the stages, now maybe I'm skipping some stages or paying less attention. But I try to follow the steps. We have reading diaries in the classroom now, so automatically my colleague and I also set out why we had them, what we wanted to achieve, then we formulated a hypothesis, then we anticipated those activities. And we kept looking, succeeding, failing, that timing. I'm still applying this; I'm going to continue with the research that I did in my bachelor's thesis.* (Johanas) These statements from our research participants show that teachers are progressive, striving to continuously improve their teaching practice, and doing so with deep critical thinking. This only supplements the thought expressed by E. Blakely & D. Hemphill (2021) and M. Finch (2022) that in pedagogy, action research is meaningful insofar as it improves educational practice and yields positive results for solving problematic situations.

3.3. **Shared, positive motivation of both teachers and pupils, emotional security and the desire to achieve better learning outcomes are factors encouraging the performance of action research in the classroom.** It is important to mention that not only teachers are positive about the action research, but they also report that pupils are positive about the activities because they feel safe, good-willed, willing to be in the classroom, in the school, and to actively participate, and that this kind of environment is what allows children to perform better. This is evidenced by the teachers' ideas expressed in the focus group: *Children's feelings and emotions, how they enjoyed doing the activity and the results they get, are what motivates, and I would very much agree about the meaning. The children themselves say that it is important to them that every activity has meaning, and since I have been teaching this class since the first year, and they are now in the fourth year, I can share that I can really see how much work was put into the first year with the conversations because there was a lot of discussion, talking, sharing, and how independent they really are now.* (Elė) *The main motive is pupil achievement. I am very interested in what improves achievement. The topic of my bachelor's thesis is the interview method for developing speaking and listening abilities. I did this activity in year 1–2 and now we are in year 3, with a textbook where we came across that interview method, my pupils, they feel like kings, they know everything, it's nothing new to them.* (Ana) It is really necessary for everyone to feel good, to feel safe and to be able to engage fully in the activity without worrying or being scared that it is unexpected. Another thing is that there certainly are children in the classroom who are more engaged and who are less engaged, especially when working in groups. [...] To avoid this, we try to choose a role for everyone when the children are in groups, so that they know in advance. If, for example, we were making yoghurt. Each group had three children. Each person had their own responsibility and at a certain point they could fulfil themselves and feel needed. [...] These seem like simple steps, but the distribution of these steps also helps. For those who are perhaps less active, less brave, it helps them to be included and not left out. (Elzė) *My motivation for this is just to help the student to have the tools and to improve* *their learning. And most importantly to notice personal progress.* (Ana) I. Bojović & R. Antonijević (2017) state that primary school pupils are able to self-evaluate their academic performance, which motivates them to learn. The teacher should actively respond to all individual pupils' abilities and develop learning through a continuous cycle of observation, planning and implementation of objectives, tasks, methods and tools tailored to the individual pupil. It is essential to develop a sense of pupils' abilities, personality traits, experiences, interests, ambitions, as well as the differences arising from the overall social context. In this way, the teacher will be able to encourage and motivate pupils to learn and help them to achieve short-term goals as well as prepare for lifelong learning (Bojović & Antonijević, 2017). For most primary school pupils, factors such as feelings, teachers, teaching, subjects, learning environment, peers and well-being have both positive and negative effects on motivation (Boström et al., 2023). These factors are similar to the findings of our research, because the teachers in the research also highlighted these factors when talking about action research. The didactic context of education is important for encouraging pupils' motivation (Blomgren, 2016; Boström et al., 2023), which is what the methodology for action research covers. The teacher's sense of responsibility and the stability of the educational process have an impact on the motivation of pupils in the classroom context (Stensmo, 2008).

3.4. **Action research can be a successful factor in the implementation of teaching/learning practices, when pupil autonomy and satisfaction of individual needs is encouraged.** These aspects are significant because failing to address children's individual needs tends to lead to learning problems and difficulties, and pupils are often challenged and unable to cope, which can reduce their motivation to learn. Examples of activities to develop pupils' autonomy were given by teachers in the focus groups: *The pupils themselves took on their roles and decided who would be the leaders. They folded, glued, and worked together in a friendly way. The activity was long-term, but the important thing is that when asked what they remembered from the third year, most of them highlighted this activity.* (Milana) *Pupils constantly make observations and suggestions for improvement.* (Zita) *Pupils are engaged in a very different way when they can learn on their own, when they can plan and initiate activities; it's not the same when I just plan and ask them to do things. Children's engagement is completely different during action research.* (Elzė) *I ask what is the meaning of the activity for the child and for me as an educator. First of all, for me to make sure that what you are doing is really meaningful and* *useful, because very often teachers tend to do a lot, do a lot, and not pause. Why do I try with children? So that I can develop research-based practice, I encourage different activities when the children themselves are engaged in those activities.* (Johanas) *In addition, I have an autistic pupil, a boy, so I am very responsible in observing and analysing what helps him, looking for ways to help him understand better.* (Oksana) It is important for pupils to be independent and to be able to collaborate (Bojović & Antonijević, 2017). Pupils, who highly value their autonomy, will expend considerable effort and energy, or try harder and choose appropriate behaviours that lead to achievement and success. Education, as a liberating factor, is the key to a child's freedom and autonomy. High-quality learning can only be achieved through an effective pedagogy that takes account of children's perceptions and ideas (Cerino, 2021). The information obtained from the assessment of children helps to design and organise spaces where learners can express their potential and satisfy their desire for independence. This process contributes to teachers' learning and professional development and strengthens teachers' relationships with children and their parents (Cerino, 2021). When choosing learning environments, it is important to consider how much freedom of movement and space children will have, because this is how children learn to solve problems, take and manage risks and be independent (Watts, 2020). Attentive listening and attention to what children say shows that adults trust children and allow them to make responsible decisions. Adults, including parents, learn with and cooperate with children, rather than trying to be in charge and have all the answers. Together, they plan the initial topics for children's exploration and prepare materials and resources to stimulate children's critical thinking (Cerino, 2021).

3.5. **Action research helps pupils learn to do their work and self-evaluate according to criteria, when a culture of consultation is encouraged.** This aspect was identified by focus group participants as one of the educational problems to be addressed on the basis of action research: *I'm teaching first-year pupils this year to self-evaluate their work. This also involves correcting work and checking and correcting the work of the students themselves. They self-evaluate according to the criteria and, when they are able to self-evaluate properly, then they can help a friend. Children are very keen to help a friend and therefore try to learn to self-evaluate properly.* (Zita) *So in the same way we made a plan, we made a plan together with them about how I would have to plant a plant, what I would have to do, what measures I would have to take, how I would observe, what I would learn by observing, so that I could* *measure the length of my seedling, what sprouted, why it sprouted, how much I had to water it, and we even divided into certain groups to see what happened, for those who were watering every day, what happened, for those who were watering every second day. It's how we organise action research with the children so that they are not just participants, so that everything is not planned and done for them, but so that they make a real effort and understand for themselves what we are trying to achieve with these activities.* (Elė) When assessing activities against the criteria, it is important that the criteria are clear to the pupils and are discussed starting from the planning of the activity, and that they are revisited during the performance of and reflection on the activity (Khan & Tzortzopoulos, 2016). During action research, assessment criteria should include problem-solving, critical thinking and product development tasks. Assessment based on these criteria should be scenario-based problems that require the consideration of aspects with more than one answer from different perspectives or require the creation of unique products such as a poem, a story, a drawing, a building or other creative work (Orhan Ozen & Ozen, 2022). In order to produce the results of such tasks, pupils absolutely need to negotiate, communicate, collaborate, discuss and substantiate.

3.6. **To enable teachers in a school to perform action research, a culture of experience-sharing and constructive consultation must be created, based on trust, good will, mutual support and encouragement.** Focus group participants made the following observations about good-willed cooperation among school teachers: *In the school where I work, there is a culture and system of sharing. We observe each other's lessons.* (Zita) *We have an education manager who is an idea generator. She not only comes up with ideas, but also advises on how to implement them. We can share with her what we did, how we did it, whether it worked or not.* (Johanas) *It is also possible to consult with the deputy headteacher (vice-principal), who has checklists for certain situations and can advise on the best way to deal with a certain issue in a particular case.* (Liza) *Observing colleagues' lessons is encouraged. After the observation, there are a lot of discussions, not only with the teachers but also with the school administration, because we make certain agreements on the way forward. We discuss the most important points, what we can change.* (Violeta) Most of the time, I share my experiences with a colleague because we work in the same class. In fact, she is the only one I can share with, because we work in a gymnasium that as of now does not have any more primary classes. […] The way we talk and share as a pair has worked, because we can share the responsibility as a pair. Even when working with parents, it helps a lot when we are together, when we can support, advise and assist each other. We are good at it. (Elzė) *In our school, there are second teachers, who start out as teaching assistants and after a certain period of time themselves become main classroom teachers.* (Elė) Research has found that mid-level leaders are able to create a culture of trust in an educational institution performing action research: they are advanced teachers who lead others; they are in a recognised leadership position, or are responsible for improving the practice of colleagues, and perform an important teaching role (Edwards-Groves, Grootenboer, & Ronnerman, 2016). In order to carry out school-wide action research, it is up to school leaders to see to it, and they absolutely need to consider topics such as activity planning in teams, communication, collaboration, the process of organising group meetings, data collection, analysis and synthesis (Castro Garcés & Martínez Granada, 2016; Gordon & Solis, 2018). Data collection and analysis should take place first, to help the team decide on the target area that is most problematic and will be addressed through action research; to set objectives and develop an action plan; then to gather feedback on progress and stakeholder concerns about performance; and then to identify results and develop continuity plans (Gordon & Solis, 2018). The advantages of collaborative planning are expressed by teachers who have worked in teams to plan and implement action research. They emphasise that they were able to learn together in order to assimilate and put into practice the key constructs of the activities that supported the intended research direction (Castro Garcés & Martínez Granada, 2016). Teachers also report that working together they gained a better understanding of key concepts and theories related to the teaching of the subject by reading and discussing the content of research articles, meeting together to plan lessons, collecting and analysing data, and talking about their own teaching practice; and, through the writing of journal entries, they had the opportunity to reflect on the process of their research and to describe their own perspectives as members of a team (Castro Garcés & Martínez Granada, 2016).

3.7. **Focus group participants, speaking about action research, also identified certain problems. One of the most significant problems hindering the planning and performance of action research, is the unwillingness of the pedagogical community to change, to make efforts to work in an innovative way, and to resolve problems that arise.** In Lithuania, there is a severe shortage of primary school teachers at this time, so teachers who have already retired are often asked to return to work, or soon-to-retire teachers are asked to postpone retirement, even though the teacher himself or herself no longer wants to work, and therefore has no intention of making any effort to learn anything. On 12 August 2024, the Employment Service announced that there are currently 540 vacancies for education professionals on its job portal, of which 53 are for primary school teachers (Teacher shortage at a record level: sends an ominous message, 2024). In fact, the true figures are even higher, because some school leaders are looking for teachers on their own and do not contact the Employment Service. This is confirmed by Unė Kaunaitė, Director of EDU Vilnius and a representative of Vilnius City Municipality, the capital of Lithuania, who says that there are 450 advertisements for teachers in the city of Vilnius alone. And the Ministry of Education, Science and Sport claims that around 500 schools are looking for teachers (Is there a shortage of teachers in Kaunas, 2024). Indeed, it is very difficult to talk about the quality of education when there is such a shortage of teachers, because the school administration must first ensure that the school has all the necessary staff, and only then can quality education be discussed. A similar situation was described by research participant Milana, emphasising the deficiencies of such an environment, that there is nobody to talk with and consult, because colleagues do not want any innovative activities and show no willingness to collaborate: I am in an environment with colleagues who are in the last year or two of their career, and they already know that, and there is no motivation there. In my environment, I was told that there is nothing to share, we are all perfect and know how to work. Even in the strategy, no areas for improvement have been identified. […] I see at work that the real values of education are no longer a concern in my school. I reflect every day with my own family members, because there is no conversation about this at school. (Milana) What our research participant said only underscores the fact that in Lithuania, it is difficult to ensure pursuit of quality education in some educational institutions. In addition, there is a worldwide shortage of teachers (UNESCO, 2023), and it is difficult to find consensus on solutions. The causes and extent of these shortages vary geographically and politically, leading to different responses, including a range of initiatives and policies, each based on a particular understanding of the problem and a solution that has had a different impact on teacher recruitment and retention (Dadvand & Lampert, 2024). In the face of severe teacher shortages, usually associated with an insufficient supply of new teachers as the number of pupils increases and teachers retire, efforts are then made to recruit many more new teachers (Dadvand & Lampert,

2024). While recruiting more teachers is essential, simply understanding the situation as a problem of supply and demand will not effectively address the root cause of the staffing problem if a significant proportion of the recruited teachers leave schools within a few years (Ingersoll & Tran, 2023). Thus, to maximise the impact of recruitment initiatives, it is essential to mitigate the conditions causing teachers to leave their jobs. In Lithuania, the improvement of working conditions is not yet progressing smoothly due to the lack of teaching materials prepared in line with the general curricula renewed in 2022, as new textbooks are not available for all classes (Murauskaitė, 2024).

Another problem encountered in Lithuania is that schools in the largest cities, including Vilnius, Kaunas, and Klaipėda, are overcrowded due to a very large number of pupils, often exceeding the limits on the number of pupils allowed in classrooms according to hygiene norms, so space is allocated in various parts of a school, sometimes without regard to the age group of the pupils, simply because a space has been found. Research participant Clareta spoke about such a situation, highlighting that her classroom is distant from the other primary classes, and the school is quite large, so it is relatively difficult for her to meet with colleagues: *The problem is that my current classroom space is very distant from the other primary classes, at the end of a completely different corridor, mixed in with the older classes, so if I want to talk with somebody about something, I have to walk down the corridor for 4–5 minutes, which is why my colleagues say they rarely see me.* (Clareta) Other studies also point to the importance of this issue for teacher well-being and recruitment. Teachers spend most of their day in school buildings, teaching in classrooms or working in offices. Their comfort and satisfaction with the physical environment of the school is very important for the progress of the learning process. The physical environment of the school has been found to affect teachers' comfort levels, which in turn affects their job satisfaction and productivity (Atyah, 2020). While the importance of pedagogy and curriculum in education is widely recognised, the impact of the physical environment is often underestimated (Schmidt, 2024). Research has shown the profound effects of the physical environment on pupils' learning outcomes, behaviour and general well-being (Gao & Lafortune, 2020; Kellum & Olson, 2023).

Lack of time for high-quality self-evaluation of pupil activity was identified by focus group participants as a third problematic aspect: *The problem I face is the lack of time for quality self-evaluation.* (Ilona) This can indeed be a problem for teachers at the start of their careers, because it can be difficult to time pupils' activities, but in Lithuania, this is also a problem for experienced teachers, who often schedule too many activities for too little time. That teachers lack the time to organise high-quality self-evaluation of pupils' achievements has also been found in other research (Adawiah, 2023), and for this reason, some teachers ignore pupil self-evaluation and do not use it at all. Researchers recognise that assessment and learning should be complementary activities and that efforts to improve the quality of learning should be made through improvements in the assessment system. This area demands more attention in everyday practice (Moosa, Salleh & Hamid, 2020; Rosen, Stoeffler & Simmering, 2020).

Conclusions

Action research-based primary education practice can be linked to a high-quality match between process and outcome, taking into account the individual needs of pupils and facilitating the development of subject-specific skills and key competences. Since action research starts with the identification of an educational problem and the development of an educational plan, selecting the appropriate educational aids and individual support for each pupil, it provides a high-quality environment for learning and achieving the intended outcome. It is also important to note that the creation of such a supportive learning environment is not only beneficial and meaningful for the individual pupil, but also for the community as a whole, as it provides the necessary attention and support for each learner, both in terms of providing feedback and demonstrating that each one of them is valuable and important, and that he or she is developing his or her abilities according to personal potential.

In addition, action research by primary teachers allows them to go deeper and address issues in the educational situation that needs to be addressed, where teachers may be less experienced, i.e. they have not yet encountered similar situations, and it is natural for them to go deeper into these areas and to see how teachers in other countries have dealt with such issues in their own context. It must be acknowledged that teachers all over the world strive to provide the best possible education for their pupils, and that pupils everywhere are pupils with many similarities, but that every country, city or school in the world has different situations, which are due to the very different experiences and needs of pupils. These need to be taken into account properly, monitored and explored, and action research allows for a solution to the situation.

We can say that action research-based educational practice complements the expression of social constructivist theory in the reality of education, because learning takes place in a contingent situation of mutual trust, which obliges students to take responsibility not only for their own learning, but also for the learning of other classmates. Moreover, in such an environment, teachers are the investigators of the educational process and the problem-solvers, empowering learners to participate actively and to base their learning on arguments and evidence. In this way, the quality of education and the changes made are seen as beneficial by the whole educational community, and learners are courageous, open, confident and unafraid to make mistakes and to solve questions and problem situations.

The educational contexts explored and described in the context of action research complement and extend the epistemological field of educational science, which analyses how a particular learner is able to learn about the world and the scientific knowledge that exists in it. This is qualitatively made possible by the mastery of a systematic reflective practice in action research, i.e. a constant reflection on the concrete elements of the educational process before, during and after an action. The teacher's ability to apply the right learning strategies, at the right time and at the right pace, enables the pupil or group to benefit from learning support and to anticipate further learning priorities.

Data from the external assessment of the quality of Lithuanian general education schools show that the challenges teachers have faced for several decades, such as lesson planning that takes into account the diversity of pupils, providing feedback, and developing pupils' self-directed learning abilities, orientation to results, assessment of pupils' achievements and progress in teaching/learning, involve important elements of the process of organising teaching/learning, which are directly related to creating opportunities for each pupil to engage in learning, to develop new experiences and to consistently make progress and achieve. And all of these problematic aspects, as our research shows, are well addressed by the application of targeted action research in practice. The use of action research in practice, with the right approach and tools, tends to improve students' learning outcomes and their motivation to learn. The use of active learning methods (debates, discussions, didactic Lego materials, learning in unconventional spaces, experimental practice, learning in green spaces, outdoors, etc.) was clearly appreciated by the pupils.

Learning together, working in pairs or small groups are activities that pupils enjoy because they can interact, confer and not be left on their own. Pupils feel that the support of their classmates is important; they feel and receive respect. Experienced teachers usually advise students who are performing action research, to help them get to know the class. Prospective teachers can choose their own active learning methods that increase pupils' motivation and success. Experienced teachers also benefit from such practice placements, because they can learn from students who base their practice on methods that promote active learning and learning from each other.

Mentor-teachers usually advise prospective primary school teacher-students who are doing action research, to help them get to know the class. Prospective teachers can choose their own active learning methods that increase pupils' motivation and achievement. In addition, it is worth presenting/applying action research-based education practices in teacher professional development training, where participants can learn from existing experiences and the available methodological material. Such training would allow for a wider application of action research and a better quality of educational problem-solving in the transformation of the current situation.

In summary, it can be said that the participatory educational process in action research includes cognitive, cultural, emotional and natural environmental dimensions. It is highly dependent on the particular situation, which provides both constraints and resources, which change over time, and on the basis of which the pupil reconstructs his/her experience, interprets it, looks for connections, i.e. actively thinks, and builds up problem-solving experience which can be used and applied in other situations. Finally, in terms of the methodological approach, pupils' learning outcomes take into account their attitude towards the problem to be solved, their analysis of their own performance, and the information gathered through feedback when teachers comment on their performance. It is important to organise the educational process on the basis of action research, because well-organised activities can improve not only pupils' learning outcomes, but also their willingness to learn and their autonomy.

Our research shows that the bachelor's theses in which soon-to-be primary school teachers applied action research were of high quality: they described the classroom context in detail, identified the problems, clearly described the method used and the results achieved, and described how they changed their teaching practice. We expect that these abilities will remain and that as primary teachers they will be able to identify and address problems in the classroom by selecting and adjusting both the teaching materials and the strategies or methods of individual support.

Most of the primary teachers in the focus groups, who are already advanced in the application of action research, demonstrated a deep understanding of action research through their examples and reasoning. Action research helped them to personalise education according to the needs of the pupil. Teachers had a better understanding of pupils' needs and knew how to meet them. The social domain of pupils is evident in action research, as changes are usually associated with pupils and teachers taking more responsibility, promoting pupils' autonomy and finding solutions to problems through good-willed discussions with colleagues.

Limitations of Research

The analysis of primary education practices in Lithuania was based only on external evaluation of the quality of schools' performance, but not on the internal evaluation tools of schools themselves. The qualitative study chose a purposive sampling method, i.e. to select one of the Lithuanian universities that train primary school teachers, because teachers were approached who work and apply action research in their practice and have written a bachelor's thesis in the field of action research, but teachers are also trained by other universities in Lithuania, i.e. Vilnius University, Klaipėda University. In addition, primary school teachers are also trained in colleges, i.e. Vilnius College, Klaipėda College.

The possibilities of generalising the qualitative research data are limited, as the data from our study does not allow us to speak more broadly about action research-based practices in primary education at the national level. Based on the experiences and opinions of the research participants, it is possible to identify the most frequent situations that can be solved by action research and the contexts in which certain classroom problems were solved.

Prospects for Further Research

The theoretical and epistemic context of the study suggest the prospects for further relevant research in this area.

Presentation of our research findings and development of action research-based educational practices in Lithuanian schools at risk identified by external evaluation. The empirical research data identified by the focus group interviews should be presented to the communities of schools working in difficult conditions. Based on the good practices already developed, it is recommended that schools undertake action research in their school education process, identifying the problem area(s), the solution options, and implementing them in the education process. In addition to implementation, and monitoring through empirical research, where researchers are not only consultants but also designers of the educational process, the selected good practices could serve as a basis for learning and professional development for other members of the school community.

Action research as a tool for the implementation of the renewed educational content in schools. The priorities in the updated General Education Framework (2022), focusing on the practice of competency-based education, flexible development of educational content oriented to the needs of the specific class and the specific students, and the development of 30% of the classroom content by the class teacher, create the preconditions for the development of quality action research within the pedagogical community of a given school. We believe that if the aim is to achieve a qualitative breakthrough in the field of education in an educational institution, according to the identified problem areas, the educational process should be similarly planned and a number of selected methods should be applied by all teachers working with pupils of a particular class. Therefore, the development of such practices should be based on action research, both in terms of implementation of the content and monitoring of qualitative change (according to agreed and defined criteria). New research would help to properly record and analyse all this in a scientific way, with a view to evidence-based practice.

References

30 préconisations pour améliorer l'éducation en France. (2017). Paris: Centre national d'étude des systèmes scolaires. https://www.cnesco.fr/fr/30-preconisations/.

Abiatal, L. K. S. & Howard, G. R. (2020). Erratum: Constructivism-led assistive technology: An experiment at a Namibian special primary school. *South Afr. J. Child. Educ.* 10, 1–12. https://hdl.handle.net/10520/EJC-1fa2698782.

Abraczinskas, M. & Zarrett, N. (2020). Youth participatory action research for health equity: increasing youth empowerment and decreasing physical activity access inequities in under-resourced programs and schools. *American Journal of Community Psychology*, 66(3–4), 232–243, doi: 10.1002/ajcp.12433.

Adawiah, R. (2023). Teacher's Constraints and Challenges in Implementing Student Attitude Assessment in Junior High School. *Open Education Studies*, 5(1), 20220204. https://doi.org/10.1515/edu-2022-0204.

Adelman, C. (1993). Kurt Lewin and the Origins of Action Research. *Educational Action Research*, 1:1, 7–24, DOI: 10.1080/0965079930010102.

Adomaitienė, J. & Zubrickienė, I. (2019). *Veiklos tyrimai, jų taikymo teorija ir praktika: studijų knyga* [*Action research, theory and practice: a study book*]. Klaipėda: Klaipėdos universiteto leidykla.

Aga, F. J. (2017). Motivating and/or de-motivating environments to do action research: the case of teachers of English as a foreign language in Ethiopian universities. *Educational Action Research*, *25*(2), 203–222. https://doi.org/10.1080/09650792.2016.1168310.

Agogué, M. & Clerc, N. (2016a). *De 2006 à 2016, l'évolution d'un processus d'accompagnement professionnel en formation de formateurs et en référence à la psychologie sociale clinique. Colloque*: 2006–2016, scénarios de formation 10 ans après – UCP – ESPé.

Agogué, M. & Clerc, N. (2016b). *Co-réflexivité et méta-analyse en formation de formateurs à l'accompagnement professionnel, Colloque: Ethique de l'accompagnement et agir coopératif*, Tours, 26–28 mai.

Aguhayon, H. G., Tingson, R. D. & Pentang, J. T. (2023). Addressing Students Learning Gaps in Mathematics through Differentiated Instruction. *International Journal of Educational Management and Development Studies*, 4 (1), 69–87. https://doi.org/10.53378/352967.

Akkari, A. & Radhouane, M. (2022). The Role of the Teacher in Promoting Intercultural Approaches. In: *Intercultural Approaches to Education*. Springer, Cham. https://doi.org/10.1007/978-3-030-70825-2_13.

Alexander, R. (2020). *A dialogic teaching companion*. Routledge. Available online: https://doi.org/10.4324/9781351040143-1.

Al-Huneini, H., Walker, S. A. & Badger, R. (2020). Introducing tablet computers to a rural primary school: An Activity Theory case study. Computers & Education, 143, 103648. https://doi.org/10.1016/j.compedu.2019.103648.

Al-Obaydi, L. H., Nashruddin, Rahman, F. F. & Suherman, L. O. A. (2021). The Use of Action Research in EFL Socio-professional Context: Students-teachers' Perceptions. *ELS Journal on Interdisciplinary Studies in Humanities*, 4(2), 232–240. DOI: https://doi.org/10.34050/elsjish.v4i2.10876.

Altet, M. (2013). Formes de résistance des pratiques de formation d'enseignants à la pratique réflexive et conditions de développement de la réflexivité. Dans M. Altet, J. Desjardins, R. Etienne, L. Paquay, & P. Perrenoud. (Sdr). *Former des enseignants réflexifs : obstacles et résistances* (pp. 39–59). Bruxelles: De Boeck Université.

Altrichter, H., Feldman, A., Posch, P. & Somekh, B. (2008). *Teachers investigate their work: An introduction to action research across the professions*. New York: Routledge.

Alytaus r. Pivašiūnų gimnazijos veiklos išorinio rizikos vertinimo ataskaita [*Report on the external risk assessment of Pivašiūnai Gymnasium, Alytus district*]. (2019). Vilnius: Nacionalinė mokyklų vertinimo agentūra.

Alytus r. Miroslav gimnazijos veiklos išorinio rizikos vertinimo ataskaita [*Report on the external risk assessment of Miroslavo Gymnasium, Alytus district*]. (2019). Vilnius: Nacionalinė mokyklų vertinimo agentūra.

Anderson, G. L., Herr, K. & Nihlen, A. S. (2007). *Studying Your Own School: An Educator's Guide to Practitioner Action Research*. Corwin Press A SAGE Publications Company.

Andrade, H. L. (2010). Students as the definitive source of formative assessment: Academic self-assessment and the self-regulation of learning. In H. Andrade, G. Cizek (Eds.), *Handbook of formative assessment*. Routledge, New York, pp. 90–105.

Andrade, H. L. (2019). A Critical Review of Research on Student Self-Assessment. *Front. Educ.* 4, 87. https://doi.org/10.3389/feduc.2019.00087.

Anwar, N., Kristiadi, D., Novezar, F. A., Tanto, P. A., Septha, K., Ardhia, P. & Abraham, J. (2020). Learning math through mobile game forprimary school students. *Sylwan*, 164, 346–352.

Appay, B. (2005). *La dictature du succès, le paradoxe de l'autonomie contrôlée et de la précarisation*. Paris, L'Harmattan, coll: Logiques sociales.

Appova, A. & Arbaugh, F. (2018). Teachers' Motivation to Learn: Implications for Supporting Professional Growth. *Professional Development in Education*, *44*(1), 5–21.

Ar Kaune jaučiamas mokytojų trūkumas? [*Is there a shortage of teachers in Kaunas?*] (2024). Kaunas: kaunodiena.lt https://m.kauno.diena.lt/naujienos/kaunas/miesto-pulsas/ar-kaune-jauciamas-mokytoju-trukumas-1188058.

Ari, S. & Çiftçi, S. (2022). An Action Research on the Use of Collaborative Teaching Techniques. *Journal of Qualitative Research in Education*, (29) https://doi.org/10.14689/enad.29.4.

Arsoetar, N. & Sugiman, S. (2019). Development of student worksheets based on Realistic Mathematics Education (RME) oriented to mathematical reasoning. *Journal of Physics: Conference Series-The 6th International Conference on Research, Implementation, and Education of Mathematics and Science*, Yogyakarta, Indonesia, 1397(1), 012091, IOP Publishing.

Ascroft, E. (2024). Intra-acting with the self: diffracting reflexivity in action-based research. *Educational Action Research*, 1–11. https://doi.org/10.1080/09650792.2024.2424286

Atyah, R. (2020). The Effects of the Physical Environment Design on Teachers' Workplace Comfort: A Critical Review. *The International Journal of Architectonic, Spatial, and Environmental Design*, 14(3), 17–30. doi:10.18848/2325-1662/CGP/v14i03/17-30.

Austin, R., Smyth, J., Rickard, A., Quirk- Bolt, N. & Metcalfe, N. (2010). Collaborative digital learning in schools: Teacher perceptions of purpose and effectiveness. *Technology, Pedagogy and Education*, 19(3), 327–343. https://doi.org/10.1080/1475939x.2010.513765.

Bakker, A. B., Hetland, J., Olsen, O. K. & Espevik, R. (2022). Daily transformational leadership: A source of inspiration for follower performance? *European Management Journal*. https://doi.org/10.1016/j.emj.2022.04.004.

Balakrishnan, V. & Claiborne, L. (2017). Participatory action research in culturally complex societies: opportunities and challenges. *Educational Action Research*, *25*(2), 185–202. https://doi.org/10.1080/09650792.2016.1206480.

Bauer, S. C. & Brazer, D. (2012). *Using research to lead school improvement: Turning evidence into action*. Thousand Oaks, CA: Sage.

Baumfield, V., Hall, E. & Wall, K. (2008). *Action research in the classroom*. London: Sage.

Bautista, A., Tan, L. S., Ponnusamy L. D. & Yau, X. (2016). Curriculum integration in arts education: Connecting multiple art forms through the idea of "space". *Journal of Curriculum Studies*, 48(5), 610–629. doi:10.1080/00220272.2015.1089940.

Becher, A. & Gläser, E. (2018). HisDeKo: A study about the historical thinking of primary school children. *History Education Research Journal*, 15(2), 264–75. DOI https://doi.org/10.18546/HERJ.15.2.08.

Beduchaud, D. (2021). *En Quête d'Ecole épisode 10: Faut-il supprimer les notes? Webradio Kadékol*, IFÉ ENS de Lyon. En ligne: http://ife.ens-lyon.fr/kadekol/en-quete-decole/faut-il-supprimer-les-notes.

Bendrojo ugdymo mokyklų veiklos kokybė [*Quality of activities in general education schools*]. (2015). Vilnius: Nacionalinė mokyklų vertinimo agentūra.

Bendrojo ugdymo programos [*General Education Framework*]. (2022). Vilnius: Nacionalinė mokyklų vertinimo agentūra.

Bendrųjų programų atnaujinimo gairės [*Guidelines for updating the Framework Programmes*]. (2019). Patvirtinta Lietuvos Respublikos švietimo, mokslo ir sporto ministro 2019 m. lapkričio 18 d. įsakymu Nr. V-1317, Lietuvos pažangos strategija „Lietuva 2030", patvirtinta Lietuvos Respublikos Seimo 2012 m. gegužės 15 d., nutarimu Nr. XI-2015. https://www.e-tar.lt/portal/lt/legalAct/e3e9269009e511ea9d279ea27696ab7b

Bendrųjų programų atnaujinimo vadovas [*Guide to updating the Framework Programmes*]. (2020). Vilnius: Švietimo, mokslo ir sporto ministerija. https://www.mokykla2030.lt/wp-content/uploads/2020/12/BP-vadovas_lapkricio_11_red.pdf

Benjamin, M. (2020). Preparing Learning Community Peer Mentors to Support Students' Transitions. *Learning Communities Research and Practice*, 8(2), Article 3. https://washingtoncenter.evergreen.edu/lcrpjournal/vol8/iss2/3.

Bergmark, U. (2022). The role of action research in teachers' efforts to develop research-based education in Sweden: intentions, outcomes, and prerequisite conditions. *Educational Action Research*, 30(3), 427–444. DOI: 10.1080/09650792.2020.1847155.

Bergmark, U., Dahlbäck, A.-Ch., Hagström, A.-K. & Viklund, S. (2023). Leading with care: four mentor metaphors in collaboration between teachers and researchers in action research (Translated from the Swedish and revised by the authors), *Educational Action Research*, DOI: 10.1080/09650792.2023.2229870.

Bianco, M. (2015). *Du langage oral à la compréhension de l'écrit*. Grenoble: PUG. DOI: 10.3917/pug.bianc.2016.01.

Biržų Kaštonų pagrindinės mokyklos veiklos teminio išorinio vertinimo ataskaita [*Report of the thematic external evaluation of Kaštonu primary school, Biržai city*]. (2021). Vilnius: Nacionalinė mokyklų vertinimo agentūra.

Bishara, S. (2021). The cultivation of self-directed learning in teaching mathematics. *World Journal on Educational Technology: Current Issues*, 13(1), 82–95.

Bitinas, B., Rupšienė, L. & Žydžiūnaitė, V. (2008). *Kokybinių tyrimų metodologija* [*Methodology of qualitative research*]. Klaipėda: S. Jokužio leidykla-spaustuvė.

Björklund, C. & Ahlskog-Björkman, E. (2017). Approaches to teaching in thematic work: Early childhood teachers' integration of mathematics and art. *International Journal of Early Years Education*, 25(2), 98–111. doi: 10.1080/09669760.2017.1287061.

Blagoeva, N. V. (2019). Project-based integration of contemporary art forms into teaching visual arts to primary school students in the after-school art clubs. *International Journal of Education & the Arts*, 20(18). http://doi.org/10.26209/ijea20n18.

Blagoeva, N. V., Karppinen, S. & Kairavuori, S. (2019). The integrated approach to teaching visual art in the after-school activity classes. *International Journal of Art & Design Education*, 38(1), 224–239. doi: 10.1111/jade.12173.

Blakely, E. & Hemphill, D. (2021). Opening third spaces for research in education: Challenging the limits of technocratic methods. Myers Education Press.

Blanchet-Cohen, N. & Di Mambro, G. (2015). Environmental Education Action Research with Immigrant Children in Schools: Space, Audience and Influence. *Action Research*, 13(2), 123–140. https://doi.org/10.1177/1476750314553679.

Blomgren, J. (2016). *Den svårfångade motivationen: Elever i en digital lärmiljö* [Hard-won motivation: Students in a digital learning environment]. Doctoral dissertation. Gothenburg University.

Blons-Pierre, C. (2016). Mobilités et compétences en langues étrangères et dans le domaine interculturel: outils et réflexions pour la description, l'évaluation et la reconnaissance de ces compétences. *Journal of international Mobility*, 1(4), 91–108.

Bojović, I. & Antonijević, R. (2017). Students' Motivation to Learn in Primary School. *Open Journal for Psychological Research*, 1(1), 11–20. DOI:10.32591/coas.ojpr.0101.02011b.

Borges, C. & Gervais, C. (2015). L'analyse des pratiques et l'approche de «l'argumentation pratique»: un dispositif de formation et de transformation. *Questions Vives*, 24, 1–21. DOI: 10.4000/questionsvives.1845.

Boss, S. (2020). How Teachers Can Learn Through Action Research. *Edutopia*. https://www.edutopia.org/article/how-teachers-can-learn-through-action-research/.

Boström, L., Bostedt, G., Eriksson, V. & Stenberg, I. (2023). Student conceptions of motivation to study revealed through phenomenography: Differences and similarities among primary school students. *Social Sciences & Humanities Open*, 8(1), 100505. https://doi.org/10.1016/j.ssaho.2023.100505.

Bourassa, B. & Picard, F. (2014). *Apprendre, c'est changer: codéveloppement professionnel de conseillers d'orientation du secteur scolaire*. Présentation au congrès international AIOSP, Québec, 4 juin.

Bradbury, H., Lewis, R. & Embury, D. C. (2019). Education Action Research: With and for the Next Generation. In *The Wiley Handbook of Action Research in Education*, edited by C. A. Mertler, 7–28. London: John Wiley & Sons.

Bramble, A. (2019). *Teachers' implementations of arts integration: a qualitative exploratory case study*. Doctoral dissertation, University of Phoenix.

Braun, V. & Clarke, V. (2006). Using thematic analysis in psychology. *Qualitative Research in Psychology*, *3*(2), 77–101.

Brochu, D. & Villemure, É. (2022). L'apprentissage en profondeur: une voie prometteuse pour développer les compétences du 21e siècle à l'école St-Vincent. Revue hybride de l'éducation, 6(1), 205–218. https://doi.org/10.1522/rhe.v6i1.1230.

Brodeur, M., Dion, É., Laplante, L., Mercier, J., Desrochers, A. & Bournot-Trites, M. (2011). Prévenir les difficultés d'apprentissage en lecture: mobilisation des connaissances issues de la recherche par l'implantation du modèle à trois niveaux. *Vivre le primaire, 23*(1), 30–32.

Broer, M., Bai, Y. & Fonseca, F. (2019). *Socioeconomic Inequality and Educational Outcomes Evidence from Twenty Years of TIMSS*. Publisher: Springer. DOI:10.1007/978-3-030-11991-1.

Brown, C. S. (2014). Language and Literacy Development in the Early Years: Foundational Skills that Support Emergent Readers. *The language and Literacy Spectrum*, 24, 35–49.

Bryk, A. S. (2017). Accélérer la manière dont nous apprenons à améliorer. *Éducation et didactique*, 11–2, 11–29. doi:10.4000/educationdidactique.2796.

Buchs, C. (2017). Comment organiser l'apprentissage des élèves par petits groupes? In: *Différenciation pédagogique: comment adapter l'enseignement pour la réussite de tous les élèves?* (p. 137–146). Paris: Conseil National d'évaluation du Système Scolaire. Prieiga per internetą: https://archive-ouverte.unige.ch/unige:95551.

Bureau de l'UNESCO à Dakar et Bureau régional pour l'éducation en Afrique. (2011). *Guide du planificateur pour l'introduction des langues et cultures africaines dans l'éducation*. Dakar: BREDA.

Bureau de l'UNESCO à Bangkok et Bureau régional pour l'éducation en Asie et dans le Pacifique. 2020. *Tools for planning and monitoring programmes of multilingual education in Asia*. Bangkok: UNESCO Office Bangkok.

Burns, A. & Kurtoğlu-Hooton, N. (2016). *Using action research to explore technology in language teaching: international perspectives*. London: British Council.

Burns, D. (2007). *Systematic action research: A strategy for whole system change*. Bristol, UK: Policy Press.

Burton, N., Brundett, M. & Jones, M. (2008). *Doing your education research project*. London: Sage.

Buslón, N., Gairal, R., León, S., Padrós, M. & Reale, E. (2020). The scientific self-literacy of ordinary people: Scientific dialogic gatherings. *Qualitative Inquiry*, 26(8–9), 977–982. https://doi.org/10.1177/1077800420938725.

Byrd, L. S. (2019). *A study of an arts integration curriculum and its impact on academic achievement*. Doctoral dissertation, University of South Alabama.

Cain, T. & Harris, R. (2013). Teachers' action research in a culture of performativity. *Educational Action Research*, 21(3), 343–358. doi: https://doi.org/10.1080/09650792.2013.815039 https://centaur.reading.ac.uk/37660/.

Cairns, D., Dickson, M. & McMinn, M. (2021). "Feeling Like a scientist": Factors Affecting students' Selections of Technology Tools in the Science Classroom. *Journal of Science Education and Technology*, 30(6): 766–776. https://doi.org/10.1007/s10956-021-09917-0.

Camponovo, S. & Moody, Z. (2021). Le chemin de l'école: un tiers-lieu vecteur d'apprentissages pour les enfants? In: *Schweizerische Zeitschrift für Bildungswissenschaften* 43,2,311–324. Enligne: URN:urn:nbn:de:0111-pedocs-231302 - DOI: 10.25656/01:23130.

Cannon, M. A. (2017). *Differentiated Mathematics Instruction: An Action Research Study*. Doctoral dissertation. https://scholarcommons.sc.edu/etd/4222.

Carignan, I., Beaudry, M.-Ch. & Larose, F. (2016). *La recherche-action et la recherche-développement au service de la littératie*. Les Éditions de l'université de Sherbrooke. DOI: http://dx.doi.org/10.17118/11143/8815.

Carling, J. (2019). *Research ethics and research integrity*. MIGNEX handbook, chapter 4 (v1). Oslo: Peace Research Institute Oslo.

Carrette, V. & Rey, B. (2010). L'approche par compétences. In *Savoir enseigner dans le secondaire. Didactique générale*. (pp. 63–104). Bruxelles, Belgique: De Boeck.

Castro Garcés, A. Y. & Martínez Granada, L. (2016). The role of collaborative action research in teachers' professional development. *PROFILE Issues in Teachers' Professional Development*, 18(1), 39–54. http://dx.doi.org/10.15446/profile. v18n1.49148.

Cerino, A. (2021). The importance of recognising and promoting independence in young children: the role of the environment and the Danish forest school approach. *Education 3–13*, *51*(4), 685–694. https://doi.org/10.1080/03004279.2021.2000468.

Cerna, L. (2019). *Refugee education: Integration models and practices in OECD countries*. OECD Education Working Papers, No. 203, OECD Publishing, Paris. https://doi.org/10.1787/a3251a00-en.

Chapman, Ch., Armstrong, P., Harris, A., Muijs, D., Reynolds, D. & Sammons, P. (2011). *School Effectiveness and Improvement Research, Policy and Practice*. London: Routledge. https://doi.org/10.4324/9780203136553.

Charlier, B. (2005). Parcours de recherche-action-formation. *Revue des sciences de l'éducation, XXXI*(2), 259–272.

Chartrand, S. G., Émery-Bruneau, J. & Sénéchal, K. (2015). *Caractéristiques de 50 genres pour développer les compétences langagières en français* (2e édition). Québec, Canada: Didactica.

Childress, D. M. (2019). *Teachers Engaging in Action Research to Increase Learner Agency*. Graduate Theses and Dissertations Retrieved from https://scholarworks.uark.edu/etd/3449.

Čiužas R. (2013). *Mokytojo kompetencijos. Profesinio meistriškumo siekis* [*Teacher competences. The pursuit of professional excellence*]. Vilnius: Edukologija.

Clark, I. (2012). Formative Assessment: A Systematic and Artistic Process of Instruction for Supporting School and Lifelong Learning. *Canadian Journal of Education*. Vol. 35, No. 2, 24–40. https://www.jstor.org/stable/canajeducrevucan.35.2.24.

Clerc, N. & Agogué, M. (2019). Un dispositif d'analyse de pratiques en formation universitaire de formateurs et ses effets sur leur professionnalisation. In *Revue de l'analyse de pratiques professionnelles*, No 15, 60–77. http://www.analysedepratique.org/?p=3365.

Cochran-Smith, M. & Lytle, S. L. (2009). *Inquiry as stance: Practitioner research for the next generation*. New York: Teachers College Press.

Cockerill, M., N. Craig, & Thurston, A. (2018). Teacher Perceptions of the Impact of Peer Learning in Their Classrooms: Using Social Interdependence Theory as a Model for Data Analysis and Presentation. *International Journal of Education and Practice*, *6*(1), 14–27. doi:10.18488/journal.61.2018.61.14.27.

Codina, G. & Robinson, D. (2024). Teachers' Continuing Professional Development: Action Research for Inclusion and Special Educational Needs and Disability. *Educ. Sci*, *14*(140). https://doi.org/10.3390/educsci14020140.

Collier, P. J. (2015). *Developing effective student peer mentoring programs*. Stylus.

Colvin, J. W. & Ashman, M. (2010). Roles, risks, and benefits of peer mentoring relationships in higher education. *Mentoring & Tutoring: Partnership in Learning*, 18(2), 121–134.

Connett, H. (2020). Action research to improve confidence in meeting diverse needand the quality of inclusive practice through lesson observations. *Support for Learning*, 35 (2), 178–191.

Conradie, P. W. (2014). Supporting Self-Directed Learning by Connectivism and Personal Learning Environments. *International Journal of Information and Education Technology*, 4(3), 254–259.

Contreras, D. & Aceituno, D. (2017). Learning to teach citizenship competencies through a school-university collaborative action research project. *Procedia – Social and Behavioral Sciences*, 237, 90 – 95. doi: 10.1016/j.sbspro.2017.02.035//.

Cooper, H. (2014a). *Professional Studies in Primary Education*. London: Sage.

Cooper, H. (2014b). *Writing History 7–11*. London: Routledge.

Cox, C., Jaramillo, R. & Reimers, F. (2005). Education for citizenship and democracy in the Americas: An agenda for action. Washington DC: Inter-American Development Bank.

Creswell, J. W. (2017). *Educational research: planning, conducting, and evaluating quantitative and qualitative research, global edition* (H. Eksi, Trans. Ed.). İstanbul: EDAM Yayimcilik.

Crocetti, E., Erentaitė, R. & Žukauskienė, R. (2014). Identity styles, positive youth development, and civic engagement in adolescence. *Journal of Youth and Adolescence*, 43(11), 1818–1828, doi: 10.1007/s10964-014-0100-4.

Culp, M. E. & Wayman Davis, V. (2023). Using Students' Interests in General Music (Part 1): Getting to Know Learners and Conducting Research. *Journal of General Music Education*, 36(2): 275276462311576, DOI: 10.1177/27527646231157675.

Cutting, R. & Kelly, O. (2015). *Creative teaching in primary science*. SAGE Publications. https://doi.org/10.4135/9781473910195.

Daar, G. F. (2020). Problems of English Language Learning in Context (Based on some Studies in Manggarai). Penerbit: PKBM SAMBI POLENG.

Dadvand, B. & Lampert, J. (2024). Addressing teacher shortages in hard-to-staff schools. *Asia-Pacific Journal of Teacher Education*, *52*(3), 271–275. https://doi.org/10.1080/1359866X.2024.2348261.

Dana, N. F. & Yendol-Hoppey, D. (2009). *The reflective educator's guide to classroom research: Learning to teach and teaching to learn through practitioner research* (2nd ed.). Thousand Oaks, CA: Corwin Press.

Dana, N. F. & Yendol-Hoppey, D. (2019). *The reflective educator's guide to classroom research: Learning to teach and teaching to learn through practitioner inquiry* (3rd ed.). Thousand Oaks, CA: Corwin.

Darling-Hammond, L., Flook, L., Cook-Harvey, C., Barron, B. & Osher, D. (2019). Implications for educational practice of the science of learning and development. *Applied Developmental Science*, *24*(2), 97–140. https://doi.org/10.1080/10888691.2018.1537791.

Davis, J., Clayton, C. & Broome, J. (2018). Thinking like Researchers: Action Research and Its Impact on Novice Teachers' Thinking. *Educational Action Research*, 26 (1): 59–74. doi:10.1080/09650792.2017.1284012.

Davitt. G. & Ryder, D. (2019). Dispositions of a responsible early childhood education leader: Voices from the field. *Journal of Educational Leadership, Policy and Practice*. Vol. 33 (1), 18–31. DOI: https://doi.org/10.21307/jelpp-2018-003.

Demirel, M. & Caymaz, B. (2015). Prospective Science and Primary School Teachers' Self-efficacy Beliefs in Scientific Literacy. Procedia – Social and Behavioral Sciences, 191:1903–1908. DOI:10.1016/j.sbspro.2015.04.500.

Denscombe, M. (2010). *The good research guide for small-scale social research projects*. McGraw Hill: Open University Press.

Diesel, R. & Scheepers, C. B. (2019). Innovation climate mediating complexity leadership and ambidexterity. *Personnel Review*, 48(7), 1782–1808. https://doi.org/10.1108/PR-11-2018-0445.

Díez-Palomar, J., Font Palomar, M., Aubert, A. & Garcia-Yeste, C. (2022). Dialogic Scientific Gatherings: The Promotion of Scientific Literacy Among Children. *Sage Open*, 12(4). https://doi.org/10.1177/21582440221121783.

Dimmock, C. (2016). Conceptualising the Research–practice–professional Development Nexus: Mobilising Schools as "Research-engaged" Professional Learning Communities. *Professional Development in Education*, 42 (1): 36–53. doi:10.1080/19415257.2014.963884.

Dion, É., Brodeur, M., Gosselin, C., Campeau, M.-È. & Fuchs, D. (2010). Implementing Research-Based Instruction to Prevent Reading Problems among Low-Income Students: Is Earlier Better? *Learning Disabilities Research & Practice, 25*(2), 87–96.

Dixon, A. (2023). *Student Engagement Action Research a Focus on Culturally Relevant Instructional Methods*. Doctoral dissertation. https://scholarcommons.sc.edu/etd/7286.

Dolbec, A. & Clément, J. (2000). La recherche-action. In: T. Karsenti et L. Savoie-Zajc (dir.), *Introduction à la recherche en éducation* (p. 199–224). Sherbrooke: Éditions du CRP. Dumais, C. (2011). L'oral pragmatique: un enseignement de l'oral près de la réalité des élèves. *Vivre le primaire, 24*(1), 42–44.

Domínguez, J. (2015). *Pensamiento Histórico y Evaluación de Competencias*. Barcelona: Editorial GRAÓ.

Donohoo, J. (2017). Collective efficacy: How educator's beliefs impact student learning. Thousand Oaks, CA: Corwin.

Druskininkų „Atgimimo" mokyklos veiklos teminio išorinio vertinimo ataskaita [*Report of the thematic external evaluation of the Druskininkai "Atgimimas" School*]. (2021). Vilnius: Nacionalinė mokyklų vertinimo agentūra.

Dubosas, M. (2016). *Studentų savivaldaus mokymosi skatinimas taikant interaktyviąsias technologijas* [*Promoting student self-directed learning through interactive technologies*]. Daktaro disertacija. Kaunas: Kauno technologijos universitetas.

Dumais, C. (2015). Une typologie des objets de l'oral pour la formation initiale et continue des enseignants. In R. Bergeron, C. Dumais, B. Harvey et R. Nolin (dir.), *La didactique du français oral du primaire à l'université* (p. 29–52). Côte-Saint-Luc, Canada: Peisaj, coll. Cogito.

Dumais, C. & Messier, G. (2016). L'atelier formatif: un modèle didactique pour enseigner l'oral. *Enjeux, revue de formation continuée et de didactique du français*, 90, 5–24.

Dumais, C. & Lafontaine, L. (2011). L'oral à l'école québécoise: portrait des recherches actuelles. *Revue suisse des sciences de l'éducation*, 33(2), 285–302.

Dumont, H., Istance, D. & Benavides, F. (2010). *The Nature of Learning. Using research to inspire practice*. OECD Publishing. http://www.oecd.org/education/ceri/50300814.pdf

Duran, D., Flores, M., Oller, M. & Marcela, R. (2019). Reading in Pairs, Description and Results of a Peer Tutoring Program for English as a Foreign Language. *Innovation in Language Learning and Teaching*, 13(4), 303–317. doi: 10.1080/17501229.2018.1462370.

Duran, E. & Karatas, A. (2019). Elimination of Writing Difficulty in Primary School: An Action Research. *International Journal of Progressive Education*, 15(5), 288–299. doi: 10.29329/ijpe.2019.212.19*(9)*.

Eady, M. J. & Lockyer, L. (2013). Tools for learning: technology and teaching strategies. *Learning to Teach in the Primary School*. Queensland University of Technology, Australia. pp. 71. http://ro.uow.edu.au/asdpapers/403.

Eden, C. & Ackermann, F. (2018). Theory into practice, practice to theory: Action research in method development. *European Journal of Operational Research*, 271(3), 1145–1155. https://doi.org/10.1016/j.ejor.2018.05.061.

Education and Training, Monitor, Finland. (2019). European Union: Luxembourg: Publications Office. https://education.ec.europa.eu/sites/default/files/document-library-docs/et-monitor-report-2019-finland_en.pdf.

Edwards-Groves, C., Grootenboer, P. & Ronnerman, K. (2016). Facilitating a culture of relational trust in school-based action research: recognising the role of middle leaders. *Educational Action Research*, *24*(3), 369–386. https://doi.org/10.1080/09650792.2015.1131175.

Edwards-Groves, C., Olin, A. & Karlberg-Granlund, G. (2016). Partnership and Recognition in Action Research: Understanding the Practices and Practice Architectures for Participation and Change. *Educational Action Research*, 24(3), 321–333. doi:10.1080/09650792.2015.1129983.

Efron, S. E. & Ravid, R. (2013). *Action Research in Education: A Practical Guide*. New Yourk, London: The Guilford Press.

El Islami, R. A. Z. & Nuangchalerm, P. (2020). Comparative study of scientific literacy: Indonesian and Thai pre-service science teachers report. *International Journal of Evaluation and Research in Education*, 9(2), 261–268.

Elo, S. & Kyngäs, H. (2008). The qualitative content analysis process, *Journal of Advanced Nursing*, vol. 62, no. 1, pp. 107–115.

Engeström, Y. & Sannino, A. (2021). From Mediated Actions to Heterogenous Coalitions: Four Generations of Activity-Theoretical Studies of Work and Learning. *Mind Culture and Activity*, *28*(1): 4–23. https://doi.org/10.1080/10749039.2020.1806328.

Engeström, Y., Rantavuori, P., Ruutu, P. & Tapola-Haapala, M. (2023). Finding Life Beyond the Classroom Walls: A Change Laboratory Supporting Expansive de-Encapsulation of School. *Éducation & Didactique*, *17*(2), 124–141. https://doi.org/10.4000/educationdidactique.11773.

Escorcia, D. & Fenouillet, F. (2018). Connaissances métacognitives et stratégies d'autorégulation impliquées dans la révision de textes: construction et validation d'un instrument autorapporté. *Mesure et évaluation en éducation*, 41(2), 1–36. https://doi.org/10.7202/1059171ar.

Esparza, D., Lynch-Arroyo, R. L. & Olimpo, J. T. (2022). Empowering Current and Future Educators: Using a Scalable Action Research Module as a Mechanism to Promote High-Quality Teaching and Learning in STEM. *Front. Educ.* 6:754097. doi: 10.3389/feduc.2021.754097.

Étienne, R. & Fumat, Y. (2014). Comment analyser les pratiques éducatives pour se former et agir? Bruxelles: De Boeck, coll. *Perspectives en éducation et formation*, p. 1–282. DOI: 10.4000/rechercheformation.2347.

European Commission (2017). *Communication from the Commission to the European parliament, the Council, The European economic and social committee and the Committee of the regions: School development and excellent teaching for a great start in life*. (2017). https://op.europa.eu/en/publication-detail/-/publication/aa9ffc00-4524-11e7-aea8-01aa75ed71a1/language-en/format-PDF.

European Commission/EACEA/Eurydice. (2019). *Teaching Careers in Europe: Access, Progression and Support*. https://op.europa.eu/en/publication-detail/-/publication/435e941e-1c3b-11e8-ac73-01aa75ed71a1/language-en

Eurydice. (2009). *L'éducation et l'accueil des jeunes enfants en Europe: réduire les inégalités sociales et culturelles*. Bruxelles: Commission européenne.

Eurydice. (2024). *Pradinis ugdymas: Lietuva* [*Primary education in Lithuania*]. Bruxelles: Commission européenne. https://eurydice.eacea.ec.europa.eu/lt/national-education-systems/lithuania/pradinis-ugdymas.

Feldman, A. (2023). Participatory and Critical Action Research. *Educational Action Research*, 31 (4), 611–619. https://doi.org/10.1080/09650792.2023.2252212.

Feldman, A., Altrichter, H., Posch, P. & Somekh, B. (2018). *Teachers investigate their work. An introduction to action research* (3rd ed.). New York, NY: Routledge.

Finch, M. (2022). Complexities of Practitioner Research: Seeking Hallmarks of Quality. *Impacting Education: Journal on Transforming Professional Practice*, 7(3), 1–10. DOI 10.5195/ie.2022.256.

Fine, M. & Torre, M. E. (2021). *Essentials of Critical Participatory Action Research (Essentials of Qualitative Methods)*. New York: American Psychological Association.

Fortin, M. F. (2010). *Fondements et étapes du processus de recherche: méthodes quantitatives et qualitatives*. 2e édition. Montréal: Cheneličre Éducation.

Fullan, M. (2019). *Nuance: Why some leaders succeed and others fail*. Thousand Oaks, CA: Corwin. Nuance: Why Some Leaders Succeed and Others Fail – Michael Fullan – Google Books.

Fullan, M. (2020). Learning and the pandemic: What's next? *Prospects*, Vol. 49, 25–28. https://link.springer.com/article/10.1007/s11125-020-09502-0.

Fullan, M. & Gallagher, M. J. (2020). *The devil is in the details: System solutions for equity, excellence, and student well-being*. Thousand Oaks, CA: Corwin.

Fullan, M. & Gallagher, M. J. (2020). *The devil is in the details: System solutions for equity, excellence, and student well-being*. Thousand Oaks, CA: Corwin.

Fullan, M. & Quinn, J. (2020). *How Do Disruptive Innovators Prepare Today's Students to Be Tomorrow's Workforce?: Deep Learning: Transforming Systems to Prepare Tomorrow's Citizens*. Inter-American Development Bank. http://dx.doi.org/10.18235/0002959.

Fullan, M. & Quinn, J. (2023). *The Drivers: Transforming Learning for Students, Schools, and Systems*. California: Corwin Press.

Fullan, M., Azorin, C., Harris, A. & Jones, M. (2023). Artificial intelligence and school leadership: challenges, opportunities and implications. *School Leadership & Management*. DOI: 10.1080/13632434.2023.2246856.

Fullan, M., Quinn, J., Drummy, M. & Gardner, M. (2020). Education Reimagined: The Future of Learning. Microsoft-EducationReimagined-Paper.pdf (azureedge.net).

Future of Education Skills. (2020). OECD Learning Compass 2030. http://www.oecd.org/education/2030-project/contact/OECD_Learning_Compass_2030_Concept_Note_Series.pdf.

Gandolfi, H. E. (2021). "It's a lot of people in different places working on many ideas": Possibilities from global history of science to Learning about nature of science. *Journal of Research in Science Teaching*, 58(4), 551–588.

Gao, N. & Lafortune, J. (2020). *Improving K-12 school facilities in California.* Public Policy Institute of California.

Gaučaitė, R., Masiliauskienė, E., Kazlauskienė, A. & Pocevičienė, R. (2012). *Savivaldaus mokymosi, orientuoto į inovatyvius sprendimus, sistema* [*A framework for self-directed learning focused on innovative solutions*]. Šiauliai: VšĮ Šiaulių universiteto leidykla.

Gauthier, A. (2010). *Proposition de composantes d'une situation d'apprentissage et d'évaluation (SAÉ) modèle en français écrit à la première année du deuxième cycle du secondaire* (Mémoire de maitrise inédit). Université du Québec en Outaouais.

Geros mokyklos koncepcija [*The concept of a good school*]. (2015). Patvirtinta Lietuvos Respublikos švietimo ir mokslo ministro, 2015 m. gruodžio 21 d. Nr. V-1308.

Gilbert, K. A., Voelkel, R. H., Jr & Johnson, C. W. (2018). Increasing Self-Efficacy through Immersive Simulations: Leading Professional Learning Communities. *Journal of Leadership Education*, 17(3), 154–174.

Gohard-Radenkovic, A. (2017). Contre-point. Quand la toute-mobilité peut devenir l'immobilisation des acteurs de la mobilité … et quand sociétés d'accueil et de départ produisent du "brain waste". *Journal of International Mobility, 1*(5), 157–176. Retrieved from: https://www.cairn.info/revue-journal-of-international-mobility-2017-1-page-157.htm.

Gohard-Radenkovic, A. & Veillette, J. (2016). De nouveaux espaces dans de nouvelles logiques migratoires? Entre mobilités et immobilités des acteur. *Cahiers internationaux de sociolinguistique*, *2*(8), 19–46. Prieiga per internetą: https://www.cairn.info/revue-cahiers-internationaux-de-sociolinguistique-2015-2-page-19.htm.

Goodnough, K. (2016). Professional learning of K-6 teachers in science through collaborative action research: An activity theory analyses. *Journal of Science Teacher Education*, 27, 747–767. doi:10.1007/s10972-016-9485-0.

Gordon, S. P. & Solis, R. D. (2018). Teacher Leaders of Collaborative Action Research: Challenges and Rewards. i.e.: inquiry in education, *10*(2), Article 3. https://digitalcommons.nl.edu/ie/vol10/iss2/3.

Gordon, S. P. & Solis, R. D. (2018). Teacher Leaders of Collaborative Action Research: Challenges and Rewards. *i.e.: inquiry in education*, 10(2), Article 3. https://digitalcommons.nl.edu/ie/vol10/iss2/3.

Granziera, H., Collie, R. J. & Martin, A. J. (2019). Adaptability: An important capacity to cultivate among pre-service teachers in teacher education programmes. Psychology Teaching Review, 25(1), 60–66. https://files.eric.ed.gov/fulltext/EJ1216443.pdf.

Grosstephan, V. (2015). Accompagner la mastérisation de la formation des enseignants en France: un dispositif de régulation pour les formateurs des IUFM. *Questions Vives*, N° 24, 1–19. DOI: 10.4000/questionsvives.1786.

Guay, M. H. & Prud'homme, L. (2011). La recherche-action. Dans T. Karsenti et L. Savoie-Zajc (dir.), *La recherche en éducation* (p. 183–211). Saint-Laurent, Québec: ERPI.

Guillemin, M. & Gillam, L. (2004). Ethics, Reflexivity, and "Ethically important moments" in Research. *Qualitative Inquiry*, 10, 261–280.

Guion, L. A. (2002). *Triangulation: Establishing the Validity of Qualitative Studies*. Gainesville: Department of Family, Youth and Community Sciences, Cooperative Extension Service, Institute of Food and Agricultural Sciences, University of Florida.

Haager, D., Klingner, J. & Vaughn, S. (2007). *Evidence-Based Reading Practices for Response to Intervention*. Baltimore, États-Unis: Paul H. Brookes Publishing.

Haidman, M. M., Mahinda, R., Bull, J., Carran, T. D. & Shelton, A. (2019). The Effects of arts-integrated instruction on memory for science content. *Trends in Neuroscience and Education*, 14(3), 25–32. https://doi.org/10.1016/j.tine.2019.02.002.

Håland, A., Wagner, Åse K. H. & McTigue, E. (2021). How do Norwegian second-grade teachers use guided reading? The quantity and quality of practices. *L1-Educational Studies in Language and Literature, 21*(1), 1–28. https://doi.org/10.17239/L1ESLL-2021.21.01.02.

Hargreaves, A. & Fullan, M. (2019). *Profesinis kapitalas: Ugdymo pertvarka kiekvienoje mokykloje* [*Professional capital: transforming education in every school*]. Vilnius: Eugrimas.

Harper, S. G. (2017). Engaging Karen Refugee Students in Science Learning Through a Cross-Cultural Learning Community. *International Journal of Science Education*, 39 (3): 358–376. https://doi.org/10.1080/09500693.2017.1283547.

Harris, L. R. & Brown, G. T. L. (2018). *Using self-assessment to improve student learning*. Routledge.

Hassan, R. (2012). La didactique de l'oral, d'un chantier à un autre ? *Repères*, 46, p. 11–129. DOI: 10.4000/reperes.94.

Hatfield, B. E., Burchinal, M. R., Pianta, R. C. & Sideris, J. (2016). Thresholds in the association between quality of teacher–child interactions and preschool children's school readiness skills. *Early Childhood Research Quarterly*, 36, 561–571. https://psycnet.apa.org/doi/10.1016/j.ecresq.2015.09.005.

Hattie, J. A. C. (2009). *Visible Learning*. Taylor & Francis Group: Routledge.

Hattie, J. A. C. & Donoghue, G. M. (2016). Learning strategies: a synthesis and conceptual model. *npj Science Learn* 1, 16013. https://doi.org/10.1038/npjscilearn.2016.13.

Hawamdeh, A. A. A. (2020). How Does the Role-Playing Strategy Affect the Development of Interpretive Skill for Astronomical Phenomena Among Fourth-Grade Female Students? *Action Research and Innovation in Science Education*, 3(2), 39–42. https://doi.org/10.51724/arise.34.

Häyrynen, S., Keinonen, T. & Kärkkäinen, S. (2021). Promoting environmental citizenship through local socio-cultural traditions in science education. *Discourse and Communication for Sustainable Education*, 12(2), 5–30.

Helmke, A. (2012). *Pamokos kokybė ir mokytojo profesionalumas: diagnostika, vertinimas, tobulinimas [Lesson quality and teacher professionalism: diagnosis, evaluation, improvement]*. Vilnius: Nacionalinė mokyklų vertinimo agentūra.

Hendricks, C. (2012). *Improving schools through action research: A reflective practice approach* (3rd ed.). Upper Saddle River, NJ: Pearson.

Henriksen, D., Richardson, C. & Mehta, R. (2017). Design thinking: A creative approach to educational problems of practice. *Thinking Skills and Creativity*, 26, 140–153.

Herder, A., Berenst, J., de Glopper, K. & Koole, T. (2020). Sharing knowledge with peers: Epistemic displays in collaborative writing of primary school children. *Learning, Culture and Social Interaction*, *24*, [100378]. https://doi.org/10.1016/j.lcsi.2020.100378.

Herr, K. G. & Nihlen, A. S. (2007). *Studying your own school: An educator's guide to practitioner research* (2nd ed.). Thousand Oaks, CA: Corwin Press.

Hesse-Biber, S. N. (2017). *The Practice of Qualitative Research: Engaging Students in the Research Process*, 3 rd ed. CA, USA, Los Angeles: SAGE.

Hillen, S. A. (2020). School staff-centered school development by communicative action: working methods for creating collective responsibility-from the idea to action. *Journal on Efficiency and Responsibility in Education and Science*, 13(4), 189–203.

Holly, M. L., Arhar, J. M. & Kasten, W. C. (2009). *Action research for teachers: Travelling the yellow brick road* (3rd ed.). Upper Saddle River, NJ: Pearson.

Hopwood, N. (2024). Twenty-five years of change laboratories in schools: a critical and formative review. *Educational Action Research*, 1–28. https://doi.org/10.1080/09650792.2024.2379343.

Houssaye, J. (2019). Pédagogie et sciences de l'éducation: pas facile! *Les Sciences de l'éducation – our l'Ère nouvelle*, 52(2), 11–27.

Hubalovsky, S., Hubalovska, M. & Musilek, M. (2019). Assessment of the influence of adaptive E-learning on learning effectiveness of primary school pupils. Computers in Human Behavior. Vol. 92, 691–705. https://doi.org/10.1016/j.chb.2018.05.033.

Ingersoll, R. M. & Tran, H. (2023). Teacher shortages and turnover in rural schools in the US: An organizational analysis. *Educational Administration Quarterly*, 59(2), 396–431. https://doi.org/10.1177/0013161X231159922.

Israel, M. (2015). *Research Ethics and Integrity for Social Scientists: Beyond Regulatory Compliance*. London: SAGE Publications Ltd.

Istorijos pamoka: mokyti ar mokytis? [History lesson: to teach or to learn?] (2012). *Švietimo problemos analizė*, 18(82), 1–12.

Įtraukties link. Ką turi žinoti mokykla? [*Towards inclusion. What does a school need to know?*] (2022). Vilnius: Nacionalinė mokyklų vertinimo agentūra. https://www.nsa.smm.lt/wp-content/uploads/2022/12/Itraukties-link.-Ka-turi-zinoti-mokykla.Atmintine-mokykloms.pdf.

Jacq, C. & Gibert, A. F. (2019). Travailler ensemble pour enseigner mieux. In *Édubref. L'essentiel pour comprendre les questions éducative*. https://eduveille.hypotheses.org/files/2019/01/Edubref-janvier-2019.pdf.

Jakavonytė-Staškuvienė, D. & Ignatavičiūtė, L. (2022). Experience of mentors and beginner primary school teachers in applying the principles of shared leadership during the school adaptation period: The case of Lithuania. *Cogent Education*, 9:1, 2070054, DOI:10.1080/2331186X.2022.2070054.

Jakavonytė-Staškuvienė, D. (2017). The policy of integrated languages didactics in Lithuania. *Problemy Wczesnej Edukacji*, *37*(2), 111–122. https://doi.org/10.5604/01.3001.0010.5584.

Jakavonytė-Staškuvienė, D. (2021). Development of primary schoolchildren's argumentation skills and reflection on activity through pair work. In: Initiatives collaboratives pour l'enfance: Quelles mutations de l'éducation et du travail social [Collaborative initiatives for childhood: mutations in education and social work] Sous la direction de Frédéric Torterat et Brahim Azaoui. Montpellier: Presses universitaires de la Méditerranée.

Jakavonytė-Staškuvienė, D. (2021a). A study of language and cognitive aspects in primary school pupils' and teachers' activities through cooperative learning. *Educational sciences: theory and practice*. Istanbul: EDAM-Education Consultancy Limited, 21(3), 88 – 106.

Jakavonytė-Staškuvienė, D. (2021b). The benefits of cooperative learning of language in different subject lessons as seen by primary school pupils: the case of one Lithuanian city school. *Education research international*. London: Hindawi, Vol. 2021, article ID 6441222, 1–11.

Jakavonyte-Staskuviene, D., Jašinauskas, L. & Kudinoviene, J. (2022). Some principles applied to Action Research in Lithuania. *Lirdef*, (actes n°1). 10.34745/numerev_1799.

Jakavonytė-Staškuvienė, D., Jašinauskas, L. & Kudinovienė, J. (2023). An analysis of prospective primary school teachers' action research: the case of Lithuania. *Educational Action Research*, 1–16. https://doi.org/10.1080/09650792.2023.2298744.

Jakavonytė-Staškuvienė, D., Žemgulienė, A. & Sakadolskis, E.-A. (2021). Cooperative learning issues in elementary education: A Lithuanian case study. *Journal of education culture and society*. Wroclaw: University of Wroclaw, 12(1), 445–468.

James Long, S. Ch. & Bae, Y. (2018). Action Research: First-Year Primary School Science Teachers' Conceptions on and Enactment of Science Inquiry in Singapore. *Asia-Pacific Science Education*, 4:2, 1–20. DOI 10.1186/s41029-017-0017-9.

Jarl, M., Blossing, U. & Andersson, K. (2017). Att Organisera För Skolframgång: Strategier För En Likvärdig Skola [To Organize for School Success: Strategies for an Equal School]. Malmö: Natur & Kultur.

Jašinauskas, L. (2019). Edukologinė novelė apie pamoką: ar pamokose mokome mokytis savivaldžiai? [An educational novella about the classroom: do we learn to learn in a self-managed way in the classroom?] *Švietimo naujienos*. Vilnius: Nacionalinė švietimo agentūra.

Jašinauskas, L., Lauciuvienė, A., Norkūnienė, R. E., Papšienė, P., Pavlovič-Jančis, A., Zablackė, R. & Zabulionienė, J. (2021). *Įtraukiojo ugdymo įgyvendinimo kryptingumas mokyklose, vykdančiose bendrojo ugdymo programas. Teminio išorinio vertinimo ataskaita* [*Targeting inclusive education in schools, in schools delivering general education programmes. Thematic External Evaluation Report*]. Vilnius: Nacionalinės švietimo agentūra.

Jegelevičienė, V. & Prakapas, R. (2018). *Bendrojo ugdymo mokytojų bendrųjų kompetencijų tobulinimo(si) poreikio ir turinio analizė* [*Analysis of the need for and content of general competences development for general education teachers*]. Vilnius: Ugdymo plėtotės centras.

Johannesson, P. (2020). Development of professional learning communities through action research: understanding professional learning in practice. *Educational Action Research*, 1–16. DOI: 10.1080/09650792.2020.1854100.

Johnson, A. P. (2011). *A short guide to action research* (4th ed.). Upper Saddle River, NJ: Pearson.

Johnson, D. W. & Johnson, R. T. (2015). Theoretical approaches to cooperative learning. In R. M. Gillies (Ed.), *Collaborative Learning: Developments in Research and Practice* (p. 17–46). New York: Nova Science.

Johnson, D. W., Johnson, R. T., Roseth, C. J. & Shin, T. S. (2014). The relationship between motivation and achievement in interdependent situations. *Journal of Applied Social Psychology, 44*(9), 622–633.

Jokela, T. (2019). Art-based action research for art education in the north. *Int J Art Des Educ*, 38(3): 599–609. https://doi.org/10.1111/jade.12243.

Jonnaert, P., Depover, Ch. & Malu, R. (2020). *Curriculum et situations*. Un cadre méthodologique pour le développement de programmes éducatifs. Bruxelles: De Boeck Université.

Jordan-Douglass, A. (2019). Artist/teacher partnerships: exploring pathways to arts integration in STEM Cur-riculum. Doctoral dissertation, University of Wisconsin-Madison.

Jørgensen, M. & Phillips, L. (2002). Discourse Analysis as Theory and Method. London, Thousand Oaks, New Delhi: SAGE Publications.

Jovaiša, L. (2007). *Enciklopedinis edukologijos žodynas* [*Encyclopaedic dictionary of education*]. Vilnius: Gimtasis žodis.

Julia, J., Iswara, P. D., Gunara, S., Yildiz, Y. M. & Agustian, E. (2020). Developing Elementary School Teacher Competence in Making Music Learning Media

Using Scratch Application: An Action Research. *Mimbar Sekolah Dasar*, *7*(3), 362–385. doi: https://doi.org/10.17509/mimbar-sd.v7i3.29100.

Jumriani, J., Mutiani, M., Putra, M. A. H., Syaharuddin, S. & Abbas, E. W. (2021). The urgency of local wisdom content in social studies learning: Literature review. *The Innovation of Social Studies Journal*, 2(2), 103–109.

Juškevičienė, A. (2020). *Bendrųjų kompetencijų ugdymasis skirtingų mokomųjų dalykų kontekste: tarp fragmentiškumo ir sistemingumo* [*Developing generic competences in the context of different subjects: between fragmentation and systematicity*]. Vilnius: Nacionalinė švietimo agnetūra.

Kaišiadorių r. Palomenės pagrindinės mokyklos veiklos išorinio rizikos vertinimo ataskaita [*Report of the external risk assessment of the Palomenės basic schools, Kaišiadorys district*]. (2019). Vilnius: Nacionalinė mokyklų vertinimo agentūra.

Kalalahti, M., Silvennoinen, H., Varjo, J. & Rinne, R. (2015). Education for all? Urban parental attitudes towards universalism and selectivism in the Finnish comprehensive school system. In Seppänen, P., Carrasco, A., Kalalahti, M., Rinne, R. & Simola, H. (eds). *Contrasting Dynamics in Education Politics of Extremes: school choice in Chile and Finland*. Rotterdam: Sense Publishers, 205–224.

Kamarudin, M. Z., & Mat Noor, M. S. A. (2023). What do we know about the selection of action research methodologies in primary science education? – A systematic literature review. *Educational Action Research*, 1–23. https://doi.org/10.1080/09650792.2023.2261502.

Karakolidis, A., Duggan, A., Shiel, G. & Kiniry, J. (2021). Examining educational inequalities: insights in the context of improved mathematics performance on national and international assessments at primary level in Ireland. *Large-scale Assess Educ* 9, 5. https://doi.org/10.1186/s40536-021-00098-1.

Kardelis, K. (2005). *Mokslinių tyrimų metodologija ir metodai* [*Research methodology and methods*]. Šiauliai: Lucilijus.

Kauno rajono Raudondvario Anelės ir Augustino Kriauzų pradinės mokyklos veiklos teminio išorinio vertinimo ataskaita [*Report of the thematic external evaluation of Raudondvaris Anelė and Augustinas Kriauzai primary school, Kaunas district*]. (2022). Vilnius: Nacionalinė mokyklų vertinimo agentūra.

Kazlauskienė, A. & Gaučaitė, R. (2018). *Formuojamasis vertinimas – individualiai pažangai skatinti* [*Formative assessment – to promote individual progress*]. Vilnius: Švietimo aprūpinimo centras.

Kazragytė, V. & Kudinovienė, J. (2018). Formative Assessment in Arts Education Lessons: Episodic or Integrated with Effective Teaching? *Pedagogika: mokslo darbai*, 131 (3), p. 217–232. http://www.pedagogika.leu.lt/index.php/Pedagogika/article/view/989/413.

Kelechukwu, N. (2011). Analysis of administrative roles in private secondary schools in Aba Education Zone of Abia State. *Continental Journal of Education Research*, 4 (1), 113–142.

Kellum, S. & Olson, S. L. (2023). The impact of sustainable buildings on educational achievements in K-12 schools. *Leonardo*, 2, 1–14.

Kemmis, S. & Mutton, R. (2012). Education for sustainability (EfS): Practice and practice architectures. *Environmental Education Research*, 18(2), 187–207. doi: 10.1080/13504622.2011.596929.

Kemmis, S. & Grootenboer, P. (2008). Situating praxis in practice: Practice architectures and the cultural, social and material conditions for practice. In S. Kemmis & T. Smith (Eds.), *Enabling praxis: Challenges for education* (pp. 37–62). Rotterdam, Netherlands: Sense.

Kemmis, S., Edwards-Groves, C., Wilkinson, J. & Hardy, I. (2012). Ecologies of practices. In P. Hager, A. Lee, & A. Reich (Eds.), *Practice, learning and change: Practice-theory perspectives on professional learning* (pp. 33–49). Dordrecht, Netherlands: Springer.

Kemmis, S., Heikkinen, H., Aspfors, J., Fransson, G. & Edwards-Groves, C. (2014). Mentoring as contested practice: Support, supervision and collaborative self-development. *Teaching and Teacher Education* 43, 154–164.

Kemmis, S., McTaggart, R. & Nixon, R. (2014). *The action research planner: Doing critical participatory action research*. Singapore: Springer.

Kemmis, S., McTaggart, R. & Nixon, R. (2015). *The Action Research Planner. Doing Critical Participatory Action Research*. Springer. http://elibrary.mukuba.edu.zm:8080/jspui/bitstream/123456789/625/1/The%20Action%20Research%20Planner.pdf.

Kemmis, S., Wilkinson, J., Edwards-Groves, C., Hardy, I., Grootenboer, P. & Bristol, L. (2014). *Changing practices, changing education*. Singapore: Springer.

Kennedy, A. (2014). Understanding Continuing Professional Development: The Need for Theory to Impact on Policy and Practice. *Professional Development in Education*, 40 (5): 688–697. doi:10.1080/19415257.2014.955122.

Keymeulen, R., Henry, J. & Longlez, A. (2020). *La classe flexible: je me lance!* Paris: De Boeck Supérieur s.a.

Khan, S. & Tzortzopoulos, P. (2016). An evaluation framework for an action research study on lean design management. In: *Proc. 24th Ann. Conf. of the Int'l. Group for Lean Construction*. Boston, USA, sect.1pp. 113–122. www.iglc.net.

Kiely, M. T., Brownell, M. T., Lauterbach, A. A. & Benedict, A. E. (2015). Teachers' beliefs about students with special needs and inclusion. H. Fives, M. G. Gill (Eds.). *International handbook of research on teachers' beliefs. Educational psychology handbook*, New York: Routledge, pp. 475–491.

Kiffer, S. (2016). *La construction des compétences d'enseignement des enseignants-chercheurs novices de l'université en France*. Thèse. France: Université de Strasbourg. https://www.theses.fr/2016STRAG029.pdf.

King, F. & Stevenson, H. (2017). Generating change from below: What role for leadership from above? *Journal of Educational Administration*, 55(6), 657–670. doi:10.1108/JEA-07-2016-0074.

Kiru, E. W. (2018). Mathematics teachers' use of information and communication technologies: An international comparison. International Journal of Research in Education and Science (IJRES), 4(1), 165–177. DOI:10.21890/ijres.383119.

Kitas žvilgsnis į ugdymo procesą [*Another look at the education process*]. (2014). *Švietimo problemos analizė*, 15(120), 1–12.

Klevering, N. & McNae, R. (2019). Making sense of leadership in early childhood education: Tensions and complexities between concepts and practices. *Journal of Educational Leadership, Policy and Practice*, 33(1), 5–17. https://doi.org/10.21307/jelpp-2018-002.

Knauder, H. & Koschmieder, C. (2019). Individualized student support in primary school teaching: A review of influencing factors using the Theory of Planned Behavior (TPB). *Teaching and Teacher Education*, Vol. 77, 66–76, https://doi.org/10.1016/j.tate.2018.09.012.

Kniffin, K. M. & Baert, H. (2015). Maximizing learning through assessment in middle and high school physical education. *Journal of Physical Education, Recreation & Dance*, 86(4), 7–16.

Koc, B. & Korkmaz, I. (2019). Okuma yazma bilmeyen diskalkulik bir ogrenciye toplama ve cikarma ogretimine yonelik bir eylem arastirmasi [An action research on teaching addition and subtraction to an illiterate student with dyscalculia]. *Egitimde Nitel Arastirmalar Dergisi*, 7(2), 710–737. https://doi:10.14689/issn.2148-2624.1.7c.2s.11m.

Kokybės krepšelio skyrimo bendrojo ugdymo mokykloms tvarkos aprašas [*Description of the procedure for allocating the quality basket to general education schools*]. (2018). Patvirtinta Lietuvos Respublikos švietimo, mokslo ir sporto ministro 2018 m. rugpjūčio 29 d. įsakymu Nr. V-707.

Kretingos rajono Kurmaičių pradinės mokyklos išorinio vertinimo ataskaita [*Report of the external evaluation of Kurmaičių primary school, Kretinga district*]. (2018). Vilnius: Nacionalinė mokyklų vertinimo agentūra.

Kurshumlia, R. & Vula, E. (2021). Using reciprocal teaching for improving students' skills in mathematical word problem solving – A project of participatory action research. *European Journal of Educational Research, 10*(3), 1371–1382. https://doi.org/10.12973/eu-jer.10.3.1371.

Kyriakides, L., Christoforidou, M., Panayiotou, A. & Creemers, B. P. M. (2017). The impact of a three-year teacher professional course on quality of teaching: Strengths and limitations of the dynamic approach. *European Journal of Teacher Education*, 40(4), 465–486. doi:10.1080/02619768.2017.1349093.

Lacelle, N. & Boultif, A. (2016). Intégration de la multimodalité dans les projets d'innovation de stagiaires en formation. In: *La recherche-action et la recherche-développement au service de la littératie*. Les Éditions de l'université de Sherbrooke. DOI: http://dx.doi.org/10.17118/11143/8814.

Lafontaine, L. (2011). *Activités de production et de compréhension orales.* Montréal, Canada: Chenelière.

Lafontaine, L. (2016). Recherche-action-formation au préscolaire et au 1er cycle du primaire: pistes méthodologiques. *La recherche-action et la recherche-développement au service de la littératie.* Les Éditions de l'université de Sherbrooke, pp. 41–67. Doi : http://dx.doi.org/10.17118/11143/8809.

Lafontaine, L., Dumais, Ch. & Pharand, J. (2016). L'oral au 1er cycle de l'école primaire québécoise: assises théoriques et démarche d'enseignement et d'évaluation. *Repères recherches en didactique du français langue maternelle,* 54, 101–119. https://doi.org/10.4000/reperes.1096.

Lafortune, L. (2006). Accompagnement-recherche-formation d'un changement en éducation: un processus exigeant une démarche de pratique réflexive. *Formation et pratiques d'enseignement en questions, 5,* 187–202.

Laidlaw, J. (2022). An action research study to enhance a music teacher's creative pedagogies with children. *Canadian Journal of Action Research, 22*(2), 72–90.

Lambert, V. A. & Lambert, C. E. (2012). Qualitative descriptive research: An acceptable design. Pacific Rim International Journal of Nursing Research, *16*(4), 255–256.

Lara Nieto-Márquez, N., Baldominos, A., Cardeña Martínez, A. & Pérez Nieto, M. Á. (2020). An Exploratory Analysis of the Implementation and Use of an Intelligent Platform for Learning in Primary Education. *Applied Sciences. 10*(3), 983. https://doi.org/10.3390/app10030983.

Lasnier, F. (2014). *Les compétences de l'apprentissage à l'évaluation.* Montréal, Québec: Guérin.

Le Boterf, G. (2010). *Construire les compétences individuelles et collectives.* Paris: Eyrolles Éditions d'Organisation.

Lefebvre, P., Bruneau, J. & Desmarais, C. (2012). Analyse conceptuelle de la compréhension inférentielle en petite enfance à partir d'une recension des modèles théoriques. *Revue des sciences de l'éducation, 38*(3), 533–553. DOI: 10.7202/1022711ar.

Leutenegger, F. (1999). Construction d'une clinique pour le didactique. *Une étude des phénomènes temporels de l'enseignement. Recherches en didactique des mathématiques, 20*(2), 209–250.

LeVasseur, L. (2012). L'école québécoise et la « culture scolaire: développement intégral de l'enfant, développement cognitif de l'élève et contextes éducatifs. *Phronesis,* 1(4), 71–83. https://doi.org/10.7202/1013238ar.

Levine, E. & Patrick, S. (2019). *What is competency-based education?* An updated definition. Vienna, VA: Aurora Institute.

Lewin, K. (1948). Action research and minority problems. In: G. W. Lewin (Ed.) *Resolving Social Conflicts.* New York: Harper & Row.

Lewin, K., Lippett, R. & White, R. K. (1939). Patterns of aggressive behaviour in experimentally created social climates. *Journal of Social Psychology*, 10, 271–301.

Lietuva. Švietimas šalyje ir regionuose [*Lithuania. Education in the country and regions*]. (2016). Vilnius: Švietimo aprūpinimo centras.

Lietuva. Švietimas šalyje ir regionuose [*Lithuania. Education in the country and regions*]. (2019). Vilnius: Švietimo aprūpinimo centras.

Lietuvos pažangos strategija „Lietuva 2030" [*Lithuania's progress strategy "Lithuania 2030"*]. (2012). Lietuvos Respublikos Seimo gegužės 15 d., nutarimas Nr. XI-2015, https://e-seimas.lrs.lt/portal/legalAct/lt/TAD/TAIS.425517.

Macaire, D. (2007). Didactique des langues et recherche-action. Recherches en Didactique des Langues et Cultures. *Les Cahiers de l'Acedle, Association des chercheurs et enseignants didacticiens des langues étrangères*, 4, 93–119. hal-00554863.

Mahon, K., Francisco, S., & Kemmis, S. (2017). *Exploring Education and Professional Practice: Through the Lens of Practice Architectures*. Singapore: Springer.

Maleyrot, E. (2013). *Les professeurs des écoles maîtres formateurs saisis par les épreuves professionnelles*. Notes du CREN n° 16.

Maleyrot, E. (2015). La visée réflexive des dispositifs d'accompagnement à l'entrée dans le métier des enseignants du premier degré: étude diachronique par les missions des maîtres formateurs. *Questions Vives*, 24, 1–20. DOI: 10.4000/questionsvives.1796.

Malorni, A., Lea, C. H., Richards-Schuster, K. & Spencer, M. S. (2022). Facilitating youth participatory action research (YPAR): a scoping review of relational practice in U.S. Youth development & out-of-school time projects. *Children and Youth Services Review*, 106399, doi: 10.1016/j.childyouth.2022.106399.

Manalo, E. (2020). *Deeper Learning, Dialogic Learning, and Critical Thinking: Research-based Strategies for the Classroom*. London and New York: Routledge.

Manfra, M. M. (2019). Action Research and Systemic, Intentional Change in Teaching Practice. *Review of Research in Education*, *43*(1), 163–196. https://doi.org/10.3102/0091732X18821132.

Maranda, M.-F., Viviers, S. & Deslauriers, J.-S. (2013). «L'école en souffrance»: recherche-action sur les situations de travail à risque pour la santé mentale en milieu scolaire. *Nouvelle revue de psychosociologie*, *15*(1), 225–240. DOI: 10.3917/nrp.015.0225.

Mariguddi, A. & Cain, T. (2022). Research-informed teaching: The case of Musical Futures. *British Educational Research Journal*, 48(3), 519–535, https://doi.org/10.1002/berj.3780.

Marijampolės Rimanto Stankevičiaus pagrindinės mokyklos išorinio vertinimo ataskaita [*Report of the external evaluation of Rimantas Stankevičius basic*

school, Marijampole city]. (2018). Vilnius: Nacionalinė mokyklų vertinimo agentūra.
Marzano, R. J. (2003). *What works in school: Translating research into action.* Alexandria, VA: Association for Supervision and Curriculum Development.
Mattatall, C. & Power, K. (2014). La collaboration des professionnels de l'enseignement et la réussite des élèves ayant des troubles d'apprentissage: Un examen de la recherche. *TA@l'école.* https://www.taalecole.ca/impact-de-la-collaboration-entre-enseignants-sur-le-rendement-scolaire-et-le-developpement-social-des-eleves-ayant-des-troubles-dapprentissage-examen-des-etudes-publiees/.
Mattavarat, S., Viseshsiri, P. & Siribanpitak, P. (2017). Proposed policy for preparation of high-quality primary school teachers in Thailand. *Kasetsart Journal of Social Sciences, 38*(2), 105–110. https://doi.org/10.1016/j.kjss.2016.04.005.
Maurel, M. (2008). La psycho-phénoménologie, théorie de l'explicitation. *Expliciter*, 77, 1–29.
Maurel, M. (2009). The explicitation interview: examples and applications. *Journal of Consciousness Studies*, 16(10–12), 58–89.
Maurer, B. (2001). *Une didactique de l'oral du primaire au lycée.* France, Paris: Bertrand Lacoste.
Mayer, R., Ouellet, F., Saint-Jacques, M. C. & Turcotte, D. (2000). *Méthodes de recherche en intervention sociale.* Montréal: Gaëtan Morin.
Mayring, P. (2019). Qualitative Content Analysis: Demarcation, Varieties, Developments. *Forum Qualitative Sozialforschung/Forum: Qualitative Social Research, 20*(3). https://doi.org/10.17169/fqs-20.3.3343.
McComas, W. F. & Clough, M. P. (2020). Nature of science in science instruction. In *Nature of Science in Science Instruction Rationales and Strategies* (pp. 3–22). Springer.
McConnell, C., Conrad, B. & Uhrmacher, B. (2020). *Lesson Planning with Purpose: Five Approaches to Curriculum Design.* New York: Teachers College Press.
McNiff, J. & Whitehead, J. (2010). *You and your action research project* (3rd ed.). Oxford, UK: Routledge.
Meninio ugdymo pamoka: ką reikėtų keisti? [*Art lesson: what needs to change?*] (2012). *Švietimo problemos analizė*, 2(33), 1–12.
Menter, I., Eliot, D., Hulme, M. & Lewin, J. (2011). *A guide to practitioner research in education.* London: Sage.
Merriam, S. B. & Tisdell, E. J. (2016). *Qualitative Research: A Guide to Design and Implementation.* CA, USA, San Francisco: Jossey-Bass.
Mertler, C. A. (2009). *Action Research. Teachers as Researchers in the Classroom.* Second Edition. SAGE: Los Angeles.
Mertler, C. A. (2012). *Action research: Improving schools and empowering educators* (3rd ed.). Thousand Oaks, CA: Sage.

Mertler, C. A. (2018). *Action research communities: Professional learning, empowerment, and improvement through collaborative action research*. London/New York: Routledge.
Mertler, C. A. (2020). *Action research: Improving schools and empowering educators* (6th ed.). Thousand Oaks, CA: SAGE.
Mertler, C. A. (2021). Action Research as Teacher Inquiry: A Viable Strategy for Resolving Problems of Practice. *Practical Assessment, Research, and Evaluation, 26*(19). Available at: https://scholarworks.umass.edu/pare/vol26/iss1/19.
Mertler, C. A. & Hartley, A. J. (2017). Classroom-based, teacher-led action research as a process for enhancing teaching and learning. *Journal of Educational Leadership in Action*, 4(2), 1–16. DOI: https://doi.org/10.62608/2164-1102.1056
Mesci, G., Schwartz, R. S. & Pleasants, B. A. S. (2020). Enabling factors of pre-service science teachers' pedagogical content knowledge for nature of science and nature of scientific inquiry. *Science & Education*, 29(2), 263–297.
Middleton, T. R. F. (2024). Layering Reflexivity into Participatory Research. *Participatory Research in Sport and Physical Activity*, edited by Audrey R. Giles, 31–43. 1st ed. London: Routledge. https://doi.org/10.4324/9781003430339-4.
Miehakanda, M. B. (2014). *L'encadrement éducatif à l'école: Vers une implication de l'apprenant*. France: Lille.
Mills, G. E. (2011). *Action research: A guide for the teacher researcher* (4th ed.). Upper Saddle River, NJ: Pearson.
Mills, K. A. & Doyle, K. (2019). Visual arts: a multimodal language for Indigenous education. *Language and Education*, 33(6), 521–543. https://doi.org/10.1080/09500782.2019.1635618.
Miskovic, M., Efron, E. S. & Ravid, R. (2012). Action Research in Action: From University to School Classrooms. *Education Research International*, Hindawi Publishing Corporation, Vol. 2012, Article ID 389736, 1–11. doi:10.1155/2012/389736.
Mohan, P. P., Chand, D. D., & Lingam, G. I. (2017). Teachers' perceptions of the impact of professional development on learning and teaching in a developing nation. *Australian Journal of Teacher Education*, 42(11), 18–33. doi:10.14221/ajte.2017v42n11.2
Mokinių, kurie mokosi pagal bendrojo ugdymo programas, mokymosi pasiekimų vertinimo ir vertinimo rezultatų panaudojimo tvarkos aprašas [*Description of the procedures for assessing the learning achievements of pupils enrolled in general education programmes and the use of assessment results*]. (2023). Patvirtintas Lietuvos Respublikos švietimo, mokslo ir sporto ministro 2023 m. rugpjūčio 31d. įsakymu Nr. V-1125. Vilnius: ŠMSM. https://www.e-tar.lt/portal/lt/legalAct/e536295047ec11ee9de9e7e0fd363afc.
Mokyklos, įgyvendinančios bendrojo ugdymo programas, veiklos kokybės įsivertinimo metodika. Ugdymas(is) paradigmų kaitoje [*Methodology for assessing the quality of a school implementing general education programmes. Education(is) in*

a paradigm shift]. (2016). Vilnius: Švietimo ir mokslo ministerijos Švietimo aprūpinimo centras.

Mokyklų, siekiančių gauti kokybės krepšelį, skirtą mokinių ugdymo pasiekimams gerinti, sąrašas [*List of schools applying for a quality basket to improve pupils' educational achievement*]. (2021). Patvirtinta Lietuvos Respublikos švietimo, mokslo ir sporto ministro 2021 m. liepos 22 d. įsakymu Nr. V-888. Vilnius: ŠMSM.

Mokyklų, vykdančių bendrojo ugdymo programas, veiklos išorinio vertinimo organizavimo ir vykdymo tvarkos aprašas [*Description of the procedure for organising and conducting external evaluations of the performance of schools delivering general education programmes*]. (2007, 2018). Patvirtinta Lietuvos Respublikos švietimo, mokslo ir sporto ministro 2007 m. balandžio 2 d. įsakymu Nr. ISAK-587 (Lietuvos Respublikos švietimo, mokslo ir sporto ministro 2018 m. gruodžio 3 d. įsakymo Nr. V-962 redakcija). Vilnius: ŠMSM.

Mokyklų, vykdančių bendrojo ugdymo programas, veiklos išorinio vertinimo statistika. 2019 m. rizikos išorinio vertinimo rezultatai [*Statistics on the external evaluation of the performance of schools delivering general education programmes. Results of the 2019 external risk assessment*]. (2019). Vilnius: Nacionalinė švietimo agentūra.

Mokyklų, vykdančių bendrojo ugdymo programas, veiklos išorinio vertinimo statistika. 2022 m. rizikos išorinio vertinimo rezultatai. [*Statistics on the external evaluation of the performance of schools delivering general education programmes. Results of the 2022 external risk assessment*]. (2023). Vilnius: Nacionalinė švietimo agentūra.

Mokyklų, vykdančių bendrojo ugdymo programas, veiklos išorinio vertinimo statistika. 2021–2022 m. rizikos išorinio vertinimo rezultatai [*Statistics on the external evaluation of the performance of schools delivering general education programmes. Results of the 2021–2022 external risk assessment*]. (2022). Vilnius: Nacionalinė švietimo agentūra.

Mokyklų, vykdančių bendrojo ugdymo programas, veiklos kokybė. Metinis pranešimas 2018 [*Quality of schools delivering general education programmes. Annual Report 2018*]. (2018). Vilnius: Nacionalinė mokyklų vertinimo agentūra. https://www.nmva.smm.lt/wp-content/uploads/2019/04/Bendrojo-ugdymo-mokykl%C5%B3-veiklos-kokyb%C4%971-1.pdf.

Mokyklų, vykdančių bendrojo ugdymo programas, veiklos teminio išorinio vertinimo, organizuojamo 2021–2022 metais analizuojamos temos – „įtraukiojo ugdymo įgyvendinimo kryptingumas mokyklose, vykdančiose bendrojo ugdymo programas" vertinimo rodikliai [*Indicators for the thematic external evaluation of schools delivering general education programmes in 2021–2022 on the theme "focus on inclusive education in schools delivering general education programmes"*]. (2021). Patvirtinta Lietuvos Respublikos švietimo, mokslo ir sporto ministro 2018 m. liepos 29 d. įsakymu Nr. V-1254. Vilnius: ŠMSM.

Mokymasis bendrojo ugdymo mokykloje: ką atspindi visuminio ir rizikos išorinio vertinimo duomenys? Bendrojo ugdymo mokyklų išorinio rizikos vertinimo rezultatai [*Learning in mainstream school: what does the evidence from the comprehensive and external risk assessment show? Results of the external risk assessment of mainstream schools*]. (2019). Vilnius: Nacionalinė švietimo agentūra.

Mokytojų trūkumas – rekordinis: siunčia grėsmingą žinią [*Teacher shortages at record levels: sending an ominous message*]. (2024). Vilnus: Tv3.lt https://www.tv3.lt/naujiena/lietuva/mokytoju-trukumas-rekordinis-siuncia-gresminga-zinia-n1359678.

Mondada, L. (2005). *Méthodes d'enregistrement et d'analyse de données vidéo prises en situation de formation*. Lyon: PIREF.

Monteiro, V., Mata, L. & Nóbrega Santos, N. (2021). Assessment Conceptions and Practices: Perspectives of Primary School Teachers and Students. *Front. Educ.* https://doi.org/10.3389/feduc.2021.631185.

Moosa, V., Salleh, S. & Hamid, L. (2020). Professional learning communities assessment–revised: A measure of schools as learning organisations. *Pertanika Journal of Social Sciences and Humanities*, 28(4), 3047–3068. doi: 10.47836/pjssh.28.4.31.

Moreno Sánchez, E., Castillo Viera, E. & Rodríguez Mena, J. A. (2017). A Cross-border Cooperation Project between Spain and Portugal to Improve the Quality of Life of the Population in Primary School. *Procedia – Social and Behavioral Sciences*, 237, 438–445. https://doi.org/10.1016/j.sbspro.2017.02.087.

Morin, F. (2022). Action Research, Education, and the Arts. *Canadian Journal of Action Research*, 22(2), 1–4.

Morin, A. (1985). Critères de « scientificité » de la recherche-action. Revue des sciences de l'éducation, 11(1), 31–49. https://doi.org/10.7202/900478ar

Morin, A. (2004a). Pourquoi un numéro sur la systémique et la recherche-action? *In questions vives n°3, Lambesc*, 11–13.

Morin, A. (2004b). De l'anthropopédagogie à la recherche-action intégrale. *In questions vives n°3, Lambesc*, 15–26.

Morin, A. & Cardinal, P. (2004). La recherche-action intégrale systémique. *In questions vives n°3, Lambesc*, 27–36.

Morris, T. H. & Rohs, M. (2023). The potential for digital technology to support self-directed learning in formal education of children: A scoping review. *Interactive Learning Environments*, 31(4), 1974–1987. https://doi.org/10.1080/10494820.2020.1870501.

Morrissette, J. & Charara, Y. (2015). Le groupe de codéveloppement: un levier de réflexivité des enseignants en transition professionnelle? *Questions Vives*, 24, 1–17. DOI:10.4000/questionsvives.1805.

Muijs, D., Kyriakides, L., van der Werf, G., Creemers, B., Timperley, H. & Earl, L. (2014). State of the Art – Teacher Effectiveness and Professional

Learning. *School Effectiveness and School Improvement*, 25 (2): 231–256. doi: 10.1080/09243453.2014.885451.
Mullis, I. V. S. & Martin, M. O. (2017). *TIMSS 2019 Assessment Frameworks*. TIMSS & PIRLS International Study Center.
Mullis, I. V. S., Martin, M. O. & Loveless, T. (2016). *20 Years of TIMSS: International Trends in Mathematics and Science Achievement, Curriculum, and Instruction*. TIMSS & PIRLS International Study Center, Lynch School of Education, Boston College and International Association for the Evaluation of Educational Achievement (IEA).
Mulyanto, B. S., Sadono, T. & Koeswanti, H. D. (2020). Evaluation of Critical Thinking Ability with Discovery Learning Using Blended Learning Approach in Primary School. *Journal of Educational Research and Evaluation*, *9*(2), 78–84. https://doi.org/10.15294/jere.v9i2.46135.
Murauskaitė, A. (2024). *Naikins pilkąsias dėmes: lopys vadovėlių stygių, pirks konspektus iš mokytojų* [*Tackling grey spots: patching textbook shortages, buying outlines from teachers*]. Vilnius: lrt.lt. https://www.lrt.lt/naujienos/lietuvoje/2/2268027/naikins-pilkasias-demes-lopys-vadoveliu-stygiu-pirks-konspektus-is-mokytoju.
Nguyen, D. & Ng, D. (2020). Teacher collaboration for change: sharing, improving and spreading. *Professional Development in Education*, 46(4), pp. 638–651. doi: 10.1080/19415257.2020.1787206.
Noble, H. & Heale, R. (2019). Triangulation in research, with examples. *Evidence-Based Nursing*, 22, 67–68.
Noddings, N. (2012). *Philosophy of Education*. Boulder, CO: Westview Press.
Noddings, N. (2013). *Caring. A Relational Approach to Ethics and Moral Education*. Berkeley, California: University of California Press.
Nokes, J. D. (2019). *Teaching History, Learning Citizenship: Tools for Civic Engagement*. New York: Teachers College Press.
Nokes-Malach, T., Zepeda, C., Richey, J. & Gadgil, S. (2019). Collaborative Learning: The Benefits and Costs. In J. Dunlosky & K. Rawson (Eds.), *The Cambridge Handbook of Cognition and Education* (Cambridge Handbooks in Psychology) (pp. 500–527). Cambridge: Cambridge University Press. https://doi.org/10.1017/9781108235631.021.
Nolin, R. (2015). Portrait des pratiques déclarées d'enseignement et d'évaluation de l'oral en classe du primaire au Québec. In R. Bergeron, C. Dumais, B. Harvey et R. Nolin (dir.), *La didactique du français oral du primaire à l'université* (pp. 69–84). Côte-Saint-Luc, Canada: Peisaj, coll. Cogito.
Nordin, N., Saadon, S. I., Saraih, U. N., Noor Azhar, M. F., Kassim, M. A., Mansor, M. F. & Hayat, H. (2021). Investigation on Volatility, Uncertainty, Complexity, and Ambiguity (VUCA) Environment in Transformational Leadership. *Proceedings of Malaysian Technical Universities Conference on Engineering and*

Technology (MUCET) 2021, 319–320. https://crim.utem.edu.my/wp-content/uploads/2022/09/157-319-3201.pdf.
Norton, L. S. (2010). *Action research in Teaching and Learning: a practical guide to conducting pedagogical research in universities*. London, New York: Routledge.
Nuangchalerm, P., El Islami, R. A. Z. & Prasertsang, P. (2022). Science attitude on environmental conservation of Thai and Indonesian novice science teacher students. *International Journal of STEM Education for Sustainability*, *2*(2), 148–155.
OCDE (2011). *Regards sur l'éducation 2011: les indicateurs de l'OCDE*. Paris: OCDE.
OECD. (2019). PISA 2018 Results (Volume II): Where All Students Can Succeed, PISA, OECD Publishing, Paris, https://doi.org/10.1787/b5fd1b8f-en.
Oestar, J. & Marzo, C. (2022). Teachers as researchers: Skills and challenges in action research making. *International Journal of Theory and Application in Elementary and Secondary School Education*, 4(2), 95–104. https://doi.org/10.31098/ijtaese.v4i2.1020
Olin, A., Almqvist, J. & Hamza, K. (2021). To recognize oneself and others in teacher-researcher collaboration. *Educational Action Research*, 31:2, 248–264, DOI: 10.1080/09650792.2021.1897949.
Orhan Ozen, S. & Ozen, S. (2022). An action research: Experiences and practices of designing 21st-century assessment activities of elementary teacher candidates. *Journal of Educational Technology & Online Learning*, 5(1), 128–143.
Pakruojo rajono Balsių pagrindinės mokyklos veiklos išorinio rizikos vertinimo ataskaita [*Report on the external risk assessment of Balsiai Primary School, Pakruojis district*]. (2019). Vilnius: Nacionalinė mokyklų vertinimo agentūra.
Palacios Mena, N., Garcia, P., Mosquera, M. L. & Alarcón, N. (2020). Development of Historical Thought in Primary Education: Analysis of An Intervention in Colombian Schools. *Australian Journal of Teacher Education*, 45(11). https://ro.ecu.edu.au/ajte/vol45/iss11/6.
Panskyi, T., Rowinska, Z. & Biedron, S. (2019). Out-of-school assistance in the teaching of visual creative programming in the game-based environment – Case study: Poland. Thinking Skills and Creativity, Vol. 34, 100593. https://doi.org/10.1016/j.tsc.2019.100593.
Patton, M. Q. (2002). Qualitative Research & Evaluation Methoods, 3 rd ed. USA, CA, Thousand Oaks: SAGE.
Pavlin, J. & Čampa, T. (2021). Is peer instruction in primary school feasible?: The case study in Slovenia. *European Journal of Educational Research*, 10(2), 785–798. https://doi.org/10.12973/eu-jer.10.2.785.
Paydar, S. & Doğan, A. (2021). An Action Research on Teaching Natural Numbers to the First Grade Primary School Student with Low Readiness. *Journal of Qualitative Research in Education*, 27. https://doi.org/10.14689/enad.27.3.

Perez-Roux, T. (2013). Les enseignants en formation à l'épreuve de la réflexivité: tensions, ajustements, évolutions. Dans M. Altet, J. Desjardins, R. Etienne, L. Paquay, & P. Perrenoud. (Dir.). *Former des enseignants réflexifs : obstacles et résistances* (pp. 115–134). Bruxelles: De Boeck Université.

Perez-Roux, T. (2017). Une forme de recherche collaborative impulsée par les praticiens: enjeux, démarche, déplacement(s) des acteurs. *Education et socialisation – Les cahiers du CERFEE*, Presses Universitaires de la Méditerranée. Collaborations chercheur(s)-praticien(s): nouvelles formes, nouveaux enjeux ? ‹10.4000/edso.2494›. ‹hal-01714813›.

Perrenoud, P. (2013). La blessure la plus rapprochée du soleil. Ambivalences et résistances face à la posture réflexive. Dans M. Altet, J. Desjardins, R. Etienne, L. Paquay & P. Perrenoud. (Dir). *Former des enseignants réflexifs: obstacles et résistances* (pp. 79–93). Bruxelles : De Boeck Université.

Phoopanna, A. & Nuangchalerm, P. (2022). Developing Grade 5 students' Scientific Habits of Mind Through Community-Based Science Learning. *Jurnal Penelitian Dan Pembelajaran IPA*, *8*(1), 1–12. https://doi.org/10.30870/jppi.v8i1.14503.

Phuntsho, T. & Dorji, Ch. (2023). Enhancing Grade Six Students' Speaking Skill through English Movies: An Action Research. *Acta Scientific Paediatrics*, 6(5), 6–13. DOI: 10.31080/ASPE.2023.06.0603.

Pine, G. J. (2008). *Action research: Building knowledge democracies*. Thousand Oaks, CA: Sage.

PISA 2009. (2010). *Results: Overcoming Social Background*. Vol. II. Paris: OECD Publishing.

Pitsia, V., Karakolidis, A. & Lehane, P. (2021). Investigating the Use of Assessment Data by Primary School Teachers: Insights from a Large-scale Survey in Ireland. *Educational Assessment*, 26(3), 145–162, DOI: 10.1080/10627197.2021.1917358.

Ponomarioviené, J. & Jakavonytė-Staškuvienė, D. (2024). Solutions for Independent Goal Setting and Implementation of Primary School Students Fostering the Competence of Learning to Learn. *Educ. Sci*, 14, 368. https://doi.org/10.3390/educsci14040368.

Posch, P. (2019). Action Research – Conceptual Distinctions and Confronting the Theory-Practice Divide in Lesson and Learning Studies. *Educational Action Research*, *27*(4): 496–510. https://doi.org/10.1080/09650792.2018.1502676.

Postholm, M. B. (2018). Teachers' professional development in school: A review study, *Cogent Education*, 5:1, 1522781, DOI: 10.1080/2331186X.2018.1522781.

Postholm, M. B., Klemp, T. & Nordbotn, M. M. (2023). Tripartite Collaboration in Student Research and Development Projects. *Scandinavian Journal of Educational Research* 1–15. https://doi.org/10.1080/00313831.2023.2250371.

Potočnik, R., Košir, T. & Devetak, I. (2022). Slovenian primary school teachers' opinion on interdisciplinary approach between fine art and science education. *European Journal of Educational Research, 11*(1), 435–443. https://doi.org/10.12973/eu-jer.11.1.435.

Priešmokyklinio, pradinio, pagrindinio ir vidurinio ugdymo bendrosios programos [Framework programmes for pre-primary, primary, primary and secondary education]. (2022). Patvirtinta Lietuvos Respublikos švietimo, mokslo ir sporto ministro 2022 m. rugpjūčio 24 d. V-1269, https://e-seimas.lrs.lt/portal/legalAct/lt/TAD/45f3b02523e311edb36fa1cf41a91fd9?positionInSearchResults=0&searchModelUUID=0930658b-09d3-4617-9b69-3e37720373e6.

Primary Education Pedagogy and Early Foreign Language Teaching. (2023). Bachelor's study programme. Lithuania: Vytautas Magnus University. https://www.vdu.lt/lt/studiju-programa/pradinio-ugdymo-pedagogika-ir-ankstyvasis-uzsienio-kalbos-mokymas/?gclid=CjwKCAjwtuOlBhBREiwA7agf1i4V1yav9QAYXw4QY2w2RuAKXmGAgLD9XKQX4IrM-0s9721U_CBcIBoCs04QAvD_BwE.

Professional Standards for Educational Leaders. (2015). Aliance for Advanced School Leadership. National Policy Board for Educational Administration. https://www.oecd.org/site/eduistp2012/49850576.pdf.

Prud'homme, L. & Guay, M.-H. (2011). La recherche-action. In: T. Karsenti et L. Savoie-Zajc (dir.). *La recherche en éducation: Étapes et approches* (3e éd.) (p. 183–211). Montréal: ERPI.

Prud'homme, L. (2007). *La différenciation pédagogique: analyse du sens construit par des enseignantes et un chercheur-formateur dans un contexte de recherche-action*. Thése. Gatineau: Université du Québec en Outaouais.

Prud'homme, L., Dolbec, A. & Guay, M.-H. (2011). Le sens construit autour de la différenciation pé¬dagogique dans le cadre d'une recherche-action-formation. *Éducation et francophonie*, XXXIX(2), 165–188.

Putra, R. M., Solekhah, S., Agustina, D. D. & Sobirov, B. (2022). Action Learning Strategy to Enhance Students Speaking Skill: A Classroom Action Research. *Anglophile Journal, 2*(1), 37–54. https://doi.org/10.51278/anglophile.v2i1.269.

Quality teaching in the European schools. (2016). Approved by the Joint Teaching Committee at its meeting of 18 and 19 February 2016, in Brussels. http://www.gudee.eu/DOC2016/2015-09-D-3-en-2-Booklet.pdf.

Raby, C., Boegner-Pagé, S., Charron, A., Gagnon, B. & Bouchard, A.-P. (2013). Le développement de la competence professionnelle des enseignants du préscolaire et du primaire à intégrer les TIC en classe: impact d'une recherche-action. *Formation et profession, 21*(2), 19–33. http://dx.doi.org/10.18162/fp.2013.2.

Ralabate, P. K. (2016). *Your UDL Lesson Planner*. Baltimore: Paul H. Brookes Publishing.

Ravanis, K. (2017). Early childhood science education: state of the art and perspectives. *Journal of Baltic Science Education*, 16(3), 284–288. https://doi.org/10.33225/jbse/17.16.284.

Read, C. (2015). Foreword. In Bland, J. (Ed), Teaching English to Young Learners. Critical Issues in Language Teaching With 3–12 Year Olds. (xi-xiii). London: Bloomsbury.

Rey, B. (2014). *La notion de compétence en éducation et formation. Enjeux et problèmes*. Bruxelles: De Boeck.

Rey, O. (2012). Le défi de l'évaluation des compétences. Dossier d'actualité Veille et Analyse. Lyon: ENS de Lyon, 76, 1–17. http://veille-et-analyses.ens-lyon.fr/DA/detailsDossier.php?parent=accueil&dossier=76&lang=fr.

Rey, O. & Feyfant, A. (2014). Évaluer pour (mieux) faire apprendre. *Dossier de veille de l'IFÉ*. Lyon: ENS de Lyon, 94, 1–41. http://veille-et-analyses.ens-lyon.fr/DA/detailsDossier.php?parent=accueil&dossier=94&lang=fr.

Riente, R. (2010). Activités d'apprentissage, SAÉ et SÉ. Quelques précisions. *Québec français, 158*, 52–53.

Robinson, P., Mourão, S. & Kang, N. J. (2015). English Learning Areas in Pre-primary Classrooms: An Investigation of Their Effectiveness. London: British Council.

Robinson, T. (2022). Building Cultural Competence in Schools Through Teacher Capacity. *Electronic Theses and Dissertations*, 2269. https://egrove.olemiss.edu/etd/2269.

Robinson, V., Lloyd, C. & Rowe, K. (2008). The Impact of Leadership on Student Outcomes: An Analysis of the Differential Effects of Leadership Types. *Educational Administration Quarterly*, 44(5), 635–674.

Rodríguez-Jiménez, C., de la Cruz-Campos, J.-C., Campos-Soto, M.-N. & Ramos-Navas-Parejo, M. (2023). Teaching and Learning Mathematicsin Primary Education: The Role ofICT-A Systematic Review of the Literature. *Mathematics* 2023, 11, 272. https://doi.org/10.3390/math11020272.

Roegiers, X. (2011). *Des situations pour intégrer les acquis scolaires*. Bruxelles: De Boeck.

Rojas-Drummond, S., Barrera Olmedo, M. J., Hernández Cruz, I. & Vélez Espinosa, M. (2020). Dialogic interactions, co-regulation and the appropriation of text composition abilities in primary school children. *Learning, Culture and Social Interaction*, 24, 100354. https://doi.org/10.1016/j.lcsi.2019.100354.

Romain, C. & Roubaud, M. N. (2013). Un observatoire des pratiques enseignantes en maternelle: vers une typologie d'activités stimulant la parole de l'enfant. *Revue des sciences de l'éducation*, 39, 2, 273–293. DOI: 10.7202/1025228ar.

Rönnerman, K. & Nordberg, A. (2024). Circle time in preschool as a practice for developing language support between teachers and children using the structured ELSA model. *Educational Action Research*, 1–16. https://doi.org/10.1080/09650792.2024.2421959.

Rosen, Y., Stoeffler, K. & Simmering, V. (2020). Imagine: Design for creative thinking, learning, and assessment in schools. *Journal of Intelligence*, 8(2), 16. doi: 10.3390/jintelligence8020016.

Roy, A., Guay, F. & Valois, P. (2013). Teaching to address diverse learning needs: Development and validation of a Differentiated Instruction Scale. *International Journal of Inclusive Education*, 17(11), 1186–1204. https://doi.org/10.1080/13603116.2012.743604.

Rupšienė, L. (2007). *Kokybinių tyrimų duomenų rinkimo metodologija* [Qualitative research data collection methodology]. Klaipėda: Klaipėdos universitetas.

Ryan, S. & Cox, J. D. (2017). Investigating student exposure to competency-based education. *Education Policy Analysis Archives, 25* (24), 1–28. http://dx.doi.org/10.14507/epaa.25.2792.

Sagnier, C. (2013). *Metacognition et Interactions en Didactique Des Langues: Perspectives Sociocognitives*. Berne: Peter Lang.

Sagor, R. (2011). *The action research guidebook: A four-stage process for educators and school teams*. Thousand Oaks, CA: Corwin Press.

Sahlberg, P. (2011). Paradoxes of educational improvement: The Finnish experience. *Scottish Educational Review*, 43 (1), 3–23.

Salihović, N. & Dizdarević, A. (2020) Methodology in Action Research on Provision of Education and Rehabilitation Support to Children with Special Needs in Regular Classrooms. In N. Salihović & A. Dizdarević (Ed.). *Theory and Methodology in International Comparative Classroom Studies* (pp.280–288/pp.307–315 in print edition). Cappelen Damm Akademisk. https://doi.org./10.23865/noasp.130.

Salite, I. (2008). Educational action research for sustainability: constructing a vision for the future in teacher education. *Journal of Teacher Education for Sustainability*, 10, 5–16. DOI: 10.2478/v10099-009-0021-6.

Salite, I., Drelinga, E., Iliško, D., Olehnoviča, E. & Zarina, S. (2016). Sustainability from the Transdisciplinary Perspective: An Action Research Strategy for Continuing Education Program Development. *Journal of Teacher Education for Sustainability*, *18*(2), 135–152. DOI: 10.1515/jtes-2016-0020.

Samuelsson, J. (2021). Developing students' relationships with mathematics. *Educational Action Research*, *31*(2), 180–194. DOI: 10.1080/09650792.2021.1899012.

Santamaría-Villar, M. B., Gilar-Corbi, R., Pozo-Rico, T. & Castejón, J. L. (2021). Teaching Socio-Emotional Competencies Among Primary School Students: Improving Conflict Resolution and Promoting Democratic Co-existence in Schools. *Front. Psychol*, 12:659348. doi: 10.3389/fpsyg.2021.659348.

Sanzo, K., Sherman, W. H. & Clayton, J. K. (2011). Leadership practices of successful middle school principals. *Journal of Educational Administration*, *49*(1), 31–45. DOI: 10.1108/09578231111102045.

Šarskuvienė, A. (2019). *Diferencijavimas, individualizavimas, suasmeninimas: kodėl svarbu akcentuoti ugdymo organizavimą, remiantis mokinių poreikiais? Bendrojo ugdymo mokyklų išorinio rizikos vertinimo rezultatai* [*Differentiation, individualisation, personalisation: why is it important to focus on organising*

education around students' needs? The results of the external risk assessment of general education schools]. Vilnius: Nacionalinė mokyklų vertinimo agentūra.
Scaradozzi, D., Sorbi, L., Pedale, A., Valzank, M. & Vergine, C. (2015). Teaching Robotics at the Primary School: An Innovative Approach.*Procedia – Social and Behavioral Sciences*, 174, 3838–3846. https://doi.org/10.1016/j.sbspro.2015.01.1122.
Schmidt, R. J. (2024). The Impact of the Physical Environment on K-12 Students. https://www.linkedin.com/pulse/impact-physical-environment-k-12-students-dr-raymond-j-schmidt-auutf.
Schmuck, R. A. (2006). *Practical Action Research for change*. London: Corwin Press.
Schurmans, M. N. (2009). L'approche compréhensive et qualitative dans la recherche en formation. *Education permanente*, 177, 91–103.
Schwartz, L., Nakonechna , M., Campbell, G., Brunner, D., Stadler, Ch., Schmid, M., Fegert, J. M. & Bürgin, D. (2022). Addressing the mental health needs and burdens of children fleeing war: a field update from ongoing mental health and psychosocial support efforts at the Ukrainian border. *Eur J Psychotraumatol*, *13*(2), 2101759.
Seiser, A. F. & Portfelt, I. (2022). Critical aspects to consider when establishing collaboration between school leaders and researchers: two cases from Sweden. *Educational Action Research*, DOI: 10.1080/09650792.2022.2110137.
Sensevy, G., Toullec-Théry, M. & Nédelec-Trohel, I. (2006). A propos de l'enseignement des mathématiques en adaptation et intégration scolaire: une étude de cas comparative en regroupement d'adaptation. *Recherches en didactique des mathématiques*, *26*(2), 151–206.
Shotter, J. & Gustavsen, B. (1999). *The Role of Dialogue Conferences in the Development of Learning Regions: Doing from within Our Lives Together What We Cannot Do Apart*. Stockholm: Stockholm School of Economics.
Šiaulių „Juventos"progimnazijos veiklos teminio išorinio vertinimo ataskaita [*Report of the thematic external evaluation of „Juventos" pro-gymnasium, Šiauliai city*]. (2021). Vilnius: Nacionalinė mokyklų vertinimo agentūra.
SICI members map (2024). https://www.sici-inspectorates.eu/About-us/SICI-members-map.
Silpną geros mokyklos požymių raišką turinčių mokyklų sąrašas [*List of schools with weak school performance*]. (2018). Patvirtinta Lietuvos Respublikos švietimo, mokslo ir sporto ministro 2018 m. lapkričio 29 d. įsakymu Nr. V-888.
Silva, J. S., Amante, L. & Morgado, J. (2017). School climate, principal support and collaboration among Portuguese teachers. *European Journal of Teacher Education*, 40(4), 505–520. doi:10.1080/02619768.2017.1295445.
Simion, A. & Stan, C. (2020). Development Of Socio-Emotional Competence Through Collaborative Learning in Primary School. In V. Chis (Ed.).

Education, Reflection, Development – ERD 2019, 85. European Proceedings of Social and Behavioural Sciences (pp. 568–574). European Publisher. https://doi.org/10.15405/epsbs.2020.06.57.

Simola, H., Kauko, J., Varjo, J., Kalalahti, M. & Sahlström, F. (2017). *Dynamics in Education Politics – Understanding and explaining the Finnish case.* London: Routledge.

Skott, C. K. & Møller, H. (2017). The individual teacher in lesson study collaboration. *International Journal for Lesson and Learning Studies*, 6, 216–232. doi:10.1108/IJLLS-10-2016-0041.

Slavin, R. E. (2014). Cooperative learning and academic achievement: why does group work? *Anales de Psicologia, 30*(3), 785–791.

Smit, B. H. J., Meirink, J. A., Tigelaar, D. E. H., Berry, A. K. & Admiraal, W. F. (2022). Principles for school student participation in pre-service teacher action research: a practice architecture's perspective. *Educational Action Research*, DOI: 10.1080/09650792.2022.2121933.

Smith, K. (2019). *Developing a Culturally Relevant Curriculum and Breaking the Barriers of Cognitive and Cultural Dissonance.* University Manila.

Smith, K. & Lindsay, S. (2016). Building future directions for teacher learning in science education. *Research in Science Education*, 46, 243–261. doi:10.1007/s11165- 015-9510-x.

Søby, M. (2015). Finnish education system. *Nordic Journal of Digital Literacy*, 10(2), 64–68. https://www.researchgate.net/publication/303146561_Finnish_education_system.

Songsee, K. & Nuangchalerm, P. (2022). Enhancing understanding about the nature of local science: An action research in primary education. *International Online Journal of Primary Education* (IOJPE), 11(2), 312–319. https://doi.org/10.55020/iojpe.1218242.

Soucy, E. (2019). *Création et mise en pratique d'un centre de l'oral: recherche-action avec des enseignantes de 1er cycle du primaire.* These de doctorat inédite. Université du Québec en Outaouais, Saint-Jérôme.

Soucy, E., Dumais, Ch. & Moreau, A. C. (2020). Quand la recherche-action au doctorat devient possible: place ą l'artisan-chercheur. *Canadian Journal for New Scholars in Education*, 11(2), 7–18.

Soverano, J. R. SR. & Laguador, J. M. (2022). Elementary School Teachers' Attitude Towards Research as Basis for a Proposed Enhancement Plan. *International Journal of Social Science Research and Review*, 5(12), 642 651.

Spencer, C. J., Porath, S., Thiele, J. & Jobe, M, (2020). *Action Research.* Monographs. NPP eBooks, 34. https://newprairiepress.org/ebooks/34.

Stalder, P. (2016). "J'existe, car je me souviens". La réflexivité au profit du management interculturel. In Dans P. Banon & C. Blons-Pierre (éds), *Didactique du français langue étrangère et seconde dans une perspective plurilingue et pluriculturelle* (p. 241–258). Berne: Peter Lang.

Stalder, P. (2019). Creativity in intercultural teams: Which indicators, facilitators and competencies? In *IACCM-IÉSEG Research conference 31st of October to 2nd of November 2019, Paris. Conference procedings* (p. 9–27). Prieiga per internetą: https://iaccm-congress.ieseg.fr/wp-content/uploads/sites/21/2018/12/1-IACCM-IESEG-Conference-Proceedings-2019-okok.pdf.

Stensmo, C. (2008). *Ledarskap i klassrummet* [Classroom management]. Studentlitteratur.

Storey-Hurtubise, E., Forristal, J., Henning, C. & Parker, J. D. A. (2022). Developing Emotional and Social Competencies in Children: Evaluating the Impact of a Classroom-Based Program. *Canadian Journal of School Psychology*, *37*(3), 257–270. https://doi.org/10.1177/08295735211051825.

Stringer, E. T. (2007). *Action research* (3rd ed.). Thousand Oaks, CA: Sage.

Stringer, E. T. (2008). *Action research in education* (2nd ed.). Upper Saddle River, NJ: Pearson.

Sumarni, W. Wardani, S., Sudarmin, S. & Gupitasar, D. N. (2016). Project Based Learning (PBL) to Improve Psychomotoric Skills: a Classroom Action Research. *Jurnal Pendidikan IPA Indonesia*, 5(2), 157–163. DOI: 10.15294/jpii.v5i2.4402.

Sun, N., Li, K. & Zhu, X. (2016). Action Research on Visualization Learning of Mathematical Concepts Under Personalized Education Idea: Take Learning of Geometrical Concepts of Elementary Math for Example. *Blended Learning: Aligning Theory with Practices*, 9757, 348–359.

Supovitz, J., A. & Christman, J. B. (2003). Developing communities of instructional practice: Lessons for Cincinnati and Philadelphia. *CPRE Policy Briefs*, 11, 1–9. Prieiga per internetą: http://repository.upenn.edu/cpre_policybriefs/28.

Švietimo įstatymas [*Law on Education*]. (1991). Galiojanti suvestinė redakcija, 2025-01-01. Vilnius: Lietuvos Respublikos Seimas.

Syarifuddin, H. & Atweh, B. (2022). The Use of Activity, Classroom Discussion, and Exercise (ACE) Teaching Cycle for Improving Students' Engagement in Learning Elementary Linear Algebra. *European Journal of Science and Mathematics Education, 10*(1), 104–138. https://doi.org/10.30935/scimath/11405.

Syawaludin, A., Gunarhadi, G. & Rintayati, P. (2019). Enhancing Elementary School students' Abstract Reasoning in Science Learning Through Augmented Reality-Based Interactive Multimedia. *Jurnal Pendidikan IPA Indonesia*, 8(2), 288–297. https://doi.org/10.15294/jpii.v8i2.19249.

Tan, A. (2019). Creativity in music education: Moving forward. In Y. Tsubonou, A. Tan, & M. Oie (Eds). *Creativity in music education: Creativity in the twenty first century* (pp. 267–271). Springer.

Tardif, M., Borges, C. & Malo, A. (2012). *Le virage réflexif en éducation. Où en sommes-nous 30 ans après Schön?* Bruxelles: De Boeck.

Targamadzė, V. (2017). *Geros mokyklos koncepcijos įgyvendinimo linkmės* [*Towards a good school concept*]. Vilnius: Vilniaus universiteto leidykla.

Taruc, P. W. (2016). Influence of teachers' beliefs and attitude towards action research. *Liceo Journal of Higher Education*, 12 (2), 280–299. http://dx.doi.org/10.1080/09650792.2015.1062408.

Taryana, T., Budiman, A., Karyati, D. & Julia, J. (2021). Enhancing students' understanding and skills on dance music: An action research. *Cypriot Journal of Educational Science*. 16(5), 2406–2424. https://doi.org/10.18844/cjes.v16i5.6334.

Tekbiyik, A. & Çelik, M. (2019). Education for Sustainable Development in Primary School: Improvement of Students' Ecocriticism Skills. *Journal of Education in Science, Environment and Health*, 5(3), 178–191. https://doi.org/10.21891/jeseh.568716.

Tengö, M., Austin, B. J., Danielsen, F. & Fernández-Llamazares, Á. (2021). Creating synergies between citizen science and Indigenous and local knowledge. *BioScience*, *71*(5), 503–518.

Tepper, B. J., Dimotakis, N., Lambert, L. S., Koopman, J., Matta, F. K., Park, H. M. & Goo, W. (2018). Examining follower responses to transformational leadership from a dynamic, person–environment fit perspective. *Academy of Management Journal*, *61*(4), 1343–1368.

Tetikci, I., Erim, G. & Halaclar, B. B. (2021). The place and effects of technology in the visual arts course. *European Journal of Educational Research*, *10*(3), 1089–1100. https://doi.org/10.12973/eu-jer.10.3.1089.

Thaiwinkarn, D., Ngang Tang, K. & Ariratana, W. (2018). Relationship between perceived directors' leadership and classroom quality of primary schools in Thailand. *Kasetsart Journal of Social Sciences*, *39*(2), 230–235. DOI:10.1016/j.kjss.2018.03.008.

Thériault, P. & Laurin, N. (2016). Enseigner la lecture au primaire: un apercu des pratiques d'enseignants des 2e et 3e cycles du primaire. In: *La recherche-action et la recherche-développement au service de la littératie*. (pp. 21–40). Les Éditions de l'Université de Sherbrooke. DOI: http://dx.doi.org/10.17118/11143/8808.

Thoonen, E. E., Sleegers, P. J., Oort, F. J., Peetsma, T. T. & Geijsel, F. P. (2011). How to improve teaching practices, the role of teacher motivation, organizational factors, and leadership practices. *Educational Administration Quarterly*, *47*(3), 496–536. doi:10.1177/0013161X11400185.

Thorgeirsdottir, H. (2015). *Investigating the use of Action Research and Activity Theory to Promote the Professional Development of Teachers in Iceland*. Doctoral dissertation. University of Iceland. https://skemman.is/bitstream/1946/23886/1/ThorgeirsdottirH.pdf.

Thornton, K. (2010). Supporting Sefl-Directed Learning: A Framework for Teachers. *Language Education in Asia*, 1(1), 158–170.

TIMSS 2019. (2021). *Ataskaita ir užduočių pavyzdžiai. Gamtos mokslai. 4 klasė* [*Report and sample assignments. Natural sciences. Grade 4*]. Vilnius: Nacionalinė švietimo agentūra.

Tirri, K., Eisenschmidt, E., Poom-Valickis, K. & Kuusisto, E. (2021). Current Challenges in School Leadership in Estonia and Finland: A Multiple-Case Study among Exemplary Principals. Education Research International, Article ID 8855927, 1–11. https://doi.org/10.1155/2021/8855927.

Tortorella, G. L., Fogliatto, F. S., Cauchick-Miguel, P. A., Kurnia, S. & Jurburg, D. (2021). Integration of industry 4.0 technologies into total productive maintenance practices. *International Journal of Production Economics*, 240, 108224.

Toulia, A., Strogilos, V. & Avramidis, E. (2021). Peer tutoring as a means to inclusion: a collaborative action research project. *Educational Action Research*, 31:2, 213–229, DOI: 10.1080/09650792.2021.1911821.

Toullec-Théry, M. (2007). Les enseignants spécialisés à dominante pédagogique à l'école primaire : recherche, action et formation. *Carrefours de l'éducation*, 2 (24), 183–199. https://www.cairn.info/revue-carrefours-de-l-education-2007-2-page-183.htm.

Tran, H. & Buckman, D. G. (2016). The Impact of Principal Movement and School Achievement on Principal Salaries. *Leadership and Policy in Schools*, 16(1), 1–24. DOI:10.1080/15700763.2016.1197279.

Tsoumanis, K. G., Stylos, G. & Kotsis, K. T. (2024). An Investigation of Primary School Students' Scientific Literacy. *European Journal of Education Studies*, *11*(2), 107–133. DOI: 10.46827/ejes.v11i2.5195.

Turkka, J., Haatainen, O. & Aksela, M. (2017). Integrating art into science education: A survey of science teachers' practices. *International Journal of Science Education*, *39*(10), 1403–1419. doi:10.1080/09500693.2017.1333656.

Turner-Bisset, R. B. (2005). *Creative Teaching: History in the Primary Classroom*. New York: David Fulton Publishers.

Uça, S. & Saracaloğlu, A. S. (2017). The use of realistic mathematics education in students' making sense of decimals: A design research. Elementary Education Online, *16*(2), 469–496. https://doi.org/10.17051/ilkonline.2017.304712.

Ugdymas(is) pradigmų kaitoje [*Education(is) in a changing world*]. (2017). Vilnius: Švietimo aprūpinimo centras.

UNESCO. (2003). United Nations Educational, Scientific and Cultural Organization. Education in a Multilingual World. Paris: UNESCO.

UNESCO. (2021). *Planifier l'éducation et planifier le futur*. Repéré à: http://www.iiep.unesco.org/fr/education-inclusive.

UNESCO. (2023). *Global Education Monitoring Report. Technology in Education. A Tool on Whose Terms?* Paris: UNESCO.

UNESCO. (2023). *Global report on teachers: Addressing teacher shortages*. United Nations Educational, Scientific and Cultural Organization. https://teachertaskforce.org/what-we-do/Knowledge-production-and-dissemination/global-report-teachers.

UNICEF. (2022). *Start of an uncertain school year for four million schoolchildren in Ukraine.* Available online: https://www.unicef.org/press-releases/start-uncertain-school-year-four-million-schoolchildren-ukraine.

Uştu, H., Saito, T. & Mentiş Taş, A. (2022). Integration of Art into STEM Education at Primary Schools: an Action Research Study with Primary School Teachers. *Syst Pract Action Res* 35, 253–274. https://doi.org/10.1007/s11213-021-09570-z.

Valstybinės švietimo 2013–2022 metų strategijos įgyvendinimas. Medžiaga diskusijoms [Implementation of the National Education Strategy 2013–2022. Material for discussion]. (2024). Vilnius: Lietuvos Respublikos švietimo, mokslo ir sporto ministerija.

Van Deur, P. (2018). *Managing Self-Directed Learning in Primary School Education.* Hershey: IGI Global.

Vanblaere, B. & Devos, G. (2016). Relating school leadership to perceived professional learning community characteristics: A multilevel analysis. *Teaching and Teacher Education*, 57, 26–38. doi:10.1016/j.tate.2016.03.003.

Varghese, J. & Crawford, S. S. (2021). A cultural framework for indigenous, local, and science knowledge systems in ecology and natural resource management. *Ecological Monographs*, 91(1), e01431.

Varjo, J., Kalalahti, M. & Kauko, J. (2019). Overview of Primary Education (Finland). *Bloomsbury Education and Childhood Studies.* www.becs-bloomsbury.com

Varjo, J., Kalalahti, M. & Silvennoinen, H. (2014). Families, school choice and democratic iterations on the Right to Education and Freedom of Education in Finnish municipalities. *Journal of School Choice*, 8(1), 20–48.

Vasileiadou, D., & Karadimitriou, K. (2021). Examining the impact of self-assessment with the use of rubrics on primary school students' performance. *Int J Educ Res Open*, 2(January), 100031. https://doi.org/10.1016/j.ijedro.2021.100031.

Vaughan, M. & Mertler, C. A. (2020). Re-orienting our thinking away from "professional development for educators" and toward the "development of professional educators." *Journal of School Leadership*. doi:10.1177/1052684620969926.

Vilniaus Aleksandro Puškino gimnazijos veiklos teminio išorinio vertinimo ataskaita [Report of the thematic external evaluation of Aleksandras Puškinas gymnasium, Vilnius city]. (2021). Vilnius: Nacionalinė mokyklų vertinimo agentūra.

Vilniaus Šeškinės pradinės mokyklos veiklos teminio išorinio vertinimo ataskaita [Report of the thematic external evaluation of Seskine primary school, Vilnius city]. (2021). Vilnius: Nacionalinė mokyklų vertinimo agentūra.

Vilniaus Sofijos Kovalevskajos progimnzijos veiklos teminio išorinio vertinimo ataskaita [Report of the thematic external evaluation of Sofija Kovalevskaja

pro-gymnasium, Vilnius city]. (2022). Vilnius: Nacionalinė mokyklų vertinimo agentūra.

Visuotinė lietuvių enciklopedija [Universal Lithuanian Encyclopedia]. (2025). LNB Mokslo ir enciklopedijų leidybos centras. https://www.vle.lt/straipsnis/refleksija/.

Vula, E. (2019). Action research as a potent methodology for improving teaching and learning in mathematics. *Eleventh Congress of the European Society for Research in Mathematics Education*, Utrecht University, Feb 2019, Utrecht, Netherlands. ‹hal-02422769›.

Vytauto Didžiojo universiteto Senatas [Senate of Vytautas Magnus University]. (2020). *Baigiamųjų darbų rengimo ir gynimo bendrosios tvarkos aprašas*. Kaunas: Vytauto Didžiojo universitetas. https://www.vdu.lt/wp-content/uploads/2021/04/Baigiamuju-darbu-rengimo-ir-gynimo-bendrosios-tvarkos-aprasas-2020-05-14-SEN-019.pdf.

Vytauto Didžiojo universiteto Senatas [Senate of Vytautas Magnus University]. (2021). *Dėl mokslinių tyrimų atitikties pagrindiniams tyrimų profesionalumo ir etikos principams vertinimo nuostatų tvirtinimo* Nr. SEN-N-17. https://www.vdu.lt/wp-content/uploads/2021/05/SEN-N-17-De%CC%87l-Moksliniu%CC%A8-tyrimu%CC%A8-atitikties-pagrindiniams-tyrimu%CC%A8-profesionalumo-ir-etikos-principams-vertinimo-nuostatu%CC%A8-tvirtinimo.pdf.

Wagner, Å. K. H., Skaftun, A. & McTigue, E. M. (2020). Literacy practices in co-taught early years classrooms. Study protocol: The Seaside case. *Nordic Journal of Literacy Research*, Vol. 6, Hefte 4, 70–97. DOI: 10.23865/njlr.v6.2212.

Wahl, E. (2015). 5 traits of creative leaders (and how to become one). *Fast Company*. http://www.fastcompany.com/3049844/5-hallmarks-of-the-most-creative-leaders.

Watts, A. (2020). *Outdoor Learning Through the Seasons: An Essential Guide for the Early Years*. London: Routledge.

Weber, R. P. (1990). *Basic Content Analysis*. Thousand Oaks: Sage Publications.

Wei, G., Lee, H.-Y. & Chung, C.-Y. (2022). Developing Pre-Service teachers' Practical Knowledge Through Formative Interventions. *Journal of Education for Teaching*, *49*(3): 384–400. https://doi.org/10.1080/02607476.2022.2111515.

Wenger, E. (2018). A Social Theory of Learning. In *Contemporary Theories of Learning: Learning Theorists … in Their Own Words*, edited by K. Illeris, 219–228. London and New York: Routledge.

Wennergren, A.-C. (2016). Teachers as Learners – With a Little Help from a Critical Friend. *Educational Action Research*, 24 (2): 260–279. doi:10.1080/09650792.2015.1058170.

Wheeler, H. C. & Root-Bernstein, M. (2020). Informing decision-making with Indigenous and local knowledge and science. *Journal of Applied Ecology*, 57(9), 1634–1643.

Wildová, R. (2014). Initial Reading Literacy Development in Current Primary School Practice. *Procedia – Social and Behavioral Sciences*, 159, 334–339.

Williams, K. S. (2024). Understanding youth empowerment: a youth participatory action research approach. *Qualitative Research in Organizations and Management*, 19(5), 1–34. https://doi.org/10.1108/QROM-07-2023-2561.

Winberg, C., Garraway, J. & Wright, J. (2023). A Systematic Review of the Literature on Change Laboratory Interventions: Lessons from Africa. *Journal of Education 92*(92): 206–227. https://doi.org/10.17159/2520-9868/i92a12.

Wolff, L.-A., Sjöblom, P., Hofman, M. & Palmberg, I. (2017). High Performance Education Fails in Sustainability? – A Reflection on Finnish Primary Teacher Education. *Education Sciences*, *7*(1), 1–22. DOI:10.3390/educsci7010032.

Wong, H. M. (2017). Implementing self-assessment in Singapore primary schools: Effects on students' perceptions of self-assessment. *Pedagogies: An International Journal*, *12*(4), 391–409.

Yan, Z. (2022). *Student self-assessment as a process for learning*. Routledge.

Yan, Z., Panadero, E., Wang, X. & Zhan, Y. (2023). A Systematic Review on Students' Perceptions of Self-Assessment: Usefulness and Factors Influencing Implementation. *Educ Psychol Rev*, 35(81), 1–28. https://doi.org/10.1007/s10648-023-09799-1.

Yoon, K. S., Duncan, T., Lee, S. W.-Y., Scarloss, B. & Shapley, K. (2007). *Reviewing the evidence on how teacher professional development affects student achievement* (Issues & Answers Report, REL 2007–No. 033). Washington, DC: U.S. Department of Education, Institute of Education Sciences, National Center for Education Evaluation and Regional Assistance, Regional Educational Laboratory Southwest. http://ies.ed.gov/ncee/edlabs.

Yorulmaz, A. & Doğan, M. C. (2022). An Action Research to Eliminate Mistakes in Multiplication and Division Operations through Realistic Mathematics Education. *Educational Policy Analysis and Strategic Research*. *17*(3), 238–262. DOI:10.29329/epasr.2022.461.12.

Yorulmaz, A., Uysal, H. & Sidekli, S. (2021). The use of mind maps related to the four operations in primary school fourth-grade students as an evaluation tool. *Journal of Education and Learning*, 15(2), 257–266. https://doi.org/10.11591/edulearn.v15i2.19894.

Ys, S. B., Mara, M. N., Yamin, M., Suid, A. B. & Dhin, C. N. (2011). Action Research on the Implementation of Active Learning at an Elementary School in Aceh. *Excellence in Higher Education*, *2*(2), 70–78. doi: 10.5195/ehe.2011.55 | http://ehe.pitt.edu.

Yuan, G. (2023). Development of Activity-Based Language Learning of Chinese for a Primary School in Western Sydney: A Participatory Action Research Study. *Open Journal of Social Sciences*, 11, 384–403. doi: 10.4236/jss.2023.112026.

Zaranis, N. (2018). Comparing the effectiveness of using ICT for teaching geometrical shapes in kindergarten and the first grade. *Int. J. Web-Based Learn. Teach. Technol.* 13, 50–63.

Žydžiūnaitė, V. & Sabaliauskas, S. (2017). *Kokybiniai tyrimai: principai ir metodai* [*Qualitative research: principles and methods*]. Vilnius: Vaga.

Žydžiūnaitė, V., Bubnys, R., Mažuolytė, G. & Mikelskienė, L. (2009). *Mokyklos aplinkos veiksniai, lemiantys socialinę ir psichologinę pedagogų sveikatą* [*School environmental factors affecting the social and psychological health of teachers*]. Šiauliai: Šiaulių kolegijos leidybos centras.

Žydžiūnaitė, V., Teresevičienė, M., Kaminskienė, L. & Gedvilienė, G. (2012). Savivaldaus mokymosi charakteristikų diskursas veiklos ir universiteto aplinkose [*Discourse on the characteristics of self-directed learning in operational and university settings*]. *Profesinės studijos teorija ir praktika*, 10, 142–151.

ERZIEHUNGSKONZEPTIONEN UND PRAXIS

EDUCATIONAL CONCEPTS AND PRACTICE

Herausgegeben von Gerd-Bodo von Carlsburg

Edited by Gerd-Bodo von Carlsburg

Band 1	Barbara Hellinge / Manfred Jourdan / Hubertus Maier-Hein: Kleine Pädagogik der Antike. 1984.
Band 2	Siegfried Prell: Handlungsorientierte Schulbegleitforschung. Anleitung, Durchführung und Evaluation. 1984.
Band 3	Gerd-Bodo Reinert von Carlsburg: Leitbild Gesamtschule versus Gymnasium? Eine Problemskizze. 1984.
Band 4	Ingeborg Wagner: Aufmerksamkeitsförderung im Unterricht. Hilfen durch Lehrertraining. 1984.
Band 5	Peter Struck: Pädagogische Bindungen. Zur Optimierung von Lehrerverhalten im Schulalltag. 1984.
Band 6	Wolfgang Sehringer (Hrsg.): Lernwelten und Instruktionsformen. 1986.
Band 7	Gerd-Bodo Reinert von Carlsburg (Hrsg.): Kindgemäße Erziehung. 1986.
Band 8	Heinrich Walther: Testament eines Schulleiters. 1986.
Band 9	Gerd-Bodo Reinert von Carlsburg / Rainer Dieterich (Hrsg.): Theorie und Wirklichkeit – Studien zum Lehrerhandeln zwischen Unterrichtstheorie und Alltagsroutine. 1987.
Band 10	Jörg Petersen / Gerhard Priesemann: Einführung in die Unterrichtswissenschaft. Teil 1: Sprache und Anschauung. 2., überarb. Aufl. 1992.
Band 11	Jörg Petersen / Gerhard Priesemann: Einführung in die Unterrichtswissenschaft. Teil 2: Handlung und Erkenntnis. 1992.
Band 12	Wolfgang Hammer: Schulverwaltung im Spannungsfeld von Pädagogik und Gesellschaft. 1988.
Band 13	Werner Jünger: Schulunlust. Messung – Genese – Intervention. 1988.
Band 14	Jörg Petersen / Gerhard Priesemann: Unterricht als regelgeleiteter Handlungszusammenhang. Ein Beitrag zur Verständigung über Unterricht. 1988.
Band 15	Wolf-Dieter Hasenclever (Hrsg.): Pädagogik und Psychoanalyse. Marienauer Symposion zum 100. Geburtstag Gertrud Bondys. 1990.
Band 16	Jörg Petersen / Gerd-Bodo Reinert von Carlsburg / Erwin Stephan: Betrifft: Hausaufgaben. Ein Überblick über die didaktische Diskussion für Elternhaus und Schule. 1990.
Band 17	Rudolf G. Büttner / Gerd-Bodo Reinert von Carlsburg (Hrsg.): Schule und Identität im Wandel. Biographien und Begebenheiten aus dem Schulalltag zum Thema Identitätsentwicklung. 1991.
Band 18	Eva Maria Waibel: Von der Suchtprävention zur Gesundheitsförderung in der Schule. Der lange Weg der kleinen Schritte. 3. Aufl. 1994.
Band 19	Heike Biermann: Chancengerechtigkeit in der Grundschule – Anspruch und Wirklichkeit. 1992.

Band 20 Wolf-Dieter Hasenclever (Hrsg.): Reformpädagogik heute: Wege der Erziehung zum ökologischen Humanismus. 2. Marienauer Symposion zum 100. Geburtstag von Max Bondy. 1993. 2., durchges. Aufl. 1998.

Band 21 Bernd Arnold: Medienerziehung und moralische Entwicklung von Kindern. Eine medienpädagogische Untersuchung zur Moral im Fernsehen am Beispiel einer Serie für Kinder im Umfeld der Werbung. 1993.

Band 22 Dimitrios Chatzidimou: Hausaufgaben konkret. Eine empirische Untersuchung an deutschen und griechischen Schulen der Sekundarstufen. 1994.

Band 23 Klaus Knauer: Diagnostik im pädagogischen Prozeß. Eine didaktischdiagnostische Handreichung für den Fachlehrer. 1994.

Band 24 Jörg Petersen / Gerd-Bodo Reinert von Carlsburg (Hrsg.): Lehren und Lernen im Umfeld neuer Technologien. Reflexionen vor Ort. 1994.

Band 25 Stefanie Voigt: Biologisch-pädagogisches Denken in der Theorie. 1994.

Band 26 Stefanie Voigt: Biologisch-pädagogisches Denken in der Praxis. 1994.

Band 27 Reinhard Fatke / Horst Scarbath: Pioniere Psychoanalytischer Pädagogik. 1995.

Band 28 Rudolf G. Büttner / Gerd-Bodo Reinert von Carlsburg (Hrsg.): Naturschutz in Theorie und Praxis. Mit Beispielen zum Tier-, Landschafts- und Gewässerschutz. 1995.

Band 29 Dimitrios Chatzidimou / Eleni Taratori: Hausaufgaben. Einstellungen deutscher und griechischer Lehrer. 1995.

Band 30 Bernd Weyh: Vernunft und Verstehen: Hans-Georg Gadamers anthropologische Hermeneutikkonzeption. 1995.

Band 31 Helmut Arndt / Henner Müller-Holtz (Hrsg.): Schulerfahrungen - Lebenserfahrungen. Anspruch und Wirklichkeit von Bildung und Erziehung heute. Reformpädagogik auf dem Prüfstand. 2. Aufl. 1996.

Band 32 Karlheinz Biller: Bildung erwerben in Unterricht, Schule und Familie. Begründung - Bausteine - Beispiele. 1996.

Band 33 Ruth Allgäuer: Evaluation macht uns stark! Zur Unverzichtbarkeit von Praxisforschung im schulischen Alltag. 1997. 2., durchges. Aufl. 1998.

Band 34 Christel Senges: Das Symbol des Drachen als Ausdruck einer Konfliktgestaltung in der Sandspieltherapie. Ergebnisse aus einer Praxis für analytische Psychotherapie von Kindern und Jugendlichen. 1998.

Band 35 Achim Dehnert: Untersuchung der Selbstmodelle von Managern. 1997.

Band 36 Shen-Keng Yang: Comparison, Understanding and Teacher Education in International Perspective. Edited and introduced by Gerhard W. Schnaitmann. 1998.

Band 37 Johann Amos Comenius: Allverbesserung (Panorthosia). Eingeleitet, übersetzt und erläutert von Franz Hofmann. 1998.

Band 38 Edeltrud Ditter-Stolz: Zeitgenössische Musik nach 1945 im Musikunterricht der Sekundarstufe I. 1999.

Band 39 Manfred Luketic: Elektrotechnische Lernsoftware für den Technikunterricht an Hauptschulen. 1999.

Band 40 Gerhard Baltes / Brigitta Eckert: Differente Bildungsorte in systemischer Vernetzung. Eine Antwort auf das Problem der funktionellen Differenzierung in der Kooperation zwischen Jugendarbeit und Schule. 1999.

Band 41 Roswit Strittmatter: Soziales Lernen. Ein Förderkonzept für sehbehinderte Schüler. 1999.

Band 42 Thomas H. Häcker: Widerstände in Lehr-Lern-Prozessen. Eine explorative Studie zur pädagogischen Weiterbildung von Lehrkräften. 1999.

Band 43 Sabine Andresen / Bärbel Schön (Hrsg.): Lehrerbildung für morgen. Wissenschaftlicher Nachwuchs stellt sich vor. 1999.

Band 44 Ernst Begemann: Lernen verstehen – Verstehen lernen. Zeitgemäße Einsichten für Lehrer und Eltern. Mit Beiträgen von Heinrich Bauersfeld. 2000.

Band 45 Günter Ramachers: Das intrapersonale Todeskonzept als Teil sozialer Wirklichkeit. 2000.

Band 46 Christoph Dönges: Lebensweltliche Erfahrung statt empirischer Enteignung. Grenzen und Alternativen empirischer Konzepte in der (Sonder-)Pädagogik. 2000.

Band 47 Michael Luley: Eine kleine Geschichte des deutschen Schulbaus. Vom späten 18. Jahrhundert bis zur Gegenwart. 2000.

Band 48 Helmut Arndt / Henner Müller-Holtz (Hrsg.): Herausforderungen an die Pädagogik aufgrund des gegenwärtigen gesellschaftlichen Wandels. Bildung und Erziehung am Beginn des 3. Jahrtausends. 2000.

Band 49 Johann Amos Comenius: Allermahnung (Pannuthesia). Eingeleitet, übersetzt und erläutert von Franz Hofmann. 2001.

Band 50 Hans-Peter Spittler-Massolle: Blindheit und blindenpädagogischer Blick. Der *Brief über die Blinden zum Gebrauch für die Sehenden* von Denis Diderot und seine Bedeutung für den Begriff von Blindheit. 2001.

Band 51 Eva Rass: Kindliches Erleben bei Wahrnehmungsproblemen. Möglichkeiten einer selbst-psychologisch ausgerichteten Pädagogik und Psychotherapie bei sublimen und unerkannten Schwächen in der sensorischen Integration. 2002.

Band 52 Bruno Hamann: Neue Herausforderungen für eine zeitgemäße und zukunftsorientierte Schule. Unter Mitarbeit von Birgitta Hamann. 2002.

Band 53 Johann Amos Comenius: Allerleuchtung (Panaugia). Eingeleitet, übersetzt und erläutert von Franz Hofmann. 2002.

Band 54 Bernd Sixtus: Alasdair MacIntyres Tugendenlehre von *After Virtue* als Beitrag zum Disput über universalistische Erziehungsziele. 2002.

Band 55 Elke Wagner: Sehbehinderung und Soziale Kompetenz. Entwicklung und Erprobung eines Konzeptes. 2003.

Band 56 Jutta Rymarczyk / Helga Haudeck: *In Search of The Active Learner.* Untersuchungen zu Fremdsprachenunterricht, bilingualen und inter- disziplinären Kontexten. 2003.

Band 57 Gerhard W. Schnaitmann: Forschungsmethoden in der Erziehungswissenschaft. Zum Verhältnis von qualitativen und quantitativen Methoden in der Lernforschung an einem Beispiel der Lernstrategienforschung. 2004.

Band 58 Bernd Schwarz / Thomas Eckert (Hrsg.): Erziehung und Bildung nach TIMSS und PISA. 2004.

Band 59 Werner Sacher / Alban Schraut (Hrsg.): Volkserzieher in dürftiger Zeit. Studien über Leben und Wirken Eduard Sprangers. 2004.

Band 60 Dorothee Dahl: Interdisziplinär geprägte Symbolik in der visuellen Kommunikation. Tendenzen therapeutisch-kunstpädagogischer Unterrichtsmodelle vor dem Hintergrund multimedialer Zeitstrukturen. 2005.

Band 61 Gerd-Bodo von Carlsburg / Marian Heitger (Hrsg.): Der Lehrer - ein (un)möglicher Beruf. 2005.

Band 62 Bruno Hamann: Pädagogische Anthropologie. Theorien - Modelle - Strukturen. Eine Einführung. 4., überarbeitete und ergänzte Auflage. 2005.

Band 63 Airi Liimets: Bestimmung des lernenden Menschen auf dem Wege der Reflexion über den Lernstil. 2005.

Band 64 Cornelia Matz: Vorbilder in den Medien. Ihre Wirkungen und Folgen für Heranwachsende. 2005.

Band 65 Birgitta Hamann: Grundfragen der Literaturdidaktik und zentrale Aspekte des Deutschunterrichts. 2005.

Band 66 Ralph Olsen / Hans-Bernhard Petermann / Jutta Rymarczyk (Hrsg.): Intertextualität und Bildung - didaktische und fachliche Perspektiven. 2006.

Band 67 Bruno Hamann: Bildungssystem und Lehrerbildung im Fokus aktueller Diskussionen. Bestandsaufnahme und Perspektiven. 2006.

Band 68 Ingeborg Seitz: Heterogenität als Chance. Lehrerprofessionalität im Wandel. 2007.

Band 69 Margret Ruep / Gustav Keller: Schulevaluation. Grundlagen, Methoden, Wirksamkeit. 2007.

Band 70 Harald Schweizer: Krach oder Grammatik? Streitschrift für einen revidierten Sprachunterricht. Kritik und Vorschläge. 2008.

Band 71 Martina Becker / Gerd-Bodo von Carlsburg / Helmut Wehr (Hrsg.): Seelische Gesundheit und gelungenes Leben. Perspektiven der Humanistischen Psychologie und Humanistischen Pädagogik. Ein Handbuch. 2008.

Band 72 Sigvard Clasen: Bildung im Licht von Beschäftigung und Wachstum. Wohin bewegt sich Deutschland? 2009.

Band 73 Gerd-Bodo von Carlsburg: Enkulturation und Bildung. Fundament sozialer Kompetenz. 2009.

Band 74 Hermann-Josef Wilbert: Musikunterricht im Rückblick. Eine alternative Musikdidaktik. 2009.

Band 75 Britta Klopsch: Fremdevaluation im Rahmen der Qualitätsentwicklung und -sicherung. Eine Evaluation der Qualifizierung baden-württembergischer Fremdevaluatorinnen und Fremdevaluatoren. 2009.

Band 76 Leonard Wehr: Partizipatorisches Marketing privater Hochschulen. Corporate Identity als Ziel von Bildungsmarketing. 2011.

Band 77 Konstantinos D. Chatzidimou: Microteaching als erlebnis- und handlungsorientierte Methode im Rahmen der Lehrerausbildung und der Didaktik. Eine theoretische und empirische Untersuchung. 2012.

Band 78 Miriam Lange: Befähigen, befähigt werden, sich befähigen - Eine Auseinandersetzung mit dem Capability Approach. 2014.

Band 79 Eva Rass (Hrsg.): Comenius: Seiner Zeit weit voraus...! Die Entdeckung der Kindheit als grundlegende Entwicklungsphase. 2014.

Band 80 Cornelia Frech-Becker: Disziplin durch Bildung - ein vergessener Zusammenhang. Eine historisch-systematische Untersuchung aus antinomischer Perspektive als Grundlage für ein bildungstheoretisches Verständnis des Disziplinproblems. 2015.

Band 81 Rüdiger Funiok / Harald Schöndorf (Hrsg.): Ignatius von Loyola und die Pädagogik der Jesuiten. Ein Modell für Schule und Persönlichkeitsbildung. 2017.

Band 82 Lara Rodríguez Sieweke (ed.): Learning Scenarios for Social and Cultural Change. *Bildung* Through Academic Teaching. 2017.

Band 83 Fred Maurer: Leseförderung durch Kriminalliteratur. Deutschdidaktische Annäherungen an ein verkanntes und vernachlässigtes Genre. 2019.

Band 84 Otilia Clipa / Erica Cîmpan: Social-Emotional Competences of Preschoolers. The Impact of Outdoor Educational Activities. 2020.

Band 85 Mariana Sirotová / Veronika Michvocíková /Marián Host'ovecký: Serious Games in University Education of Future Teachers. 2021.

Band 86 Valdonė Indrašienė/ Violeta Jegelevičienė / Odeta Merfeldaitė / Daiva Penkauskienė / Jolanta Pivorienė /Asta Railienė / Justinas Sadauskas / Natalija Valavičienė: Critical Thinking in Higher Education and Labour Market. 2021.

Band 87 Jan Rolf Friederichs: Schulreformen als Antwort auf gesellschaftliche Veränderungen. Die Gemeinschaftsschule im Spannungsfeld der Bildungspolitik in Baden-Württemberg. 2021.

Band 88 Otilia Clipa (ed.): Challenges in Education – Policies, Practice and Research. 2021.

Band 89 Palmira Pečiuliauskienė / Lina Kaminskienė: Science Teachers' Innovative Work Behavior: Factors and Actors. 2022.

Band 90 Natalija Mazeikiene (eds.): Discovering the New Place of Learning. 2022.

Band 91 Vilma Žydžiūnaitė / Lina Kaminskienė / Vaida Jurgilė (eds.): Teacher Leadership: Learning, Teaching and Leading. Experiences of Teachers and School Administration. 2022.

Band 92 Daiva Jakavonytė-Staškuvienė, Jolita Kudinovienė and Linas Jašinauskas: Action Research-Based Practices in Primary Education. Educational Contexts and Teachers' Experiences. 2026.

www.peterlang.com

FSC
www.fsc.org
MIX
Papier | Fördert gute Waldnutzung
FSC® C083411

Kolibri 360 GmbH
Ferdinand-Jühlke-Straße 7
99095 Erfurt, Deutschland
produktsicherheit@kolibri360.de

Druck:
CPI Druckdienstleistungen GmbH
im Auftrag der
Kolibri 360 GmbH
Ferdinand-Jühlke-Str. 7
99095 Erfurt